Garfield
dishes
it out

BY JIM DAVIS

Ballantine Books Trade Paperbacks • New York

2014 Ballantine Books Trade Paperback Edition

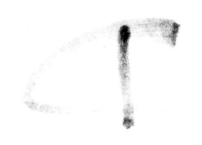

Published in the United States by Ballantine Books, an imprint of Random House, a division of Random House LLC, a Penguin Random House Company, New York.

BALLANTINE and the HOUSE colophon are registered trademarks of Random House LLC.

Originally published in slightly different form in the United States by Ballantine Books, an imprint of Random House, a division of Random House LLC, in 1994.

ISBN 978-0-345-52595-6
eBook ISBN 978-0-345-54992-1

Printed in the United States of America on acid-free paper

www.ballantinebooks.com

9 8 7 6 5 4 3 2 1

First Colorized Edition

GARFIELD'S TOP TEN COUNTRY PET TUNES

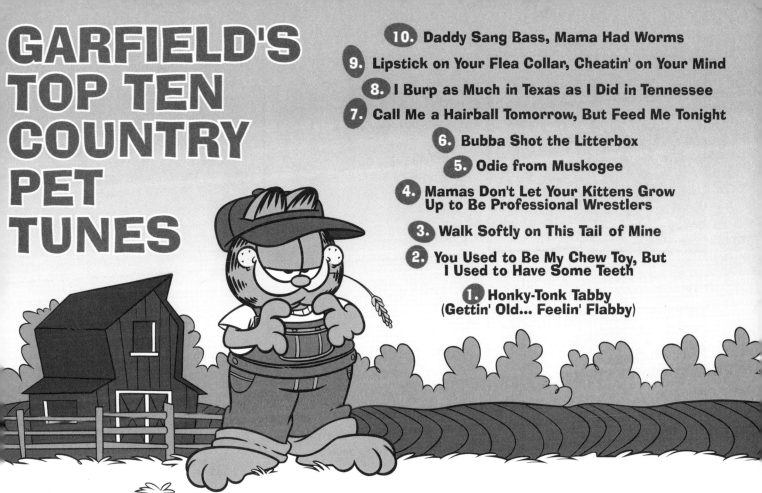

10. Daddy Sang Bass, Mama Had Worms
9. Lipstick on Your Flea Collar, Cheatin' on Your Mind
8. I Burp as Much in Texas as I Did in Tennessee
7. Call Me a Hairball Tomorrow, But Feed Me Tonight
6. Bubba Shot the Litterbox
5. Odie from Muskogee
4. Mamas Don't Let Your Kittens Grow Up to Be Professional Wrestlers
3. Walk Softly on This Tail of Mine
2. You Used to Be My Chew Toy, But I Used to Have Some Teeth
1. Honky-Tonk Tabby (Gettin' Old... Feelin' Flabby)

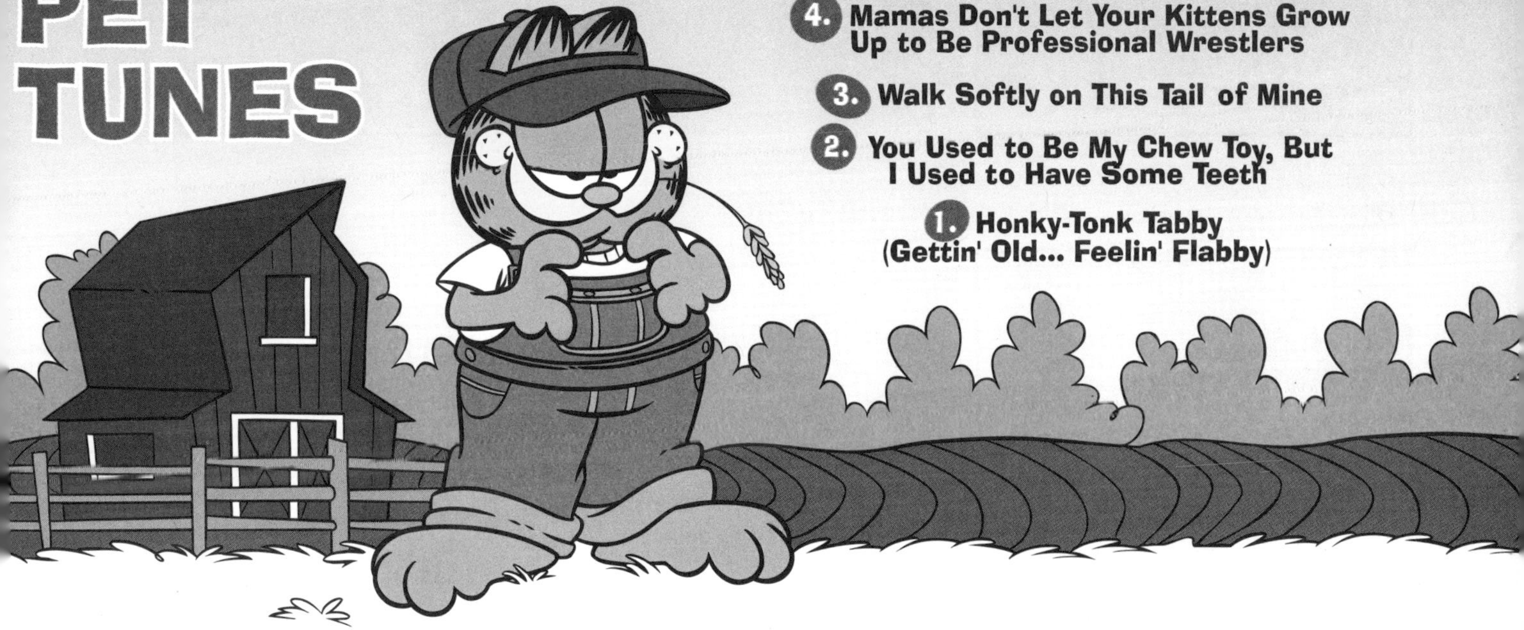

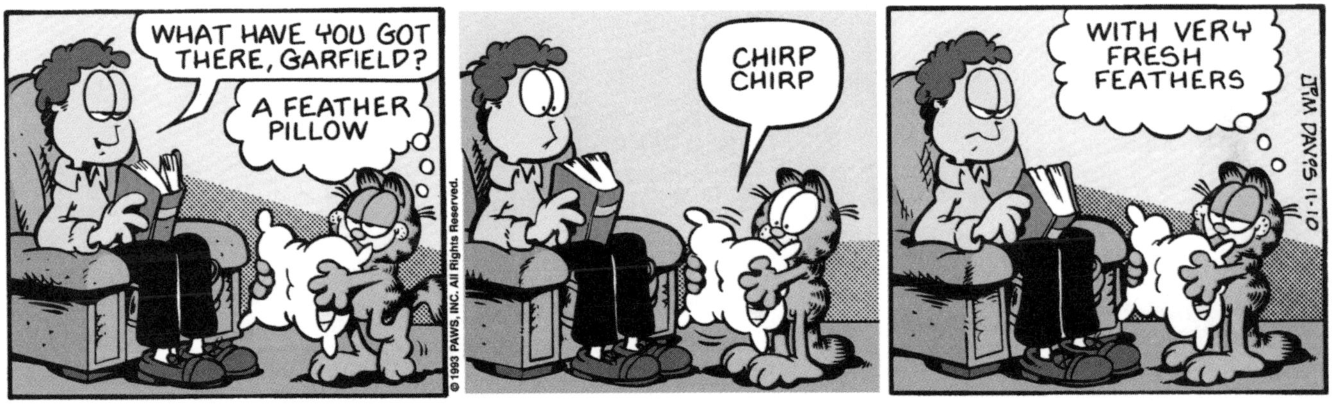
WHAT HAVE YOU GOT THERE, GARFIELD?
A FEATHER PILLOW
CHIRP CHIRP
WITH VERY FRESH FEATHERS
JIM DAVIS 11-10

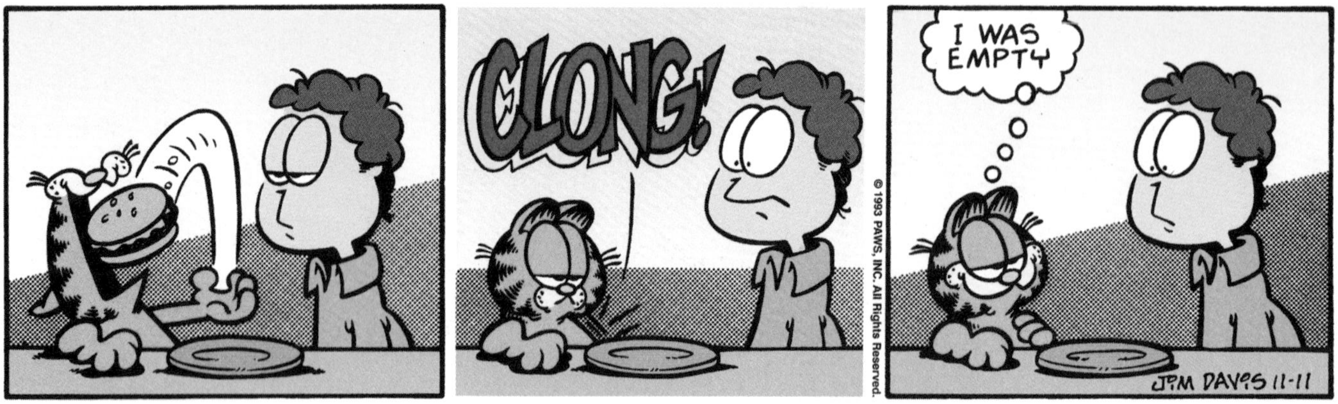
CLONG!
I WAS EMPTY
© 1993 PAWS, INC. All Rights Reserved.
JIM DAVIS 11-11

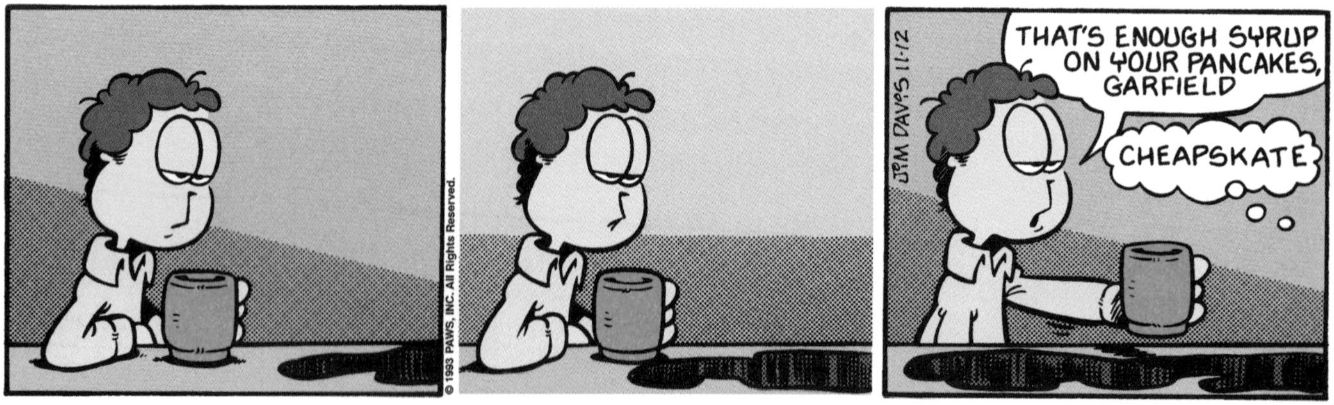
© 1993 PAWS, INC. All Rights Reserved.
JIM DAVIS 11-12
THAT'S ENOUGH SYRUP ON YOUR PANCAKES, GARFIELD
CHEAPSKATE

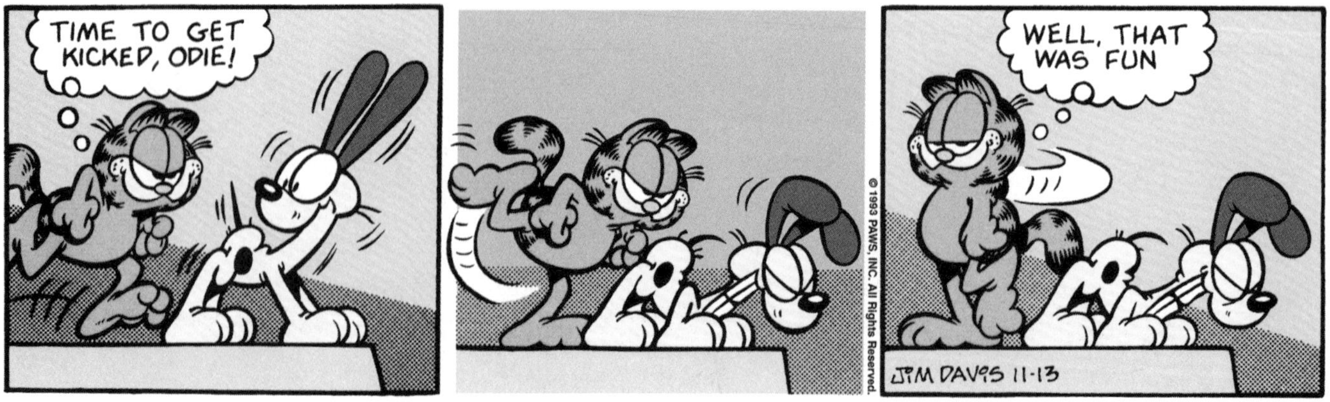
TIME TO GET KICKED, ODIE!
© 1993 PAWS, INC. All Rights Reserved.
WELL, THAT WAS FUN
JIM DAVIS 11-13

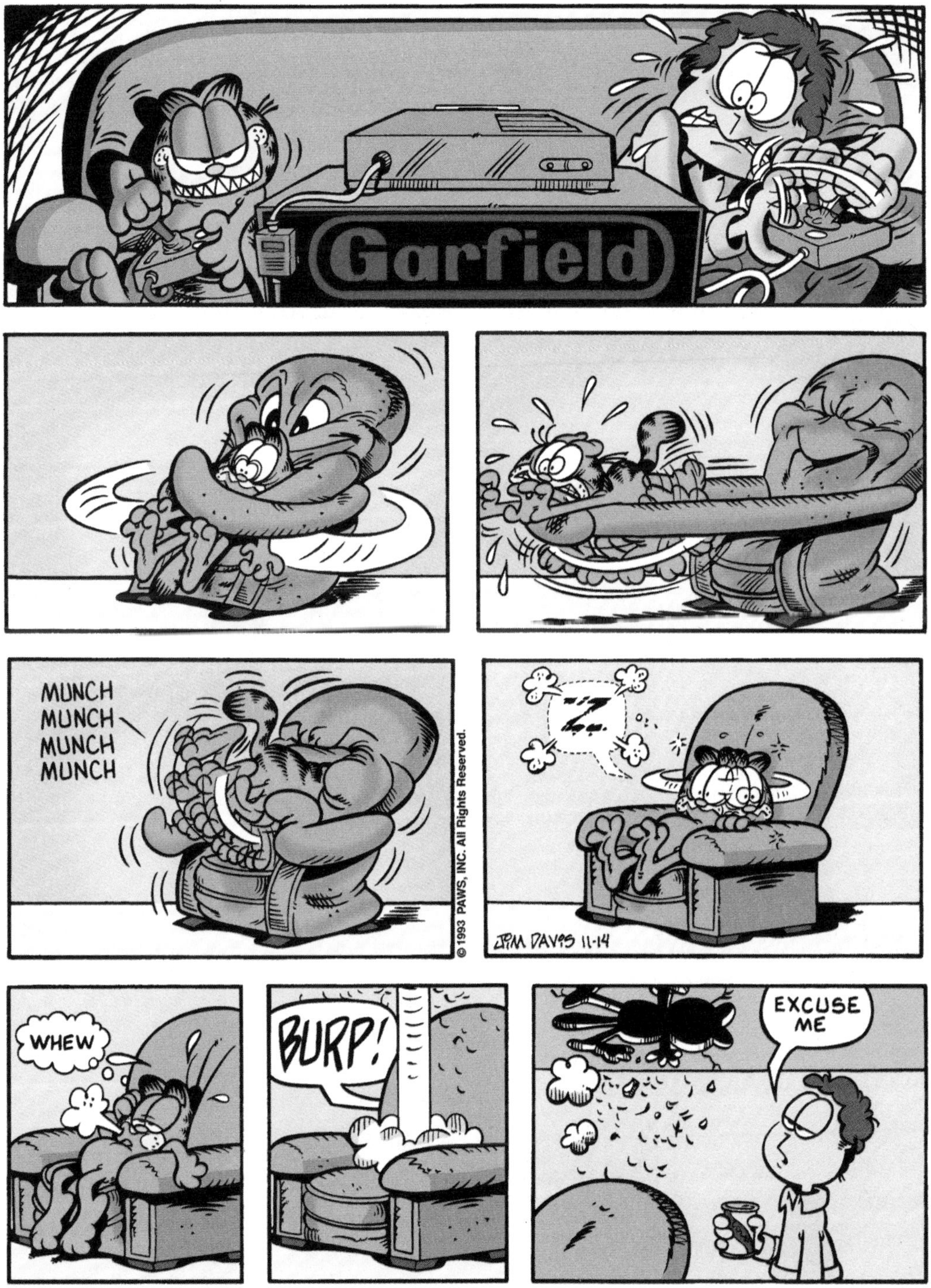
Garfield
MUNCH
MUNCH
MUNCH
MUNCH
Z
JIM DAVIS 11-14
WHEW
BURP!
EXCUSE ME

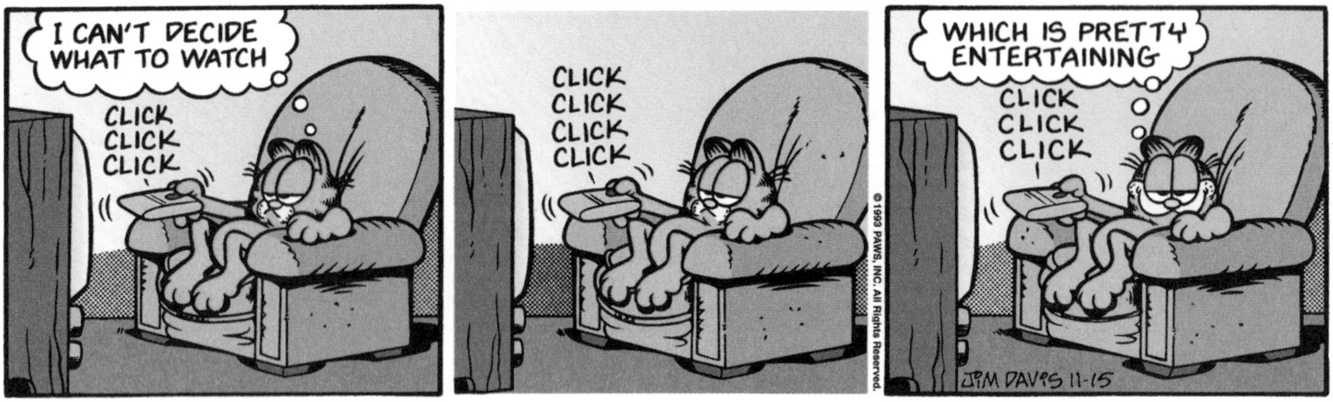
I CAN'T DECIDE WHAT TO WATCH
CLICK CLICK CLICK
CLICK CLICK CLICK CLICK
WHICH IS PRETTY ENTERTAINING
CLICK CLICK CLICK
© 1993 PAWS, INC. All Rights Reserved.
JIM DAVIS 11-15

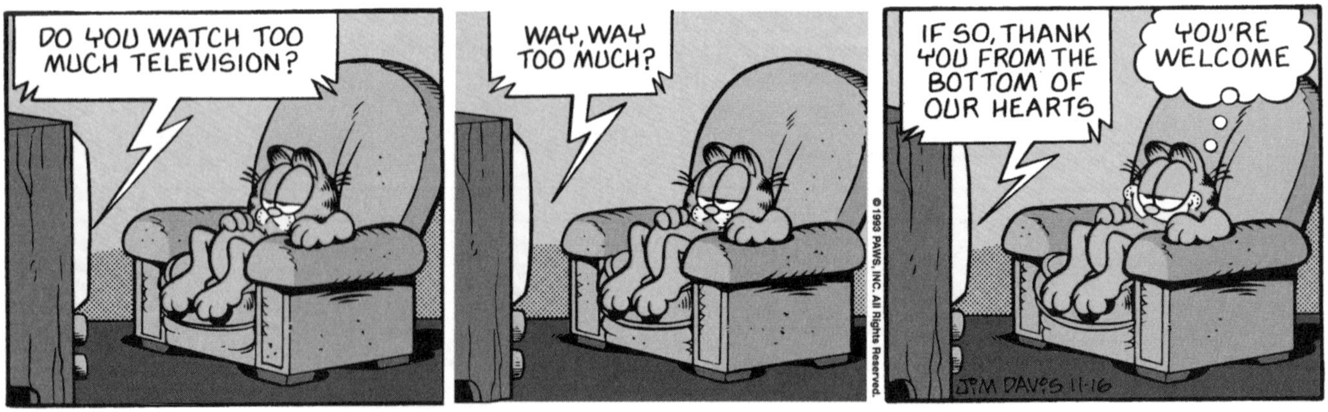
DO YOU WATCH TOO MUCH TELEVISION?
WAY, WAY TOO MUCH?
IF SO, THANK YOU FROM THE BOTTOM OF OUR HEARTS
YOU'RE WELCOME
© 1993 PAWS, INC. All Rights Reserved.
JIM DAVIS 11-16

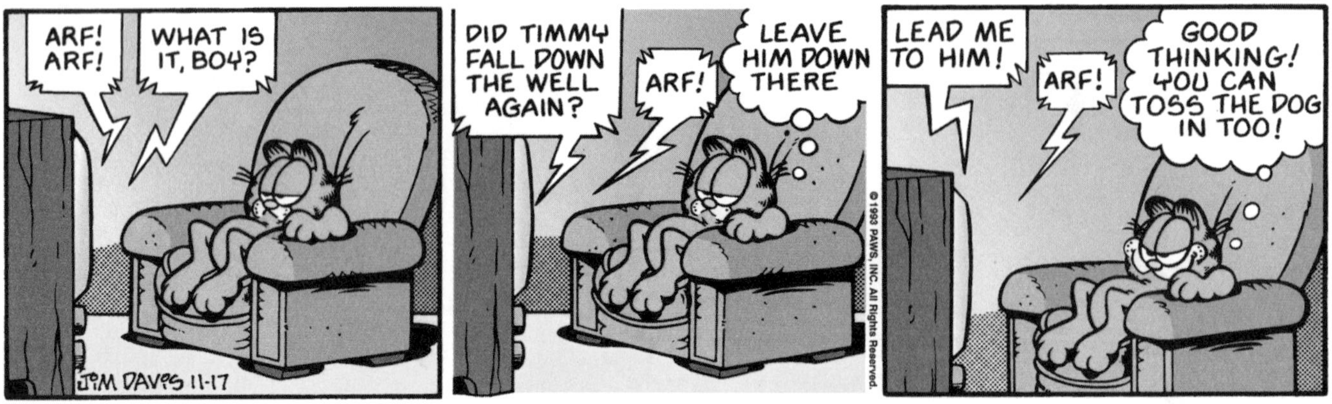
ARF! ARF!
WHAT IS IT, BOY?
JIM DAVIS 11-17
DID TIMMY FALL DOWN THE WELL AGAIN?
ARF!
LEAVE HIM DOWN THERE
© 1993 PAWS, INC. All Rights Reserved.
LEAD ME TO HIM!
ARF!
GOOD THINKING! YOU CAN TOSS THE DOG IN TOO!

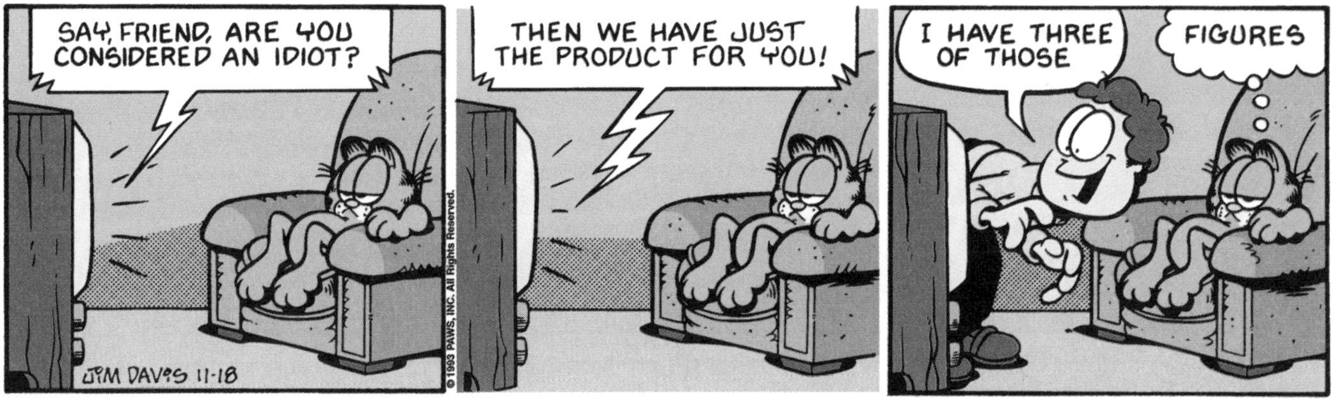
SAY, FRIEND, ARE YOU CONSIDERED AN IDIOT?
JIM DAVIS 11-18
© 1993 PAWS, INC. All Rights Reserved.
THEN WE HAVE JUST THE PRODUCT FOR YOU!
I HAVE THREE OF THOSE
FIGURES

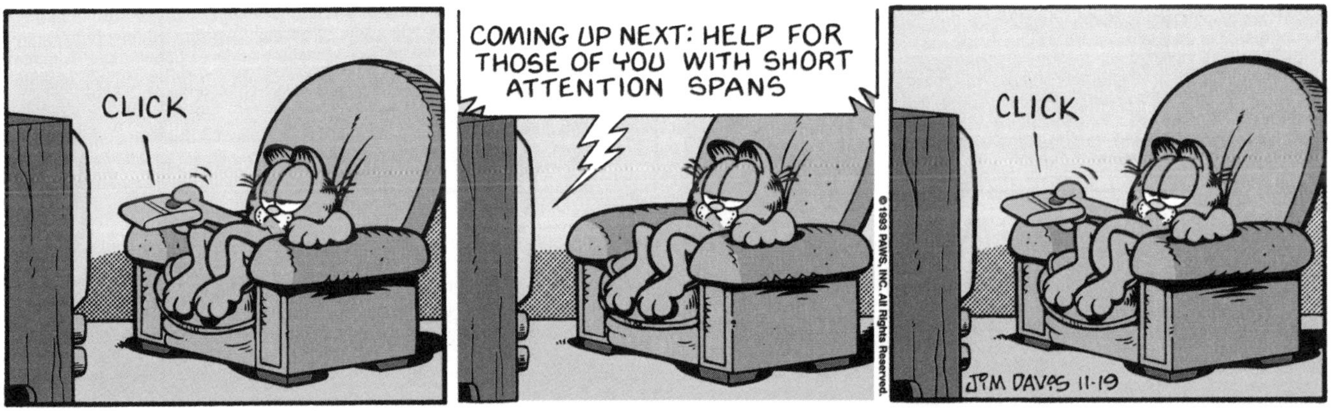
CLICK
COMING UP NEXT: HELP FOR THOSE OF YOU WITH SHORT ATTENTION SPANS
© 1993 PAWS, INC. All Rights Reserved.
CLICK
JIM DAVIS 11-19

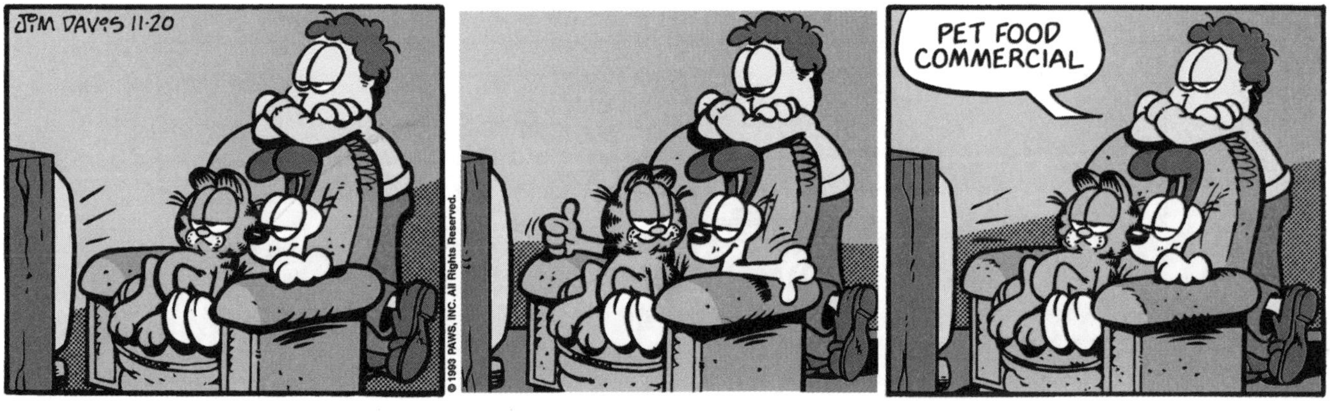
JIM DAVIS 11-20
© 1993 PAWS, INC. All Rights Reserved.
PET FOOD COMMERCIAL

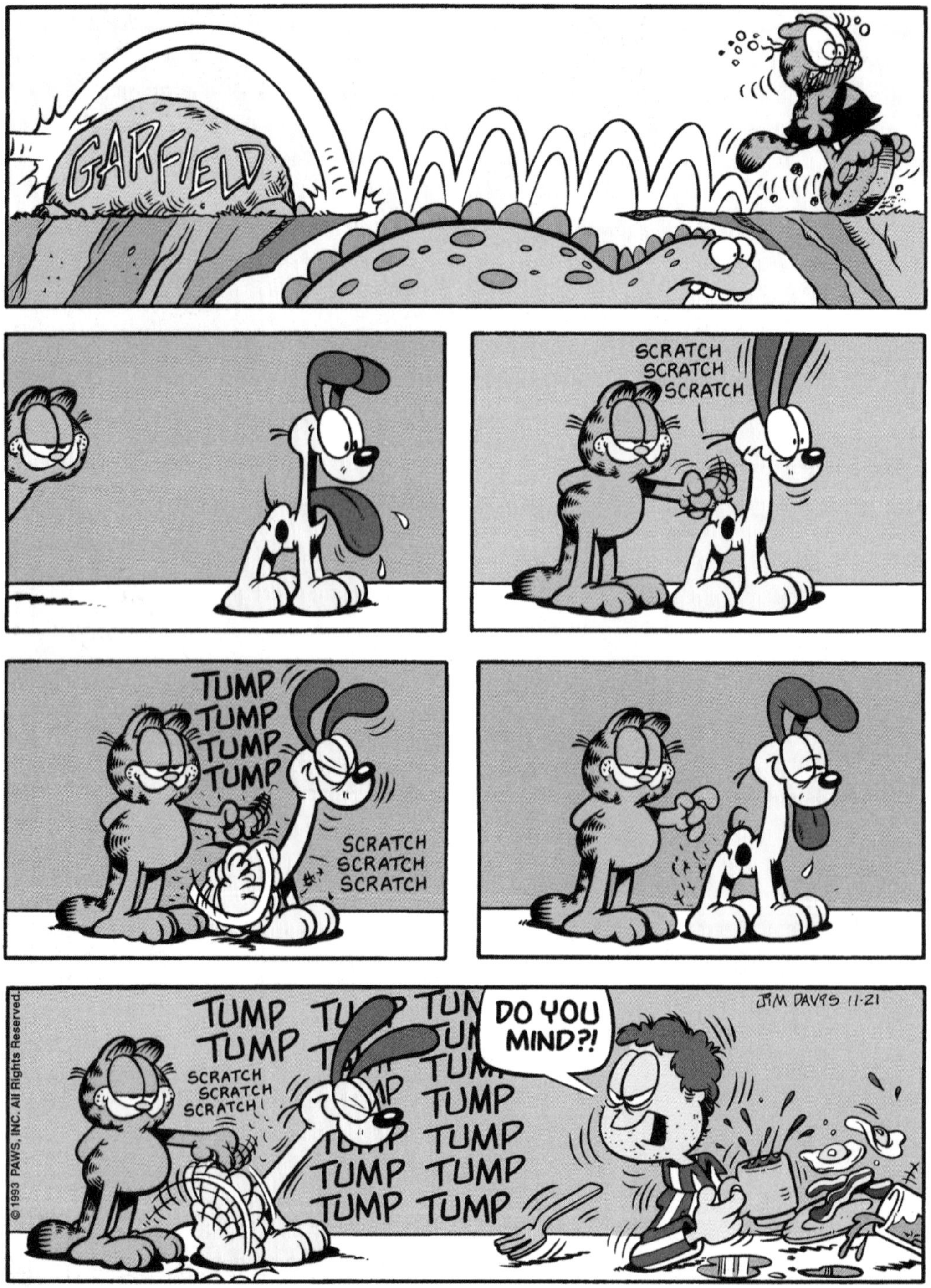
GARFIELD
SCRATCH
SCRATCH
SCRATCH
TUMP
TUMP
TUMP
TUMP
SCRATCH
SCRATCH
SCRATCH
TUMP
TUMP
SCRATCH
SCRATCH
SCRATCH
TUMP TUMP
TUMP TUMP
TUMP TUMP
TUMP
DO YOU MIND?!
JIM DAVIS 11-21

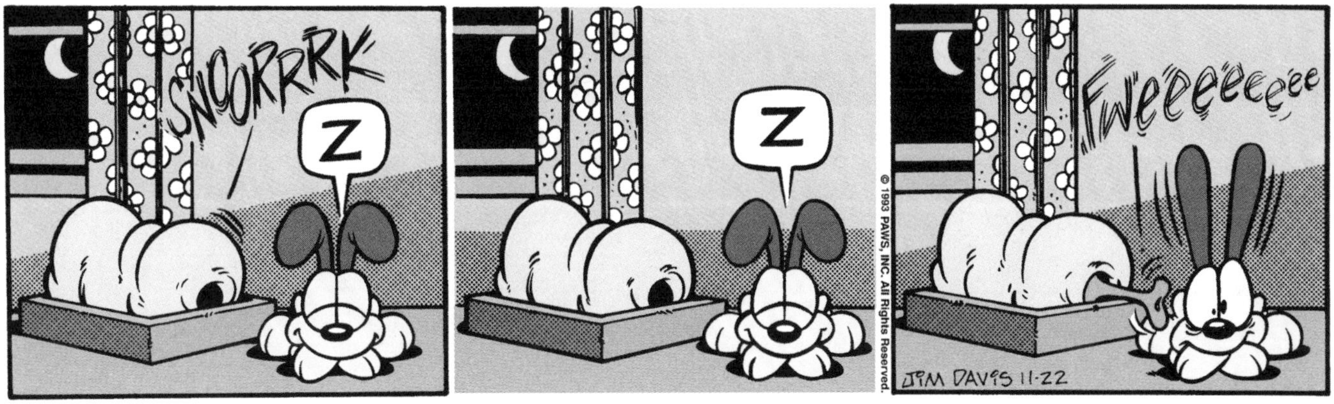
SNOORRRK
Z
Z
© 1993 PAWS, INC. All Rights Reserved.
Fweeeeeeee
JIM DAVIS 11-22

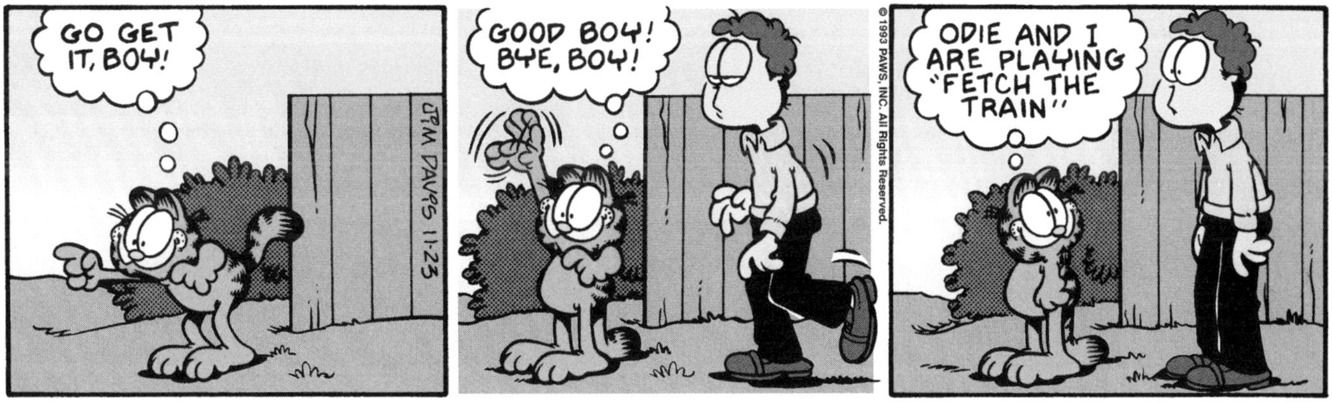
GO GET IT, BOY!
JIM DAVIS 11-23
GOOD BOY! BYE, BOY!
© 1993 PAWS, INC. All Rights Reserved.
ODIE AND I ARE PLAYING "FETCH THE TRAIN"

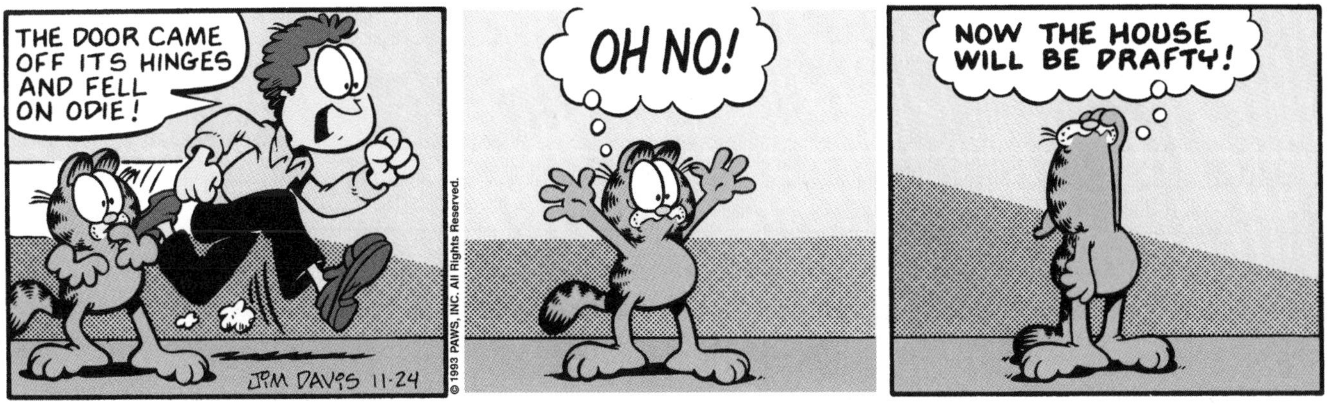
THE DOOR CAME OFF ITS HINGES AND FELL ON ODIE!
JIM DAVIS 11-24
© 1993 PAWS, INC. All Rights Reserved.
OH NO!
NOW THE HOUSE WILL BE DRAFTY!

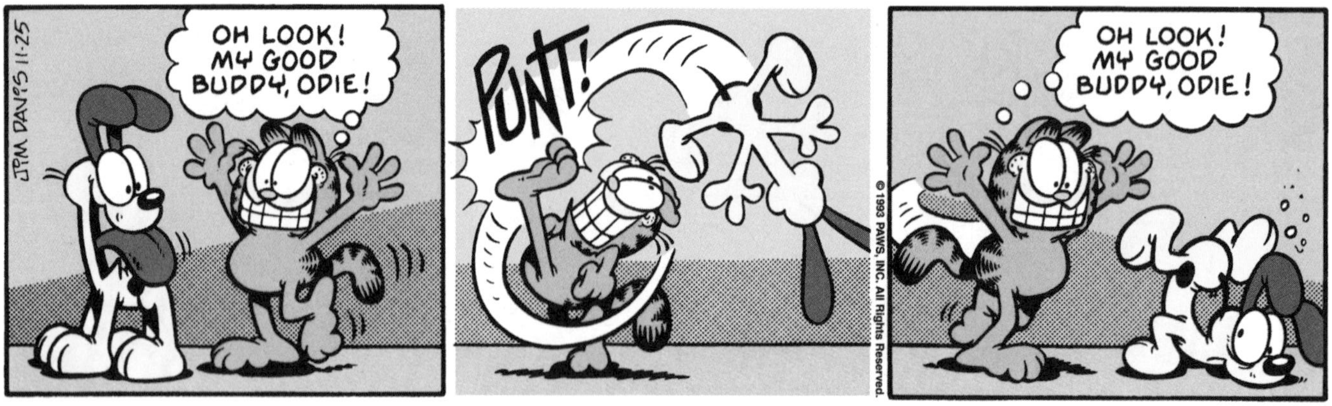
JIM DAVIS 11-25
OH LOOK! MY GOOD BUDDY, ODIE!
PUNT!
© 1993 PAWS, INC. All Rights Reserved.
OH LOOK! MY GOOD BUDDY, ODIE!

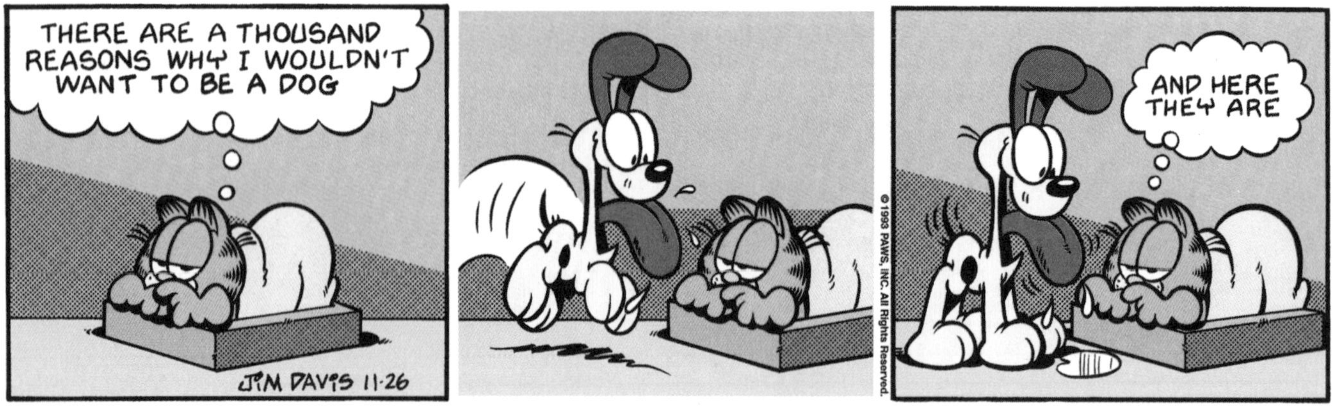
THERE ARE A THOUSAND REASONS WHY I WOULDN'T WANT TO BE A DOG
JIM DAVIS 11-26
© 1993 PAWS, INC. All Rights Reserved.
AND HERE THEY ARE

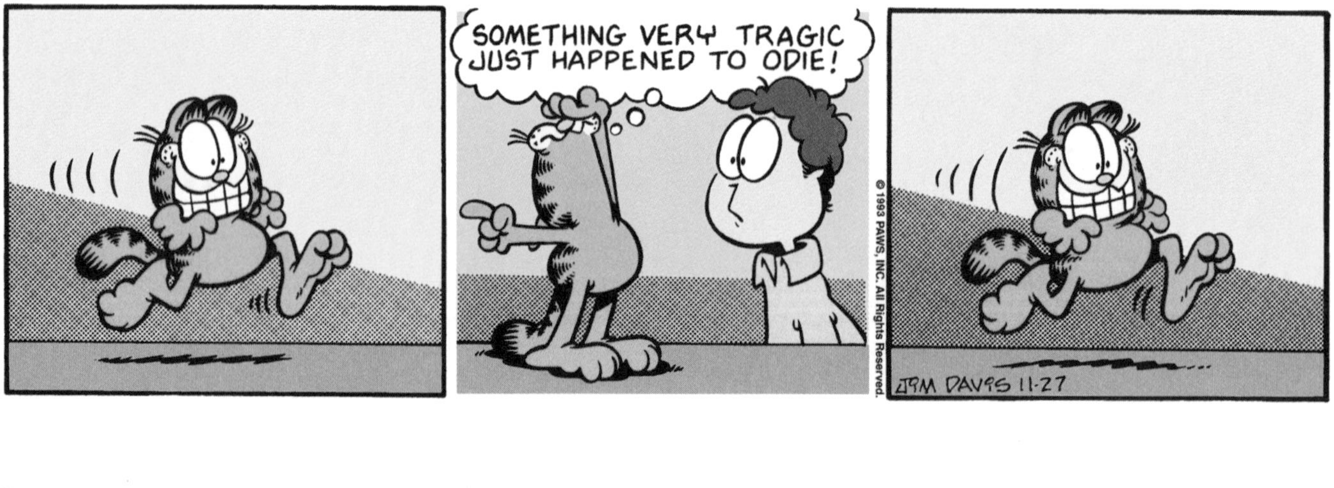
SOMETHING VERY TRAGIC JUST HAPPENED TO ODIE!
© 1993 PAWS, INC. All Rights Reserved.
JIM DAVIS 11-27

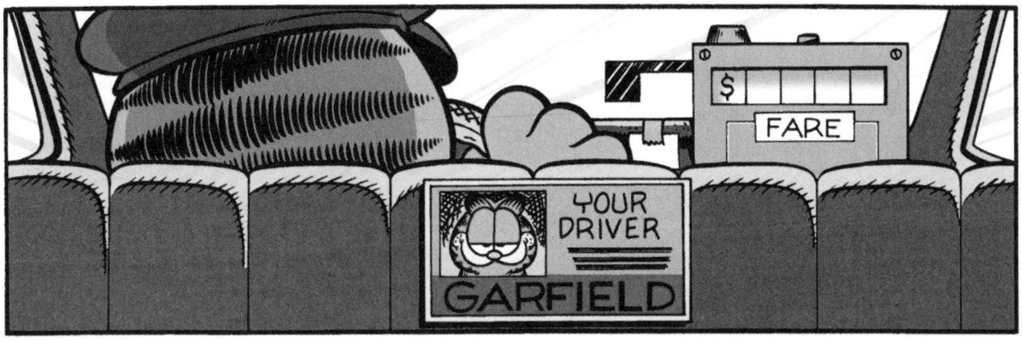

$
FARE
YOUR DRIVER
GARFIELD

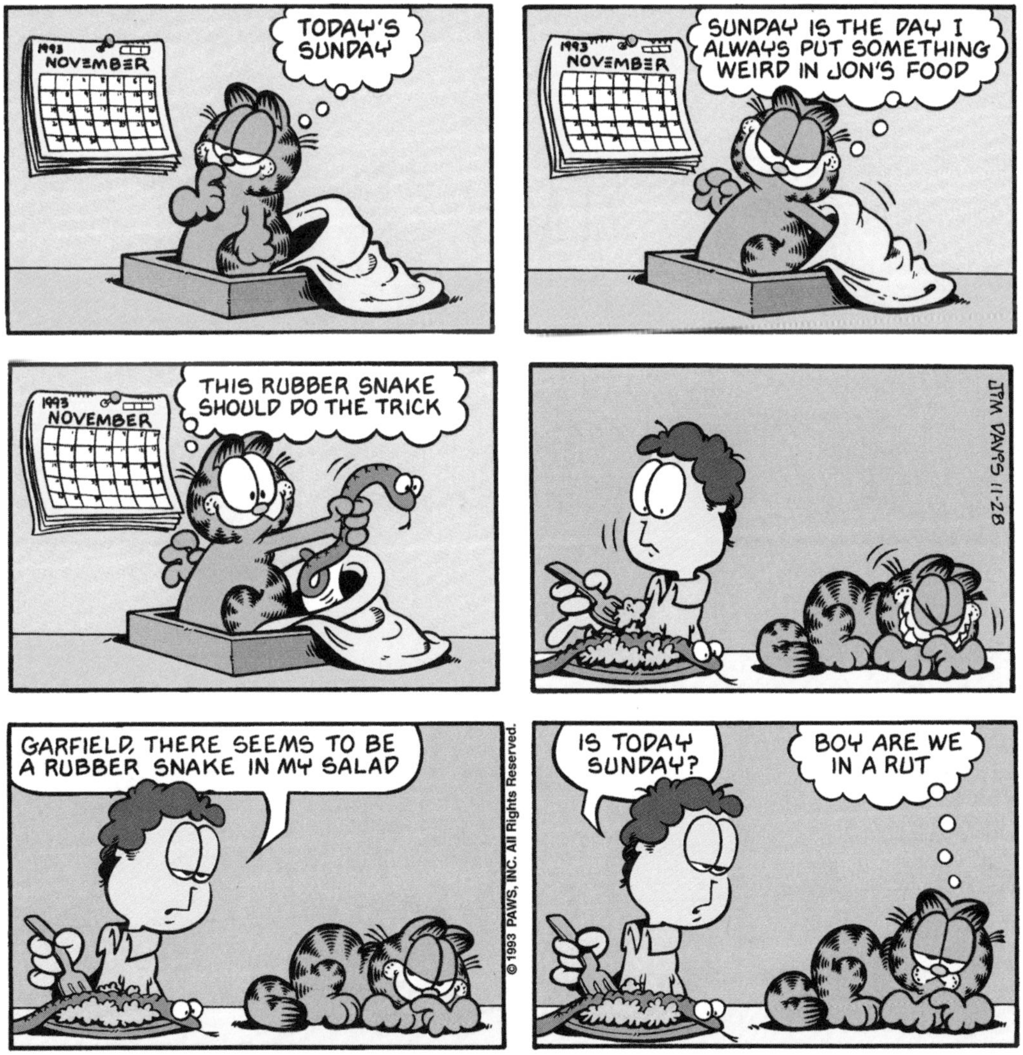

1993
NOVEMBER
TODAY'S SUNDAY
SUNDAY IS THE DAY I ALWAYS PUT SOMETHING WEIRD IN JON'S FOOD
THIS RUBBER SNAKE SHOULD DO THE TRICK
JPM DAVPS 11-28
GARFIELD, THERE SEEMS TO BE A RUBBER SNAKE IN MY SALAD
IS TODAY SUNDAY?
BOY ARE WE IN A RUT

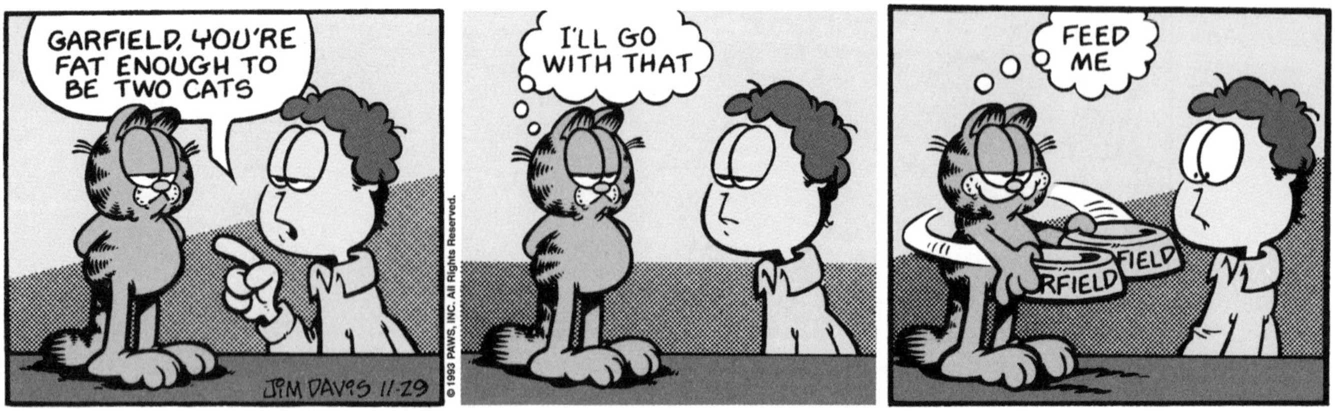
GARFIELD, YOU'RE FAT ENOUGH TO BE TWO CATS
I'LL GO WITH THAT
FEED ME
RFIELD
FIELD
JIM DAVIS 11-29
© 1993 PAWS, INC. All Rights Reserved.

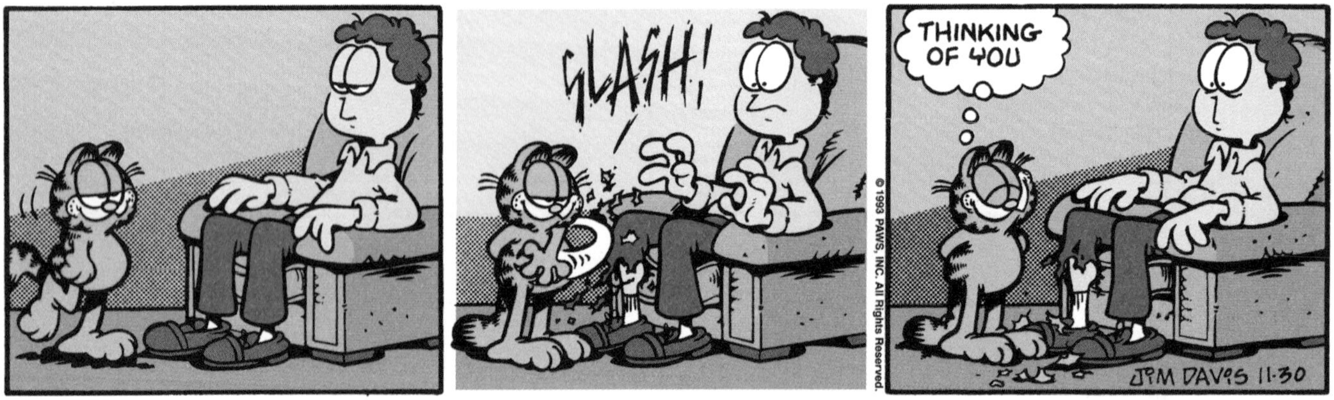
SLASH!
THINKING OF YOU
JIM DAVIS 11-30
© 1993 PAWS, INC. All Rights Reserved.

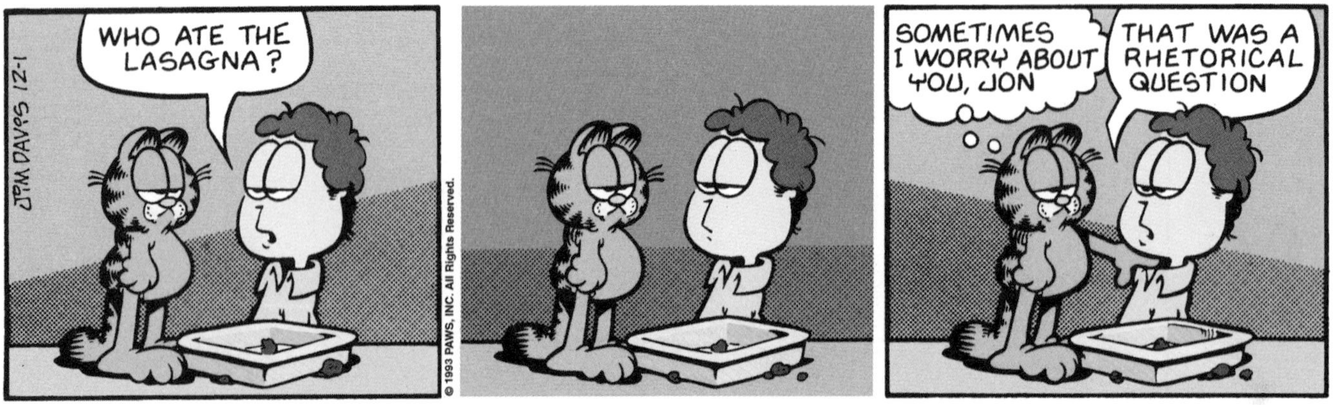
WHO ATE THE LASAGNA?
SOMETIMES I WORRY ABOUT YOU, JON
THAT WAS A RHETORICAL QUESTION
JIM DAVIS 12-1
© 1993 PAWS, INC. All Rights Reserved.

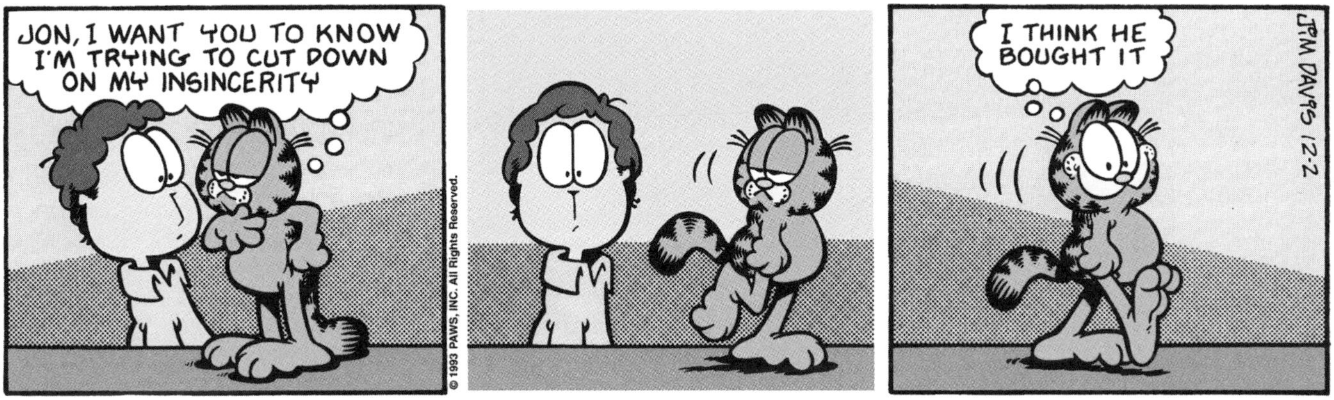
JON, I WANT YOU TO KNOW I'M TRYING TO CUT DOWN ON MY INSINCERITY
© 1993 PAWS, INC. All Rights Reserved.
I THINK HE BOUGHT IT
JIM DAVIS 12-2

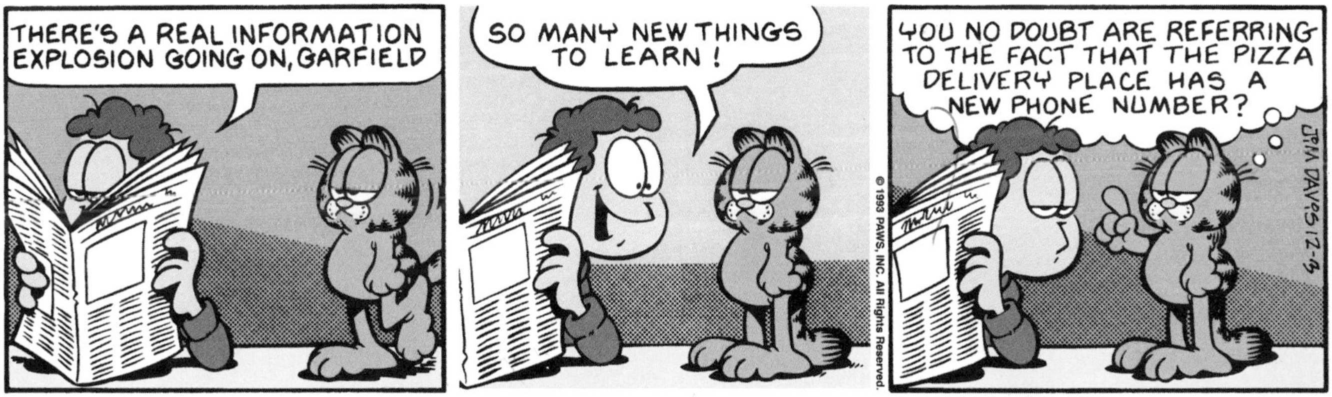
THERE'S A REAL INFORMATION EXPLOSION GOING ON, GARFIELD
SO MANY NEW THINGS TO LEARN!
© 1993 PAWS, INC. All Rights Reserved.
YOU NO DOUBT ARE REFERRING TO THE FACT THAT THE PIZZA DELIVERY PLACE HAS A NEW PHONE NUMBER?
JIM DAVIS 12-3

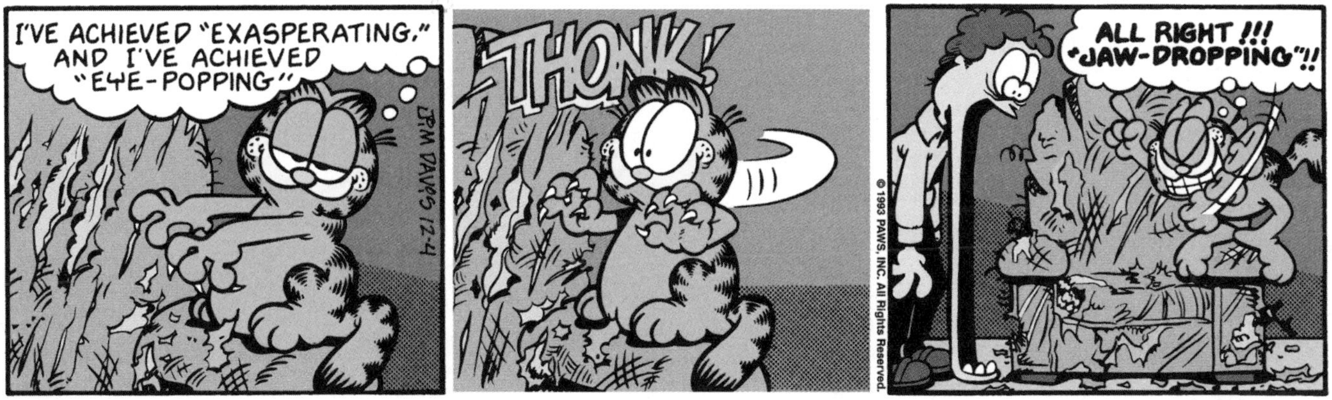
I'VE ACHIEVED "EXASPERATING," AND I'VE ACHIEVED "EYE-POPPING"
JIM DAVIS 12-4
THONK!
© 1993 PAWS, INC. All Rights Reserved.
ALL RIGHT!!! "JAW-DROPPING"!!

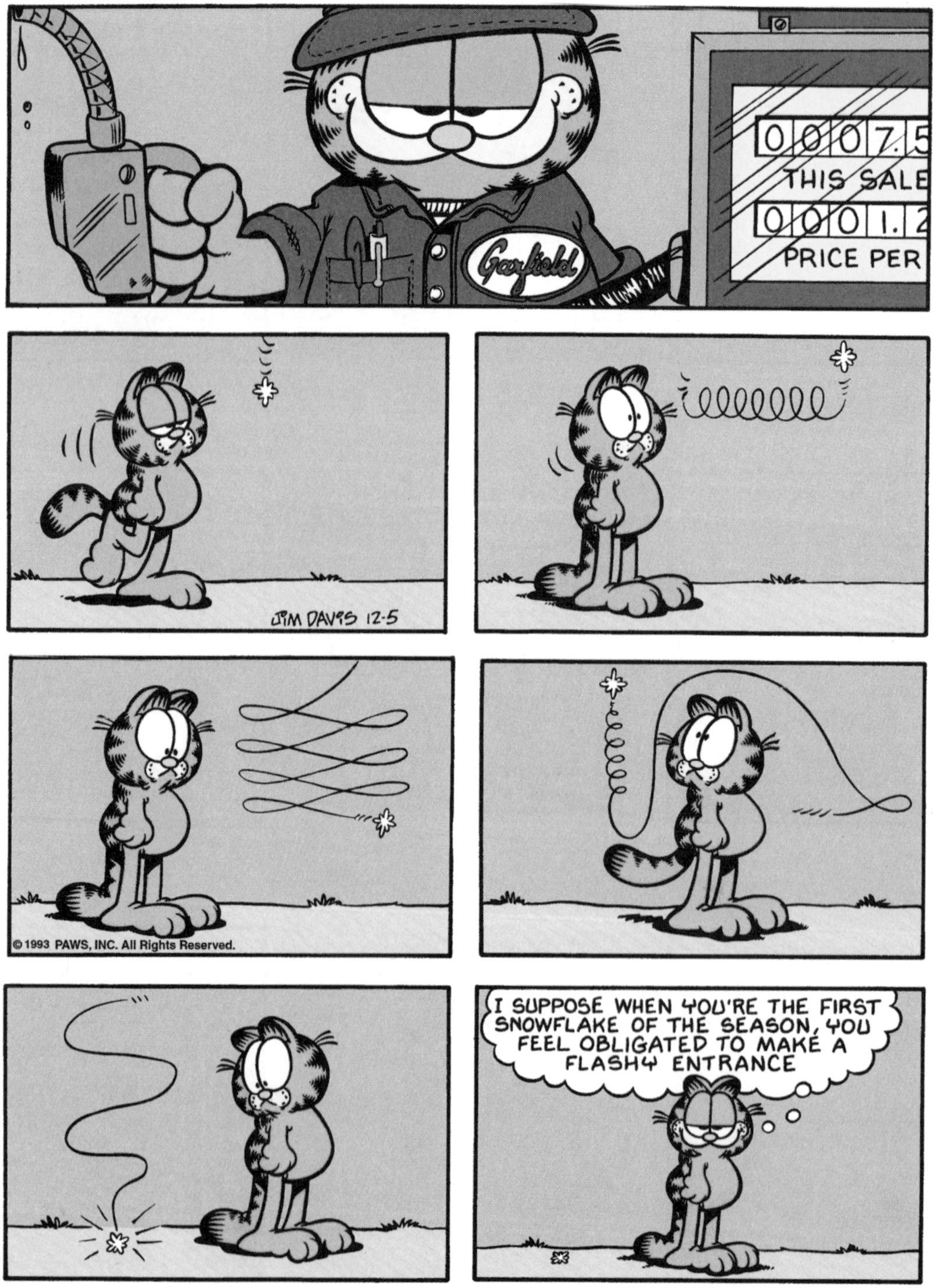

0007.5
THIS SALE
0001.2
PRICE PER
Garfield
JIM DAVIS 12-5
© 1993 PAWS, INC. All Rights Reserved.
I SUPPOSE WHEN YOU'RE THE FIRST SNOWFLAKE OF THE SEASON, YOU FEEL OBLIGATED TO MAKE A FLASHY ENTRANCE

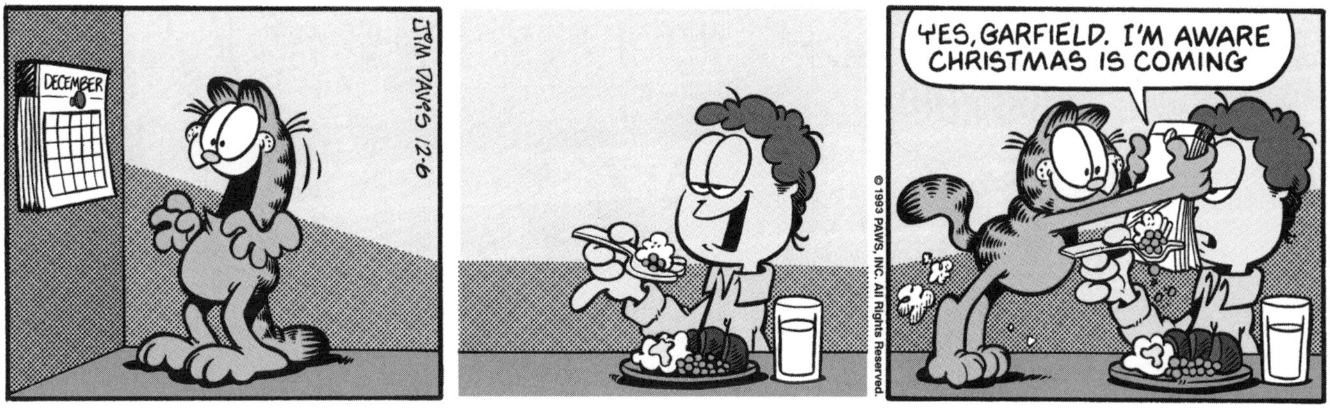
DECEMBER
JIM DAVIS 12-6
© 1993 PAWS, INC. All Rights Reserved.
YES, GARFIELD. I'M AWARE CHRISTMAS IS COMING

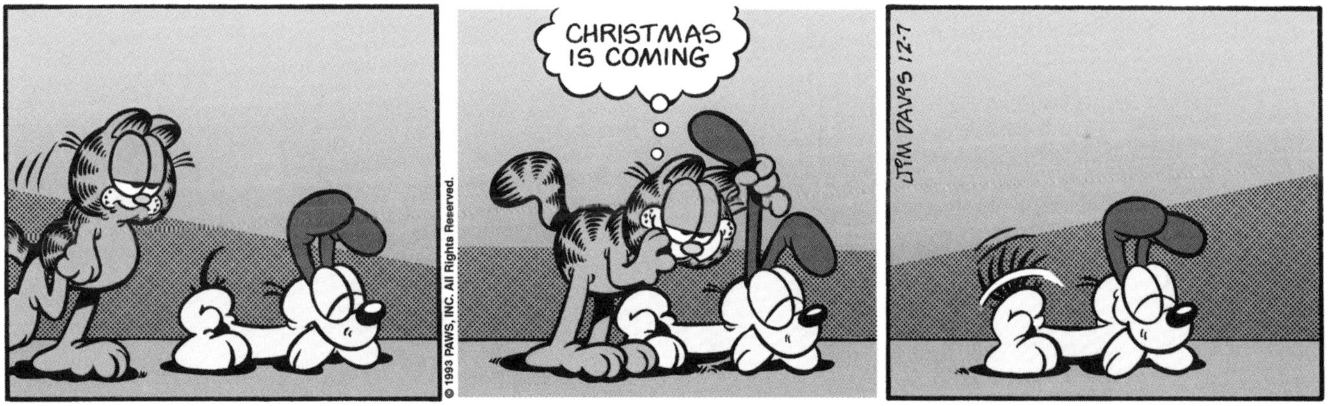
© 1993 PAWS, INC. All Rights Reserved.
CHRISTMAS IS COMING
JIM DAVIS 12-7

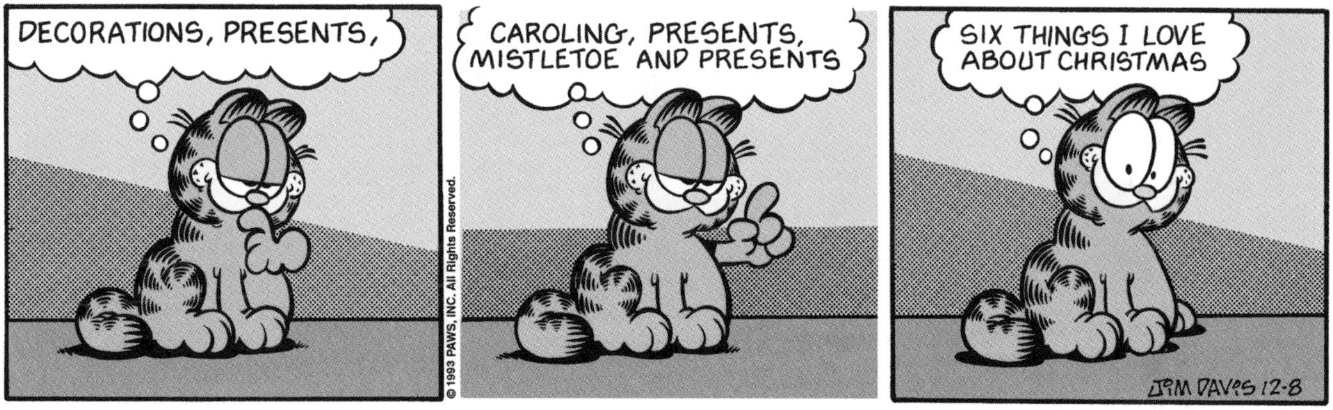
DECORATIONS, PRESENTS,
© 1993 PAWS, INC. All Rights Reserved.
CAROLING, PRESENTS, MISTLETOE AND PRESENTS
SIX THINGS I LOVE ABOUT CHRISTMAS
JIM DAVIS 12-8

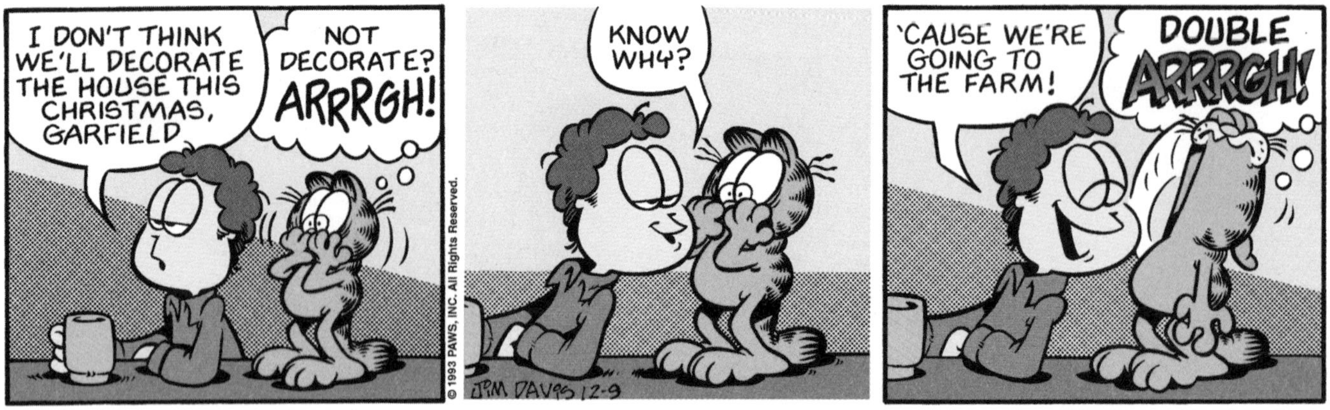
I DON'T THINK WE'LL DECORATE THE HOUSE THIS CHRISTMAS, GARFIELD
NOT DECORATE? ARRRGH!
© 1993 PAWS, INC. All Rights Reserved.
JIM DAVIS 12-9
KNOW WHY?
'CAUSE WE'RE GOING TO THE FARM!
DOUBLE ARRRGH!

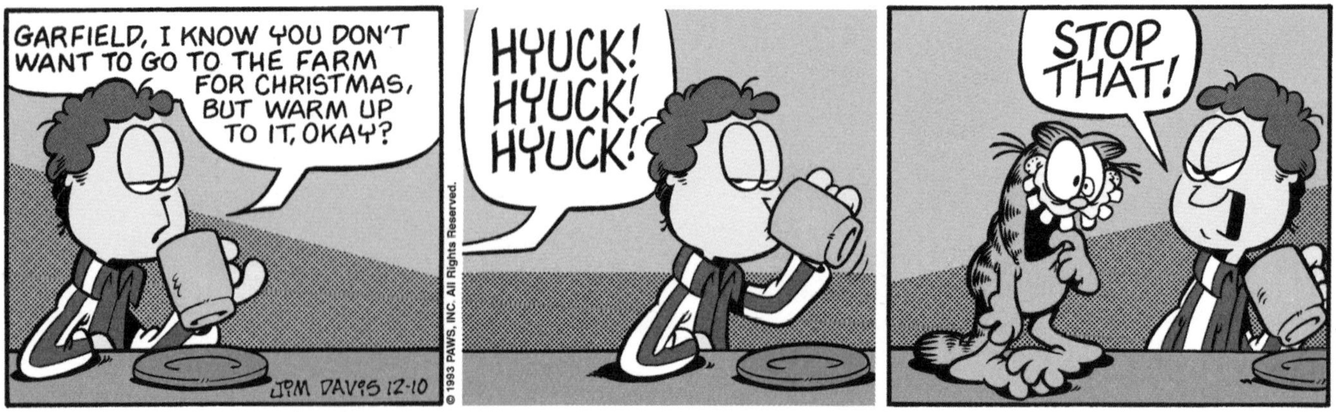
GARFIELD, I KNOW YOU DON'T WANT TO GO TO THE FARM FOR CHRISTMAS, BUT WARM UP TO IT, OKAY?
JIM DAVIS 12-10
© 1993 PAWS, INC. All Rights Reserved.
HYUCK! HYUCK! HYUCK!
STOP THAT!

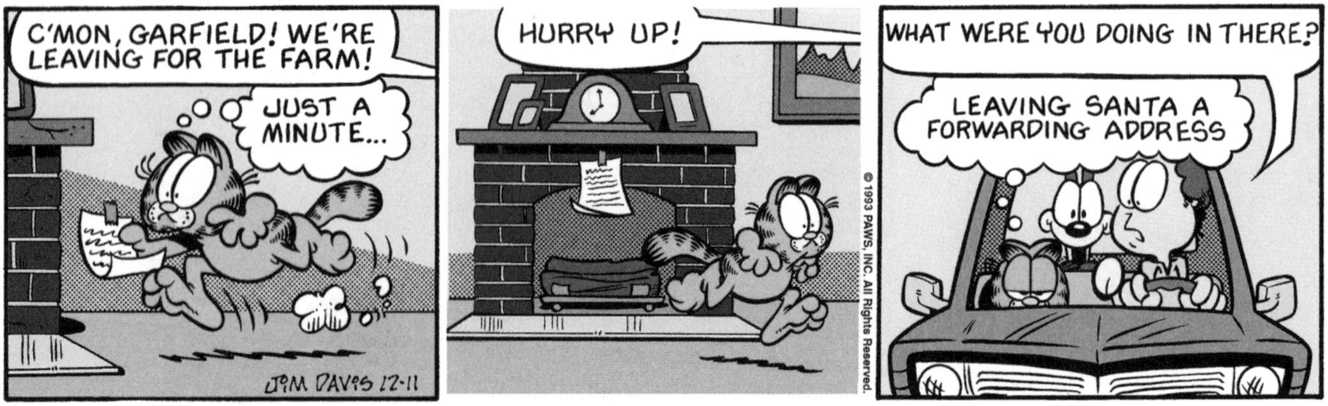
C'MON, GARFIELD! WE'RE LEAVING FOR THE FARM!
JUST A MINUTE...
JIM DAVIS 12-11
HURRY UP!
© 1993 PAWS, INC. All Rights Reserved.
WHAT WERE YOU DOING IN THERE?
LEAVING SANTA A FORWARDING ADDRESS

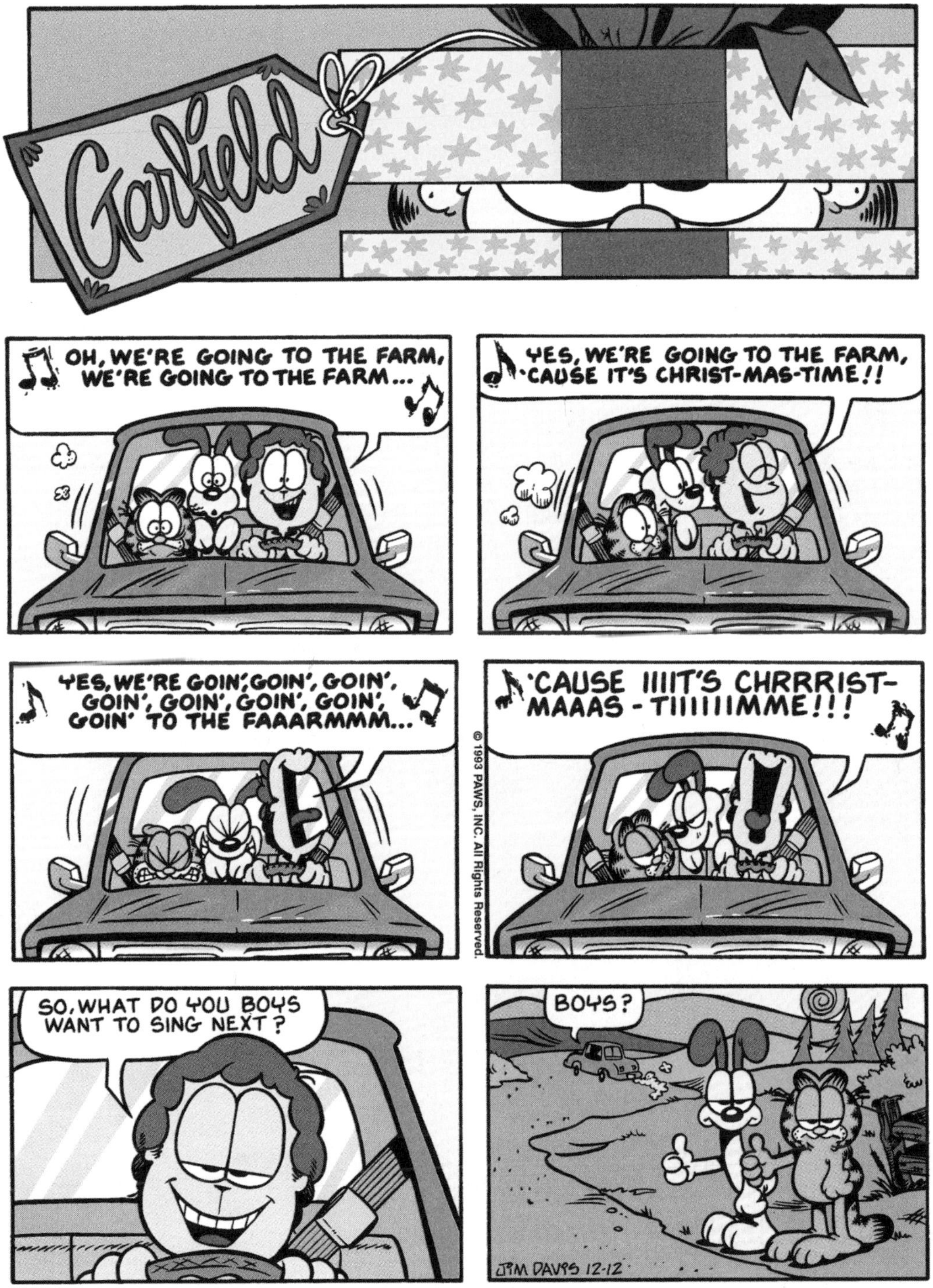
Garfield
OH, WE'RE GOING TO THE FARM, WE'RE GOING TO THE FARM...
YES, WE'RE GOING TO THE FARM, 'CAUSE IT'S CHRIST-MAS-TIME!!
YES, WE'RE GOIN', GOIN', GOIN', GOIN', GOIN', GOIN', GOIN', GOIN' TO THE FAAARMMM...
'CAUSE IIIIT'S CHRRRIST-MAAAS - TIIIIIIIMME!!!
SO, WHAT DO YOU BOYS WANT TO SING NEXT?
BOYS?
JIM DAVIS 12-12

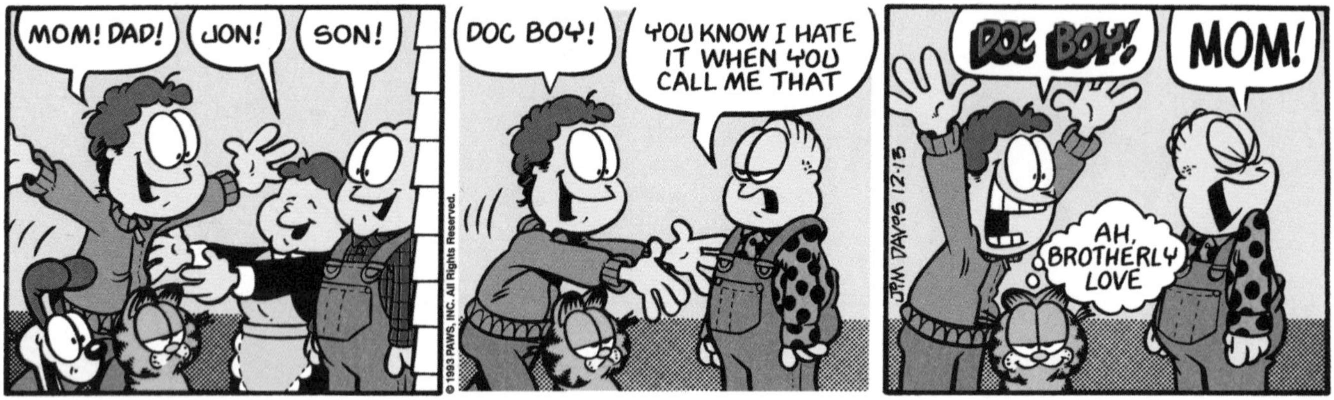
MOM! DAD!
JON!
SON!
© 1993 PAWS, INC. All Rights Reserved.
DOC BOY!
YOU KNOW I HATE IT WHEN YOU CALL ME THAT
DOC BOY!
MOM!
JIM DAVIS 12-13
AH, BROTHERLY LOVE

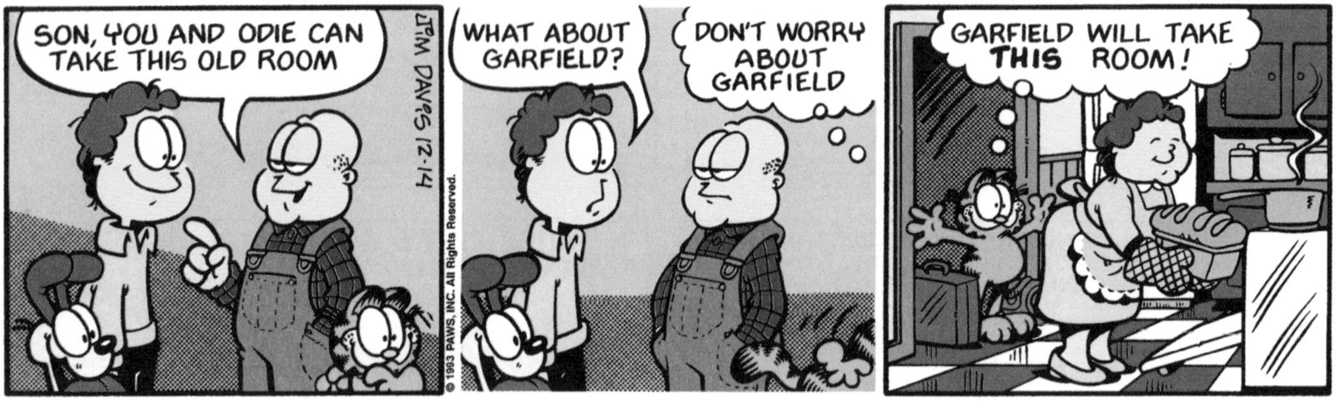
SON, YOU AND ODIE CAN TAKE THIS OLD ROOM
JIM DAVIS 12-14
© 1993 PAWS, INC. All Rights Reserved.
WHAT ABOUT GARFIELD?
DON'T WORRY ABOUT GARFIELD
GARFIELD WILL TAKE **THIS** ROOM!

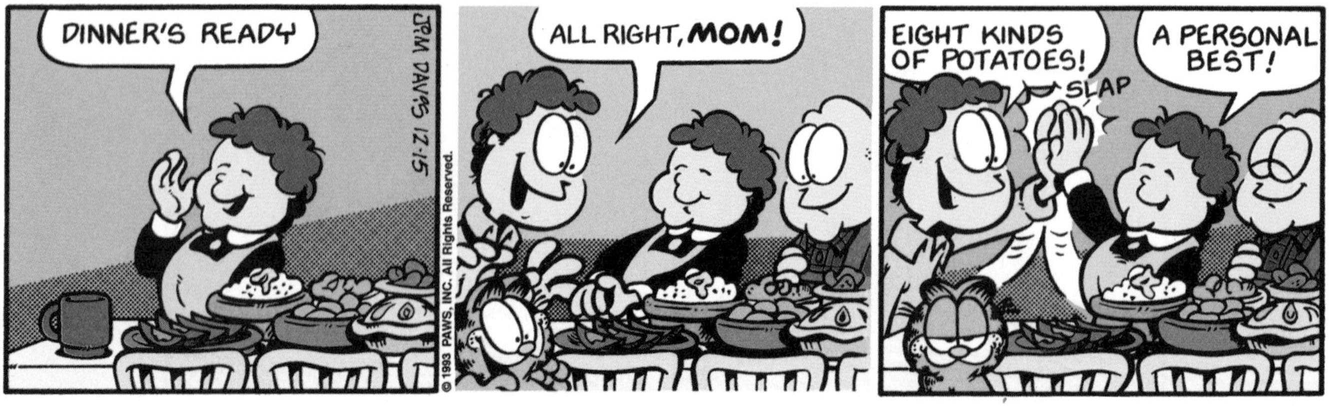
DINNER'S READY
JIM DAVIS 12-15
© 1993 PAWS, INC. All Rights Reserved.
ALL RIGHT, **MOM!**
EIGHT KINDS OF POTATOES!
SLAP
A PERSONAL BEST!

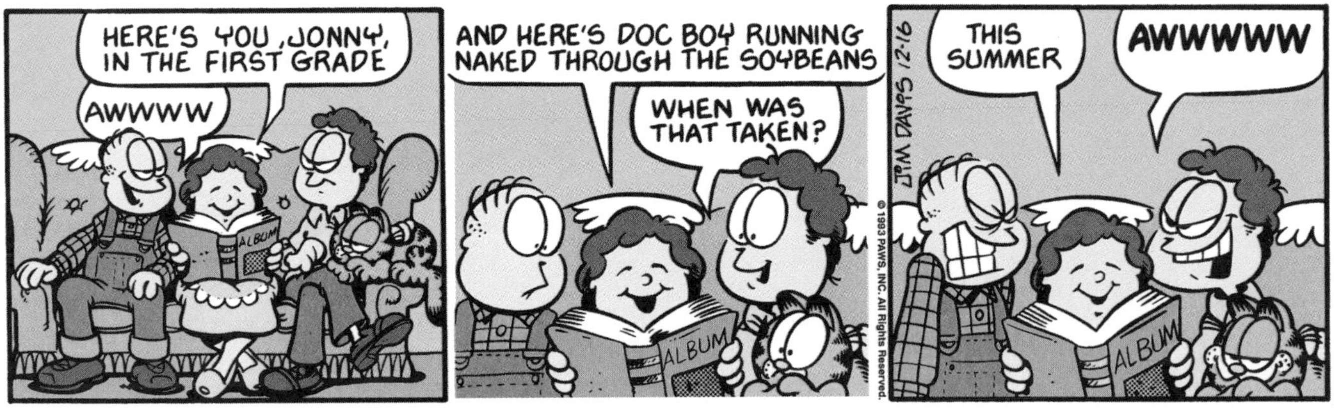
HERE'S YOU, JONNY, IN THE FIRST GRADE
AWWWW
AND HERE'S DOC BOY RUNNING NAKED THROUGH THE SOYBEANS
WHEN WAS THAT TAKEN?
THIS SUMMER
AWWWWW
JIM DAVIS 12-16
© 1993 PAWS, INC. All Rights Reserved.

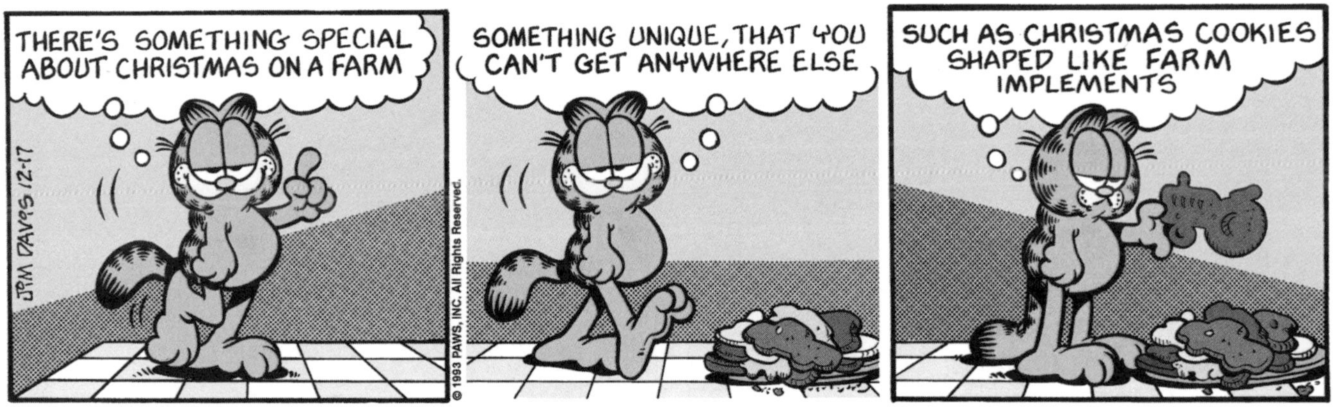
THERE'S SOMETHING SPECIAL ABOUT CHRISTMAS ON A FARM
SOMETHING UNIQUE, THAT YOU CAN'T GET ANYWHERE ELSE
SUCH AS CHRISTMAS COOKIES SHAPED LIKE FARM IMPLEMENTS
JIM DAVIS 12-17
© 1993 PAWS, INC. All Rights Reserved.

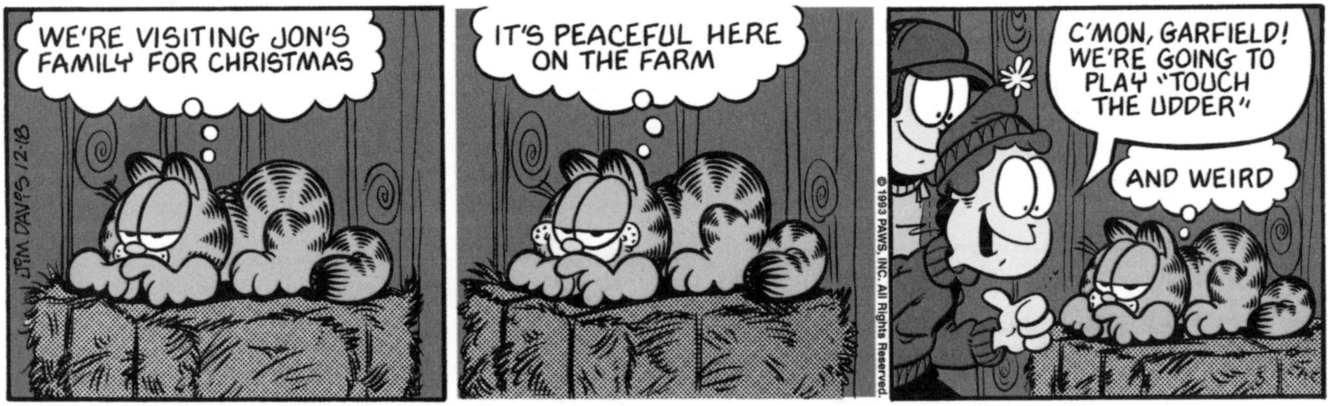
WE'RE VISITING JON'S FAMILY FOR CHRISTMAS
IT'S PEACEFUL HERE ON THE FARM
C'MON, GARFIELD! WE'RE GOING TO PLAY "TOUCH THE UDDER"
AND WEIRD
JIM DAVIS 12-18
© 1993 PAWS, INC. All Rights Reserved.

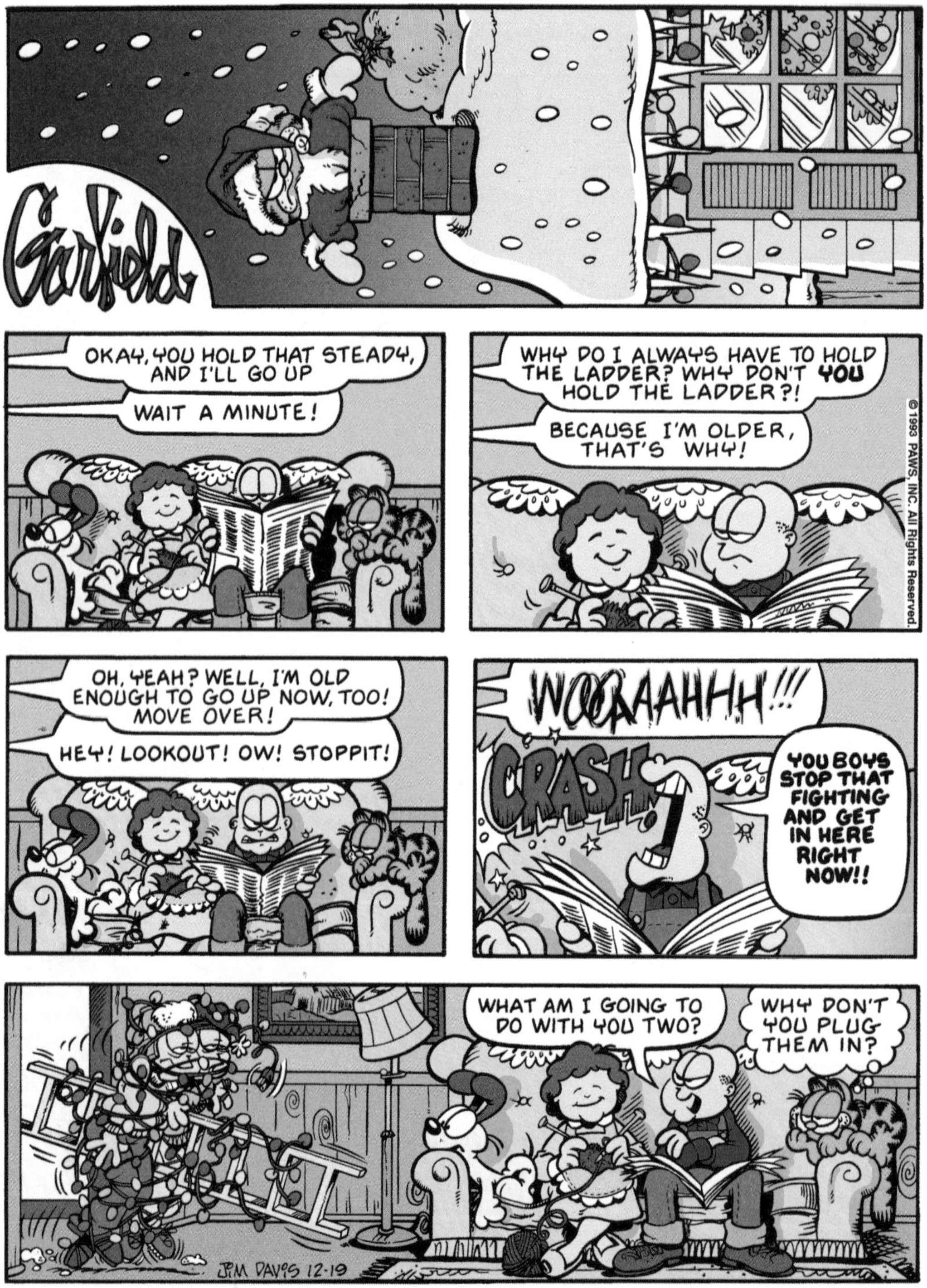

Garfield
OKAY, YOU HOLD THAT STEADY, AND I'LL GO UP
WAIT A MINUTE!
WHY DO I ALWAYS HAVE TO HOLD THE LADDER? WHY DON'T **YOU** HOLD THE LADDER?!
BECAUSE I'M OLDER, THAT'S WHY!
OH, YEAH? WELL, I'M OLD ENOUGH TO GO UP NOW, TOO! MOVE OVER!
HEY! LOOKOUT! OW! STOPPIT!
WOOAAAHHH!!!
CRASH
YOU BOYS STOP THAT FIGHTING AND GET IN HERE RIGHT NOW!!
WHAT AM I GOING TO DO WITH YOU TWO?
WHY DON'T YOU PLUG THEM IN?
JIM DAVIS 12-19

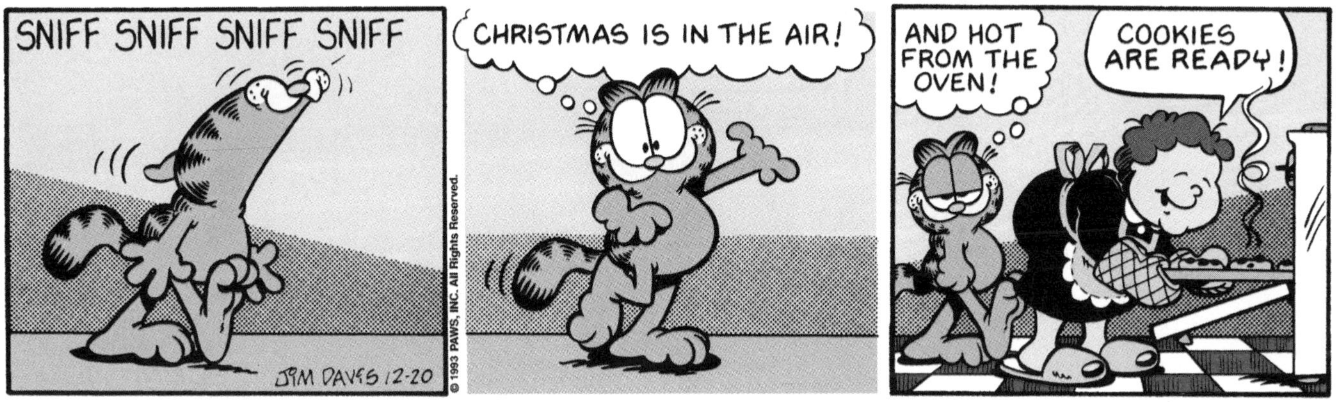
SNIFF SNIFF SNIFF SNIFF
JIM DAVIS 12-20
© 1993 PAWS, INC. All Rights Reserved.
CHRISTMAS IS IN THE AIR!
AND HOT FROM THE OVEN!
COOKIES ARE READY!

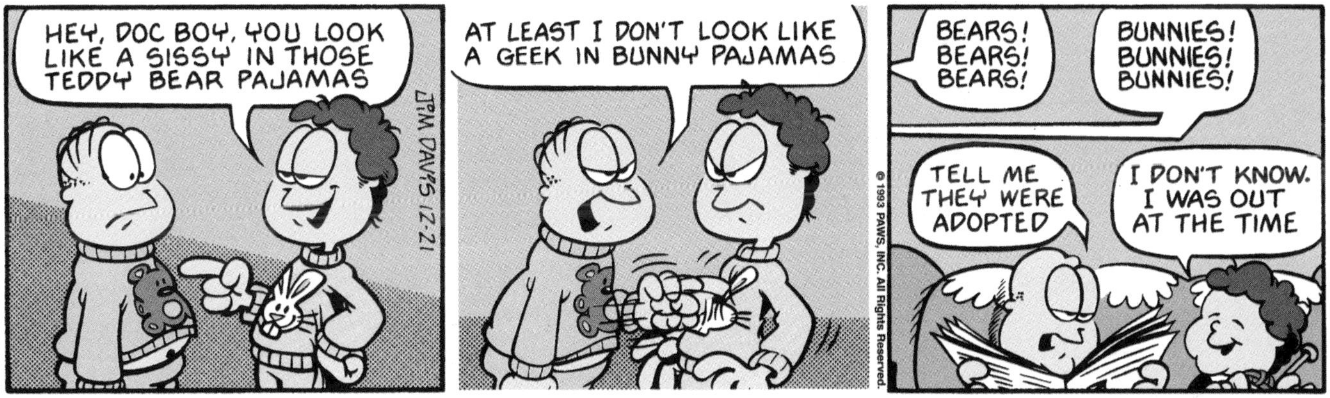
HEY, DOC BOY, YOU LOOK LIKE A SISSY IN THOSE TEDDY BEAR PAJAMAS
JIM DAVIS 12-21
AT LEAST I DON'T LOOK LIKE A GEEK IN BUNNY PAJAMAS
© 1993 PAWS, INC. All Rights Reserved.
BEARS! BEARS! BEARS!
BUNNIES! BUNNIES! BUNNIES!
TELL ME THEY WERE ADOPTED
I DON'T KNOW. I WAS OUT AT THE TIME

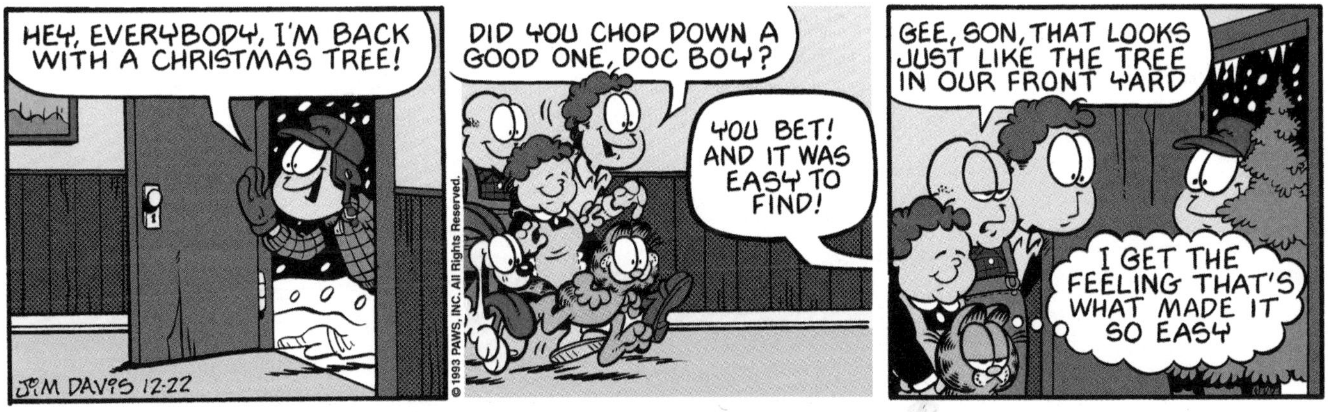
HEY, EVERYBODY, I'M BACK WITH A CHRISTMAS TREE!
JIM DAVIS 12-22
© 1993 PAWS, INC. All Rights Reserved.
DID YOU CHOP DOWN A GOOD ONE, DOC BOY?
YOU BET! AND IT WAS EASY TO FIND!
GEE, SON, THAT LOOKS JUST LIKE THE TREE IN OUR FRONT YARD
I GET THE FEELING THAT'S WHAT MADE IT SO EASY

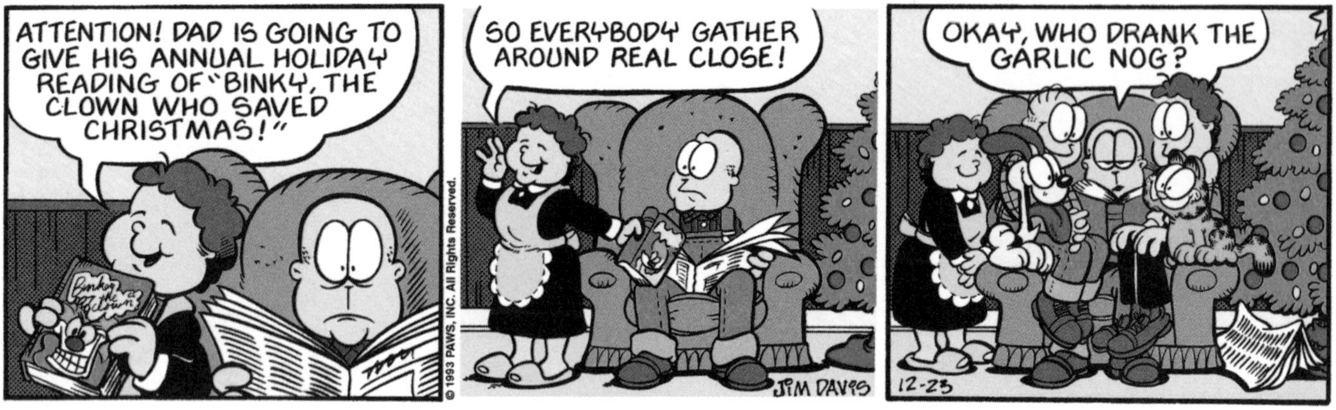
ATTENTION! DAD IS GOING TO GIVE HIS ANNUAL HOLIDAY READING OF "BINKY, THE CLOWN WHO SAVED CHRISTMAS!"
© 1993 PAWS, INC. All Rights Reserved.
SO EVERYBODY GATHER AROUND REAL CLOSE!
JIM DAVIS
OKAY, WHO DRANK THE GARLIC NOG?
12-23

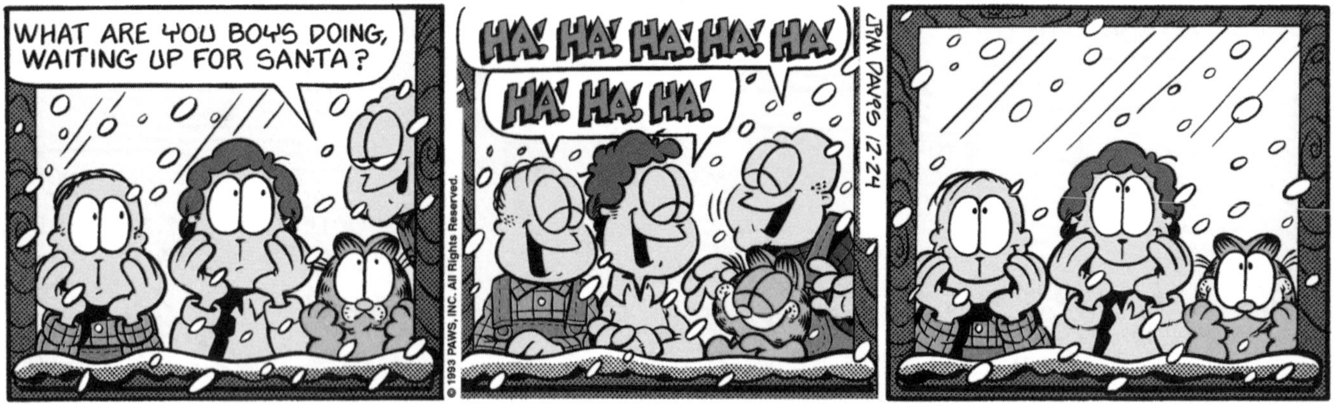
WHAT ARE YOU BOYS DOING, WAITING UP FOR SANTA?
© 1993 PAWS, INC. All Rights Reserved.
HA! HA! HA! HA! HA!
HA! HA! HA!
JIM DAVIS 12-24

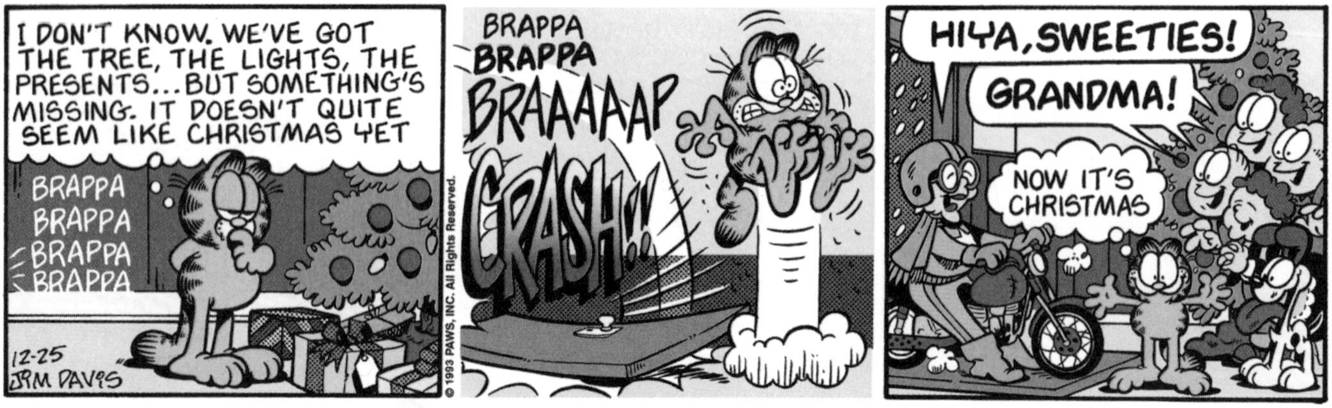
I DON'T KNOW. WE'VE GOT THE TREE, THE LIGHTS, THE PRESENTS... BUT SOMETHING'S MISSING. IT DOESN'T QUITE SEEM LIKE CHRISTMAS YET
BRAPPA
BRAPPA
BRAPPA
BRAPPA
12-25
JIM DAVIS
© 1993 PAWS, INC. All Rights Reserved.
BRAPPA
BRAPPA
BRAAAAAP
CRASH!!
HIYA, SWEETIES!
GRANDMA!
NOW IT'S CHRISTMAS

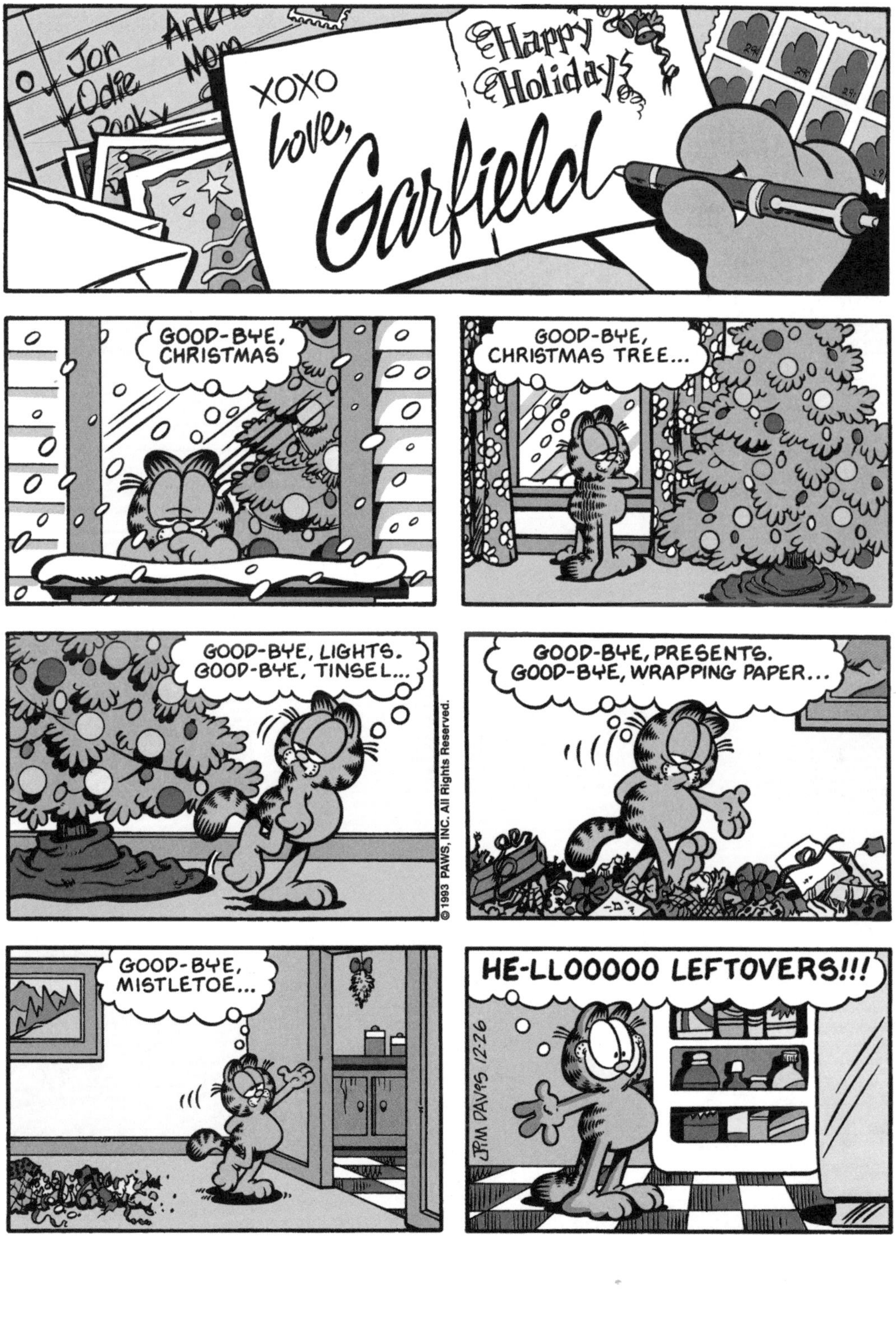
Jon
Odie
Arlene
Mom
XOXO
love,
Garfield
Happy Holidays
GOOD-BYE, CHRISTMAS
GOOD-BYE, CHRISTMAS TREE...
GOOD-BYE, LIGHTS. GOOD-BYE, TINSEL...
© 1993 PAWS, INC. All Rights Reserved.
GOOD-BYE, PRESENTS. GOOD-BYE, WRAPPING PAPER...
GOOD-BYE, MISTLETOE...
HE-LLOOOOO LEFTOVERS!!!
JPM DAVIS 12-26

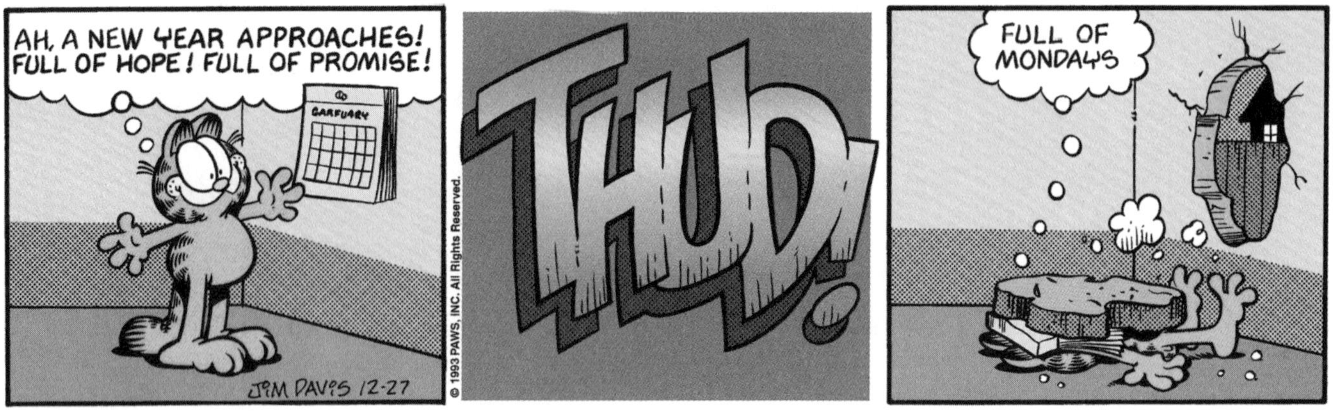
AH, A NEW YEAR APPROACHES! FULL OF HOPE! FULL OF PROMISE!
GARFUARY
JIM DAVIS 12-27
© 1993 PAWS, INC. All Rights Reserved.
THUD!
FULL OF MONDAYS

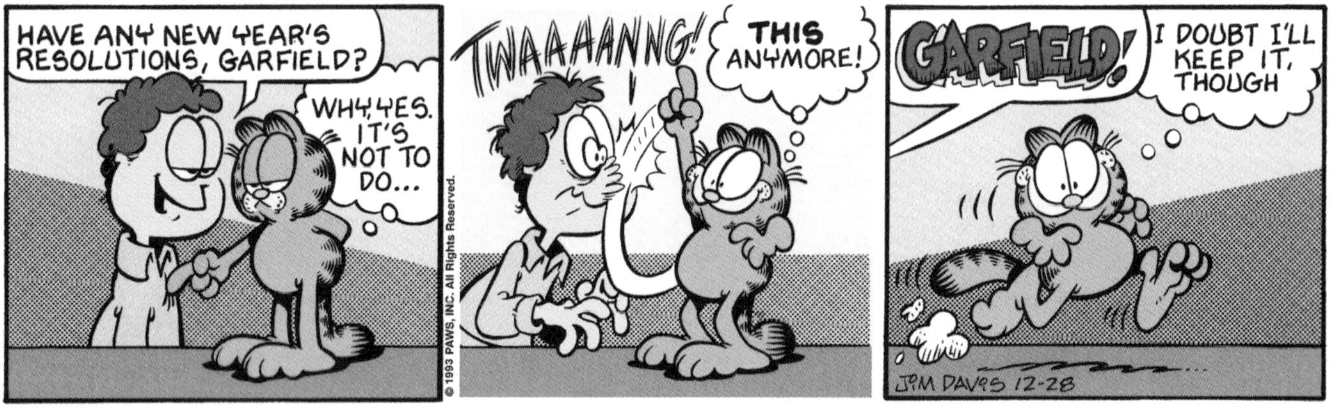
HAVE ANY NEW YEAR'S RESOLUTIONS, GARFIELD?
WHY, YES. IT'S NOT TO DO...
© 1993 PAWS, INC. All Rights Reserved.
TWAAAANNG!
THIS ANYMORE!
GARFIELD!
I DOUBT I'LL KEEP IT, THOUGH
JIM DAVIS 12-28

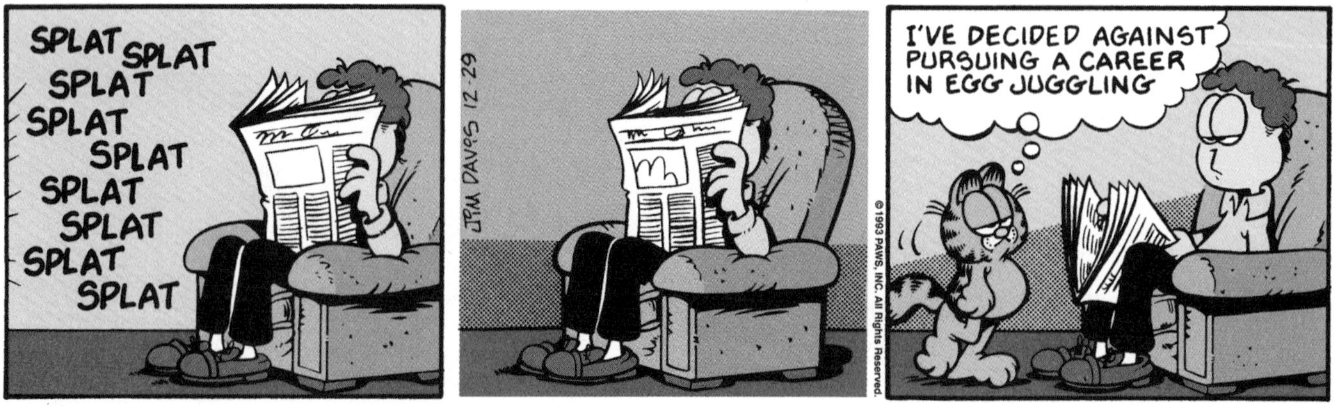
SPLAT SPLAT
SPLAT
SPLAT
SPLAT
SPLAT
SPLAT
SPLAT
SPLAT
JIM DAVIS 12-29
I'VE DECIDED AGAINST PURSUING A CAREER IN EGG JUGGLING
© 1993 PAWS, INC. All Rights Reserved.

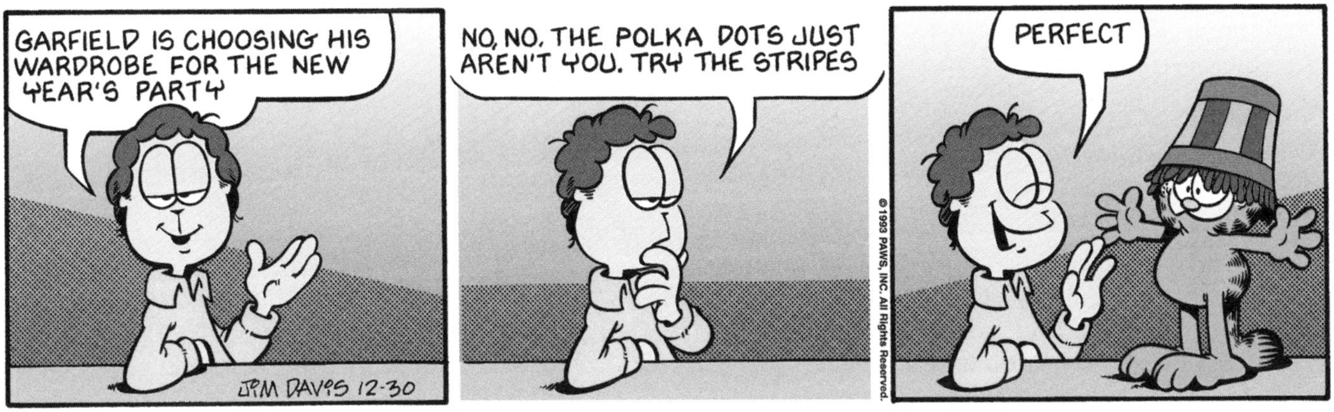
GARFIELD IS CHOOSING HIS WARDROBE FOR THE NEW YEAR'S PARTY
JIM DAVIS 12-30
NO, NO. THE POLKA DOTS JUST AREN'T YOU. TRY THE STRIPES
PERFECT

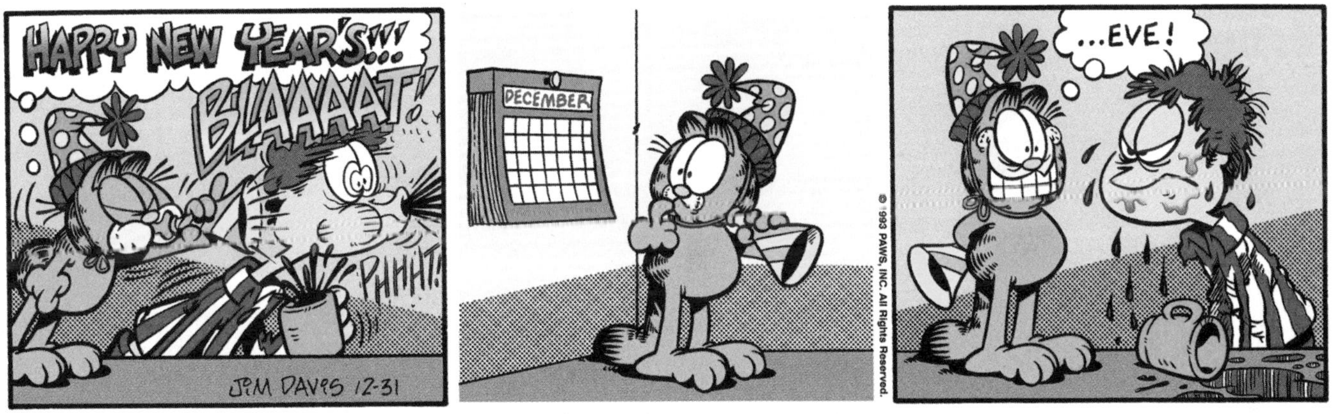
HAPPY NEW YEAR'S!!!
BLAAAAT!
PHHHT!
JIM DAVIS 12-31
DECEMBER
...EVE!

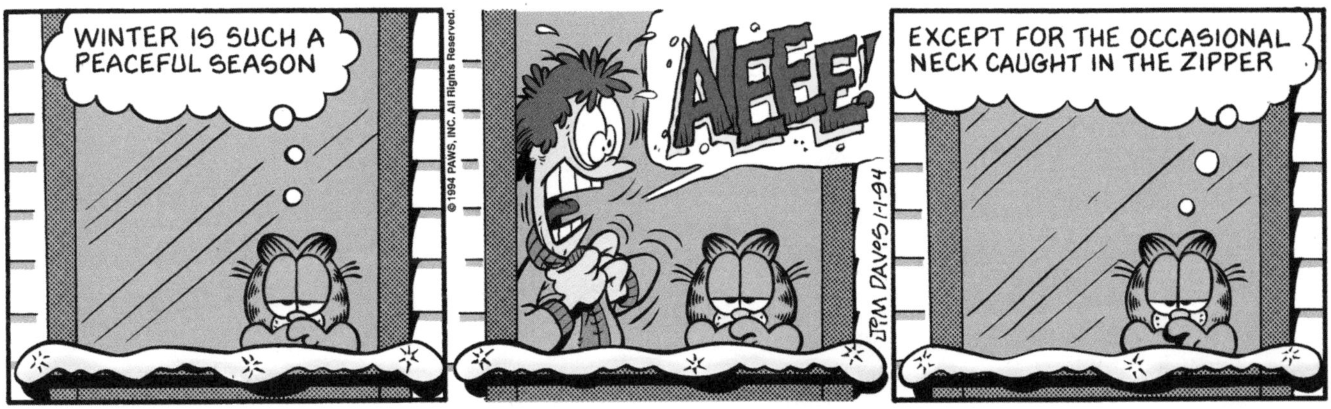
WINTER IS SUCH A PEACEFUL SEASON
AIEEE!
JIM DAVIS 1-1-94
EXCEPT FOR THE OCCASIONAL NECK CAUGHT IN THE ZIPPER

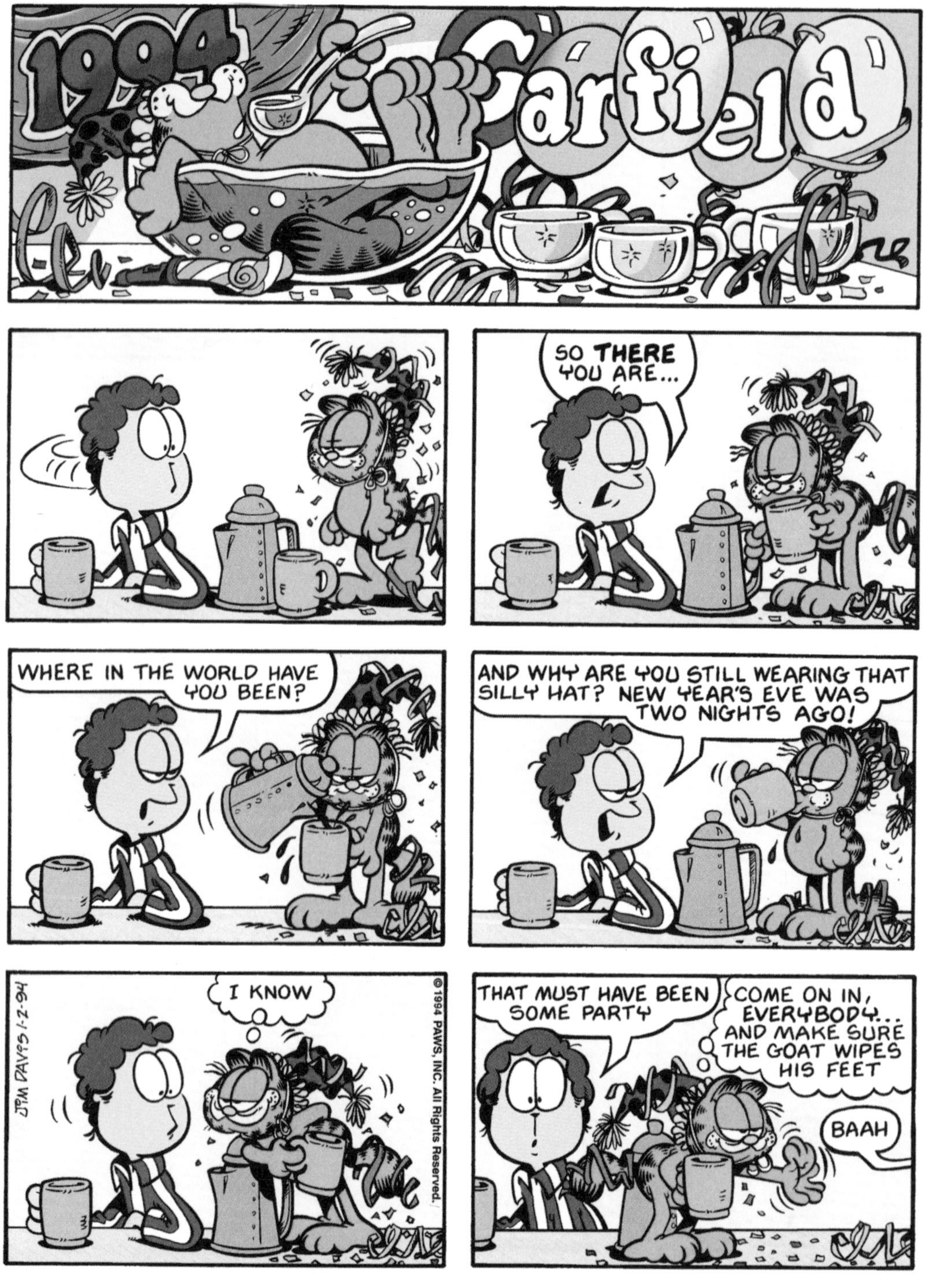
1994
Garfield
SO THERE YOU ARE...
WHERE IN THE WORLD HAVE YOU BEEN?
AND WHY ARE YOU STILL WEARING THAT SILLY HAT? NEW YEAR'S EVE WAS TWO NIGHTS AGO!
I KNOW
JPM DAVIS 1-2-94
© 1994 PAWS, INC. All Rights Reserved.
THAT MUST HAVE BEEN SOME PARTY
COME ON IN, EVERYBODY... AND MAKE SURE THE GOAT WIPES HIS FEET
BAAH

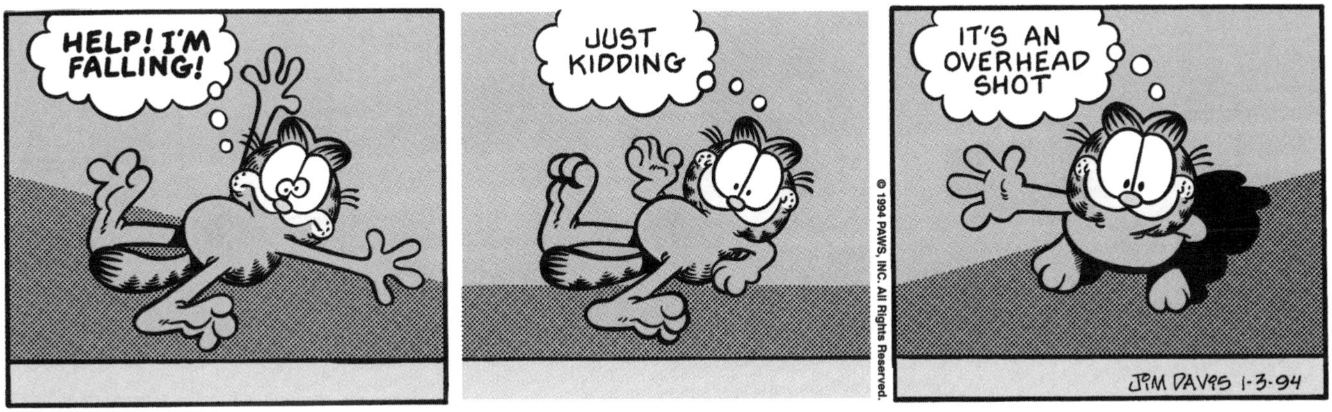
HELP! I'M FALLING!
JUST KIDDING
IT'S AN OVERHEAD SHOT
© 1994 PAWS, INC. All Rights Reserved.
JIM DAVIS 1-3-94

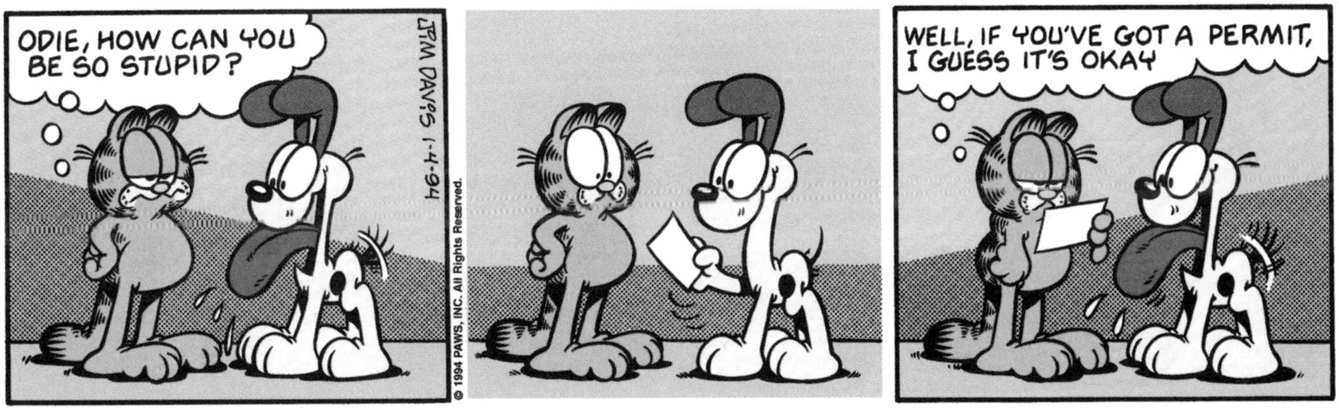
ODIE, HOW CAN YOU BE SO STUPID?
JIM DAVIS 1-4-94
© 1994 PAWS, INC. All Rights Reserved.
WELL, IF YOU'VE GOT A PERMIT, I GUESS IT'S OKAY

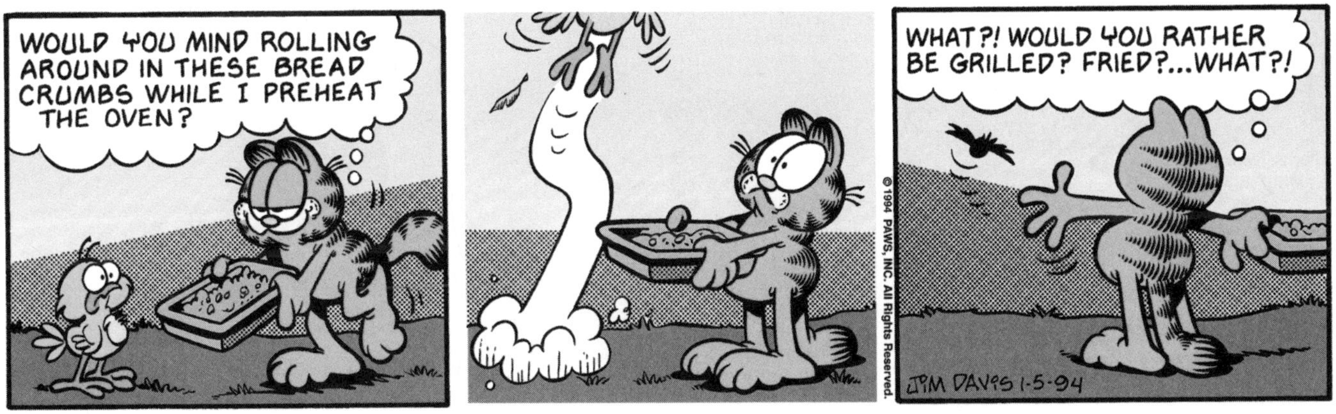
WOULD YOU MIND ROLLING AROUND IN THESE BREAD CRUMBS WHILE I PREHEAT THE OVEN?
© 1994 PAWS, INC. All Rights Reserved.
WHAT?! WOULD YOU RATHER BE GRILLED? FRIED?...WHAT?!
JIM DAVIS 1-5-94

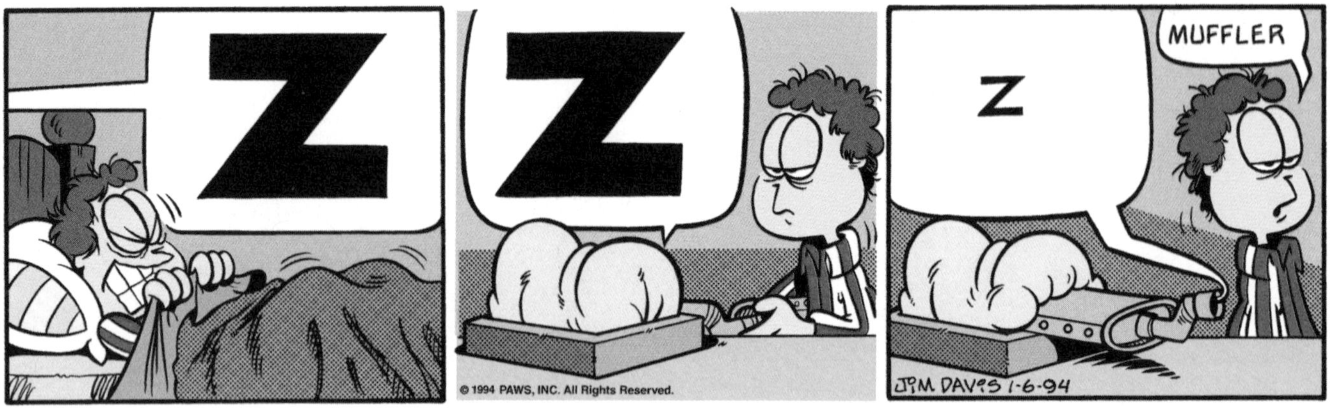
Z
Z
Z
MUFFLER
© 1994 PAWS, INC. All Rights Reserved.
JIM DAVIS 1-6-94

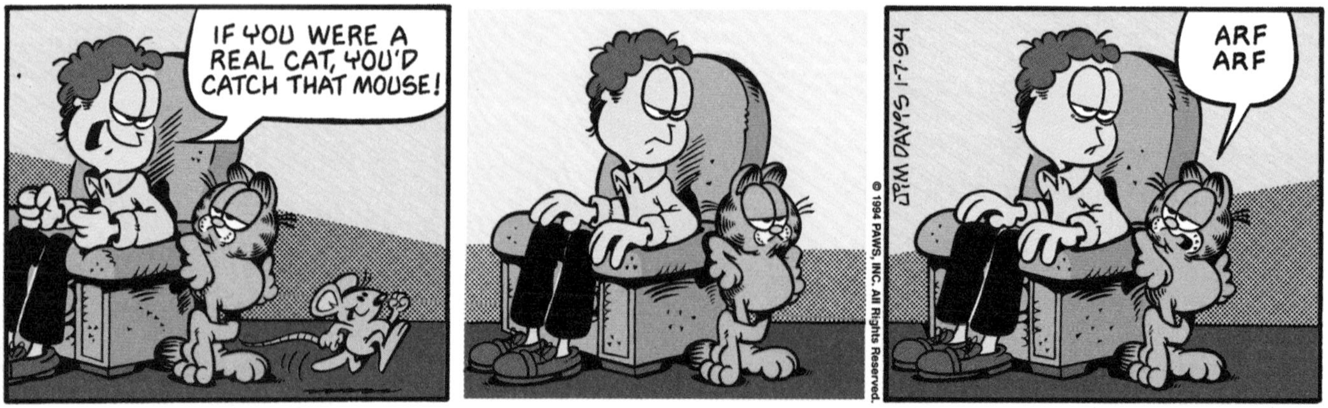
IF YOU WERE A REAL CAT, YOU'D CATCH THAT MOUSE!
JIM DAVIS 1-7-94
© 1994 PAWS, INC. All Rights Reserved.
ARF ARF

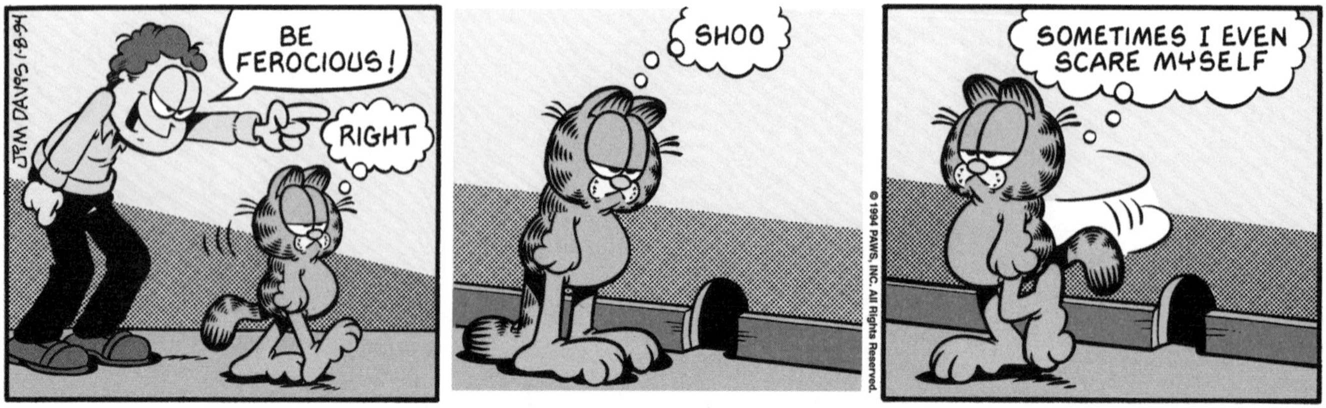
JIM DAVIS 1-8-94
BE FEROCIOUS!
RIGHT
SHOO
© 1994 PAWS, INC. All Rights Reserved.
SOMETIMES I EVEN SCARE MYSELF

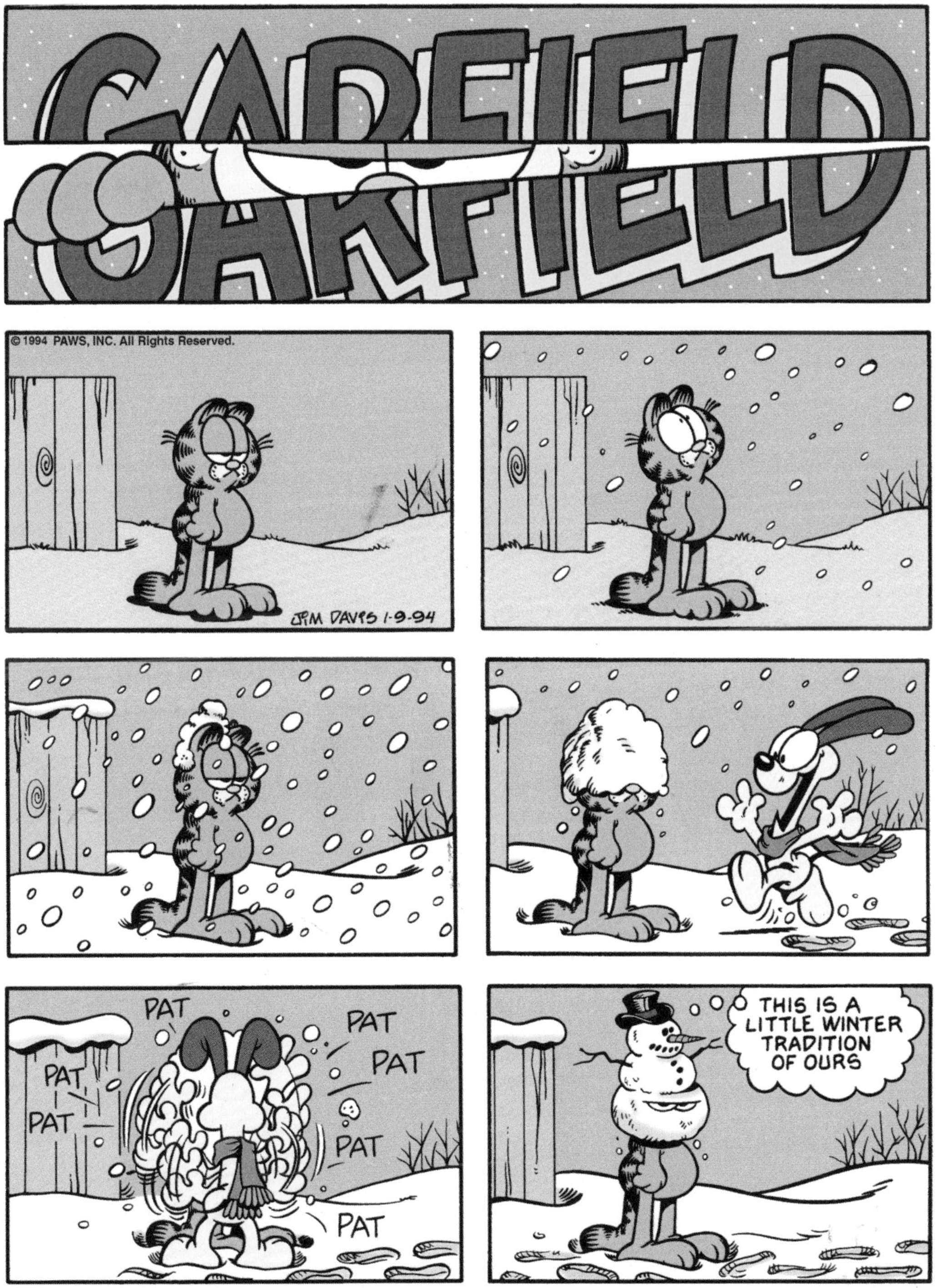
GARFIELD
© 1994 PAWS, INC. All Rights Reserved.
JIM DAVIS 1-9-94
PAT
PAT
PAT
PAT
PAT
PAT
PAT
THIS IS A LITTLE WINTER TRADITION OF OURS

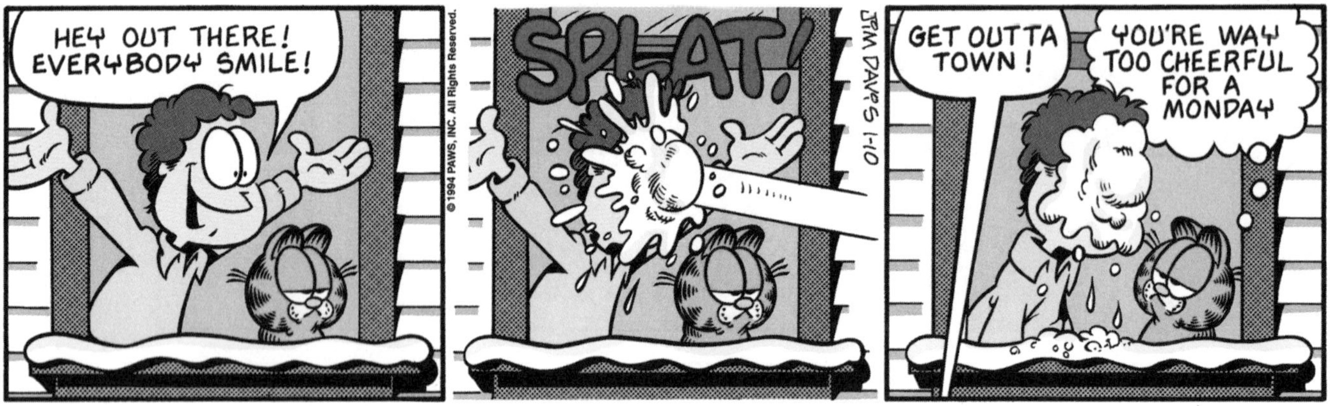
HEY OUT THERE! EVERYBODY SMILE!
© 1994 PAWS, INC. All Rights Reserved.
SPLAT!
JIM DAVIS 1-10
GET OUTTA TOWN!
YOU'RE WAY TOO CHEERFUL FOR A MONDAY

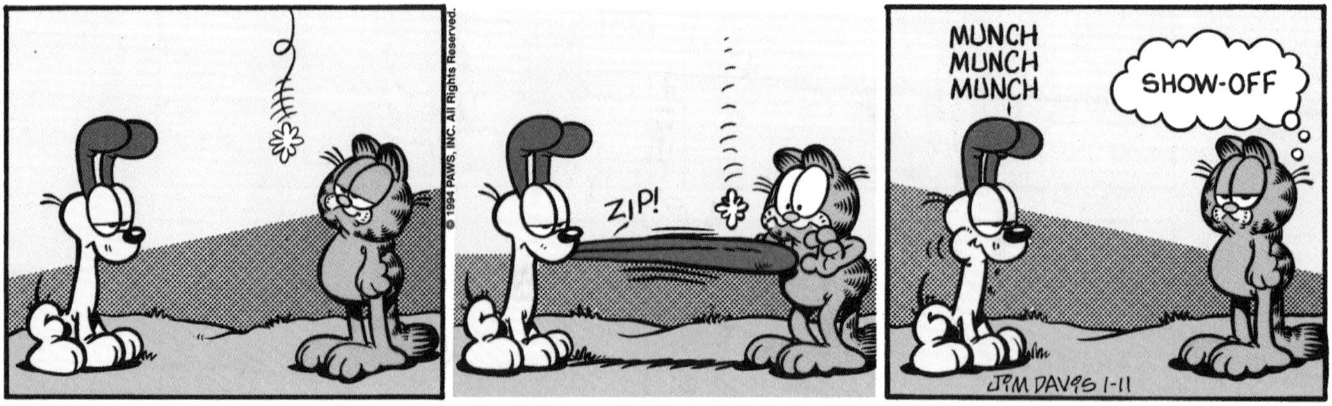
© 1994 PAWS, INC. All Rights Reserved.
ZIP!
MUNCH MUNCH MUNCH
SHOW-OFF
JIM DAVIS 1-11

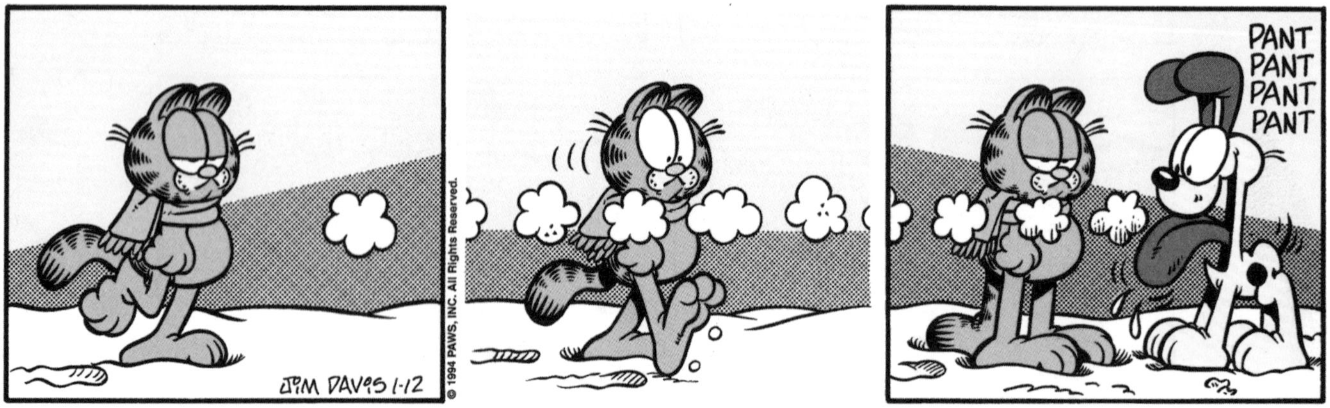
JIM DAVIS 1-12
© 1994 PAWS, INC. All Rights Reserved.
PANT PANT PANT PANT

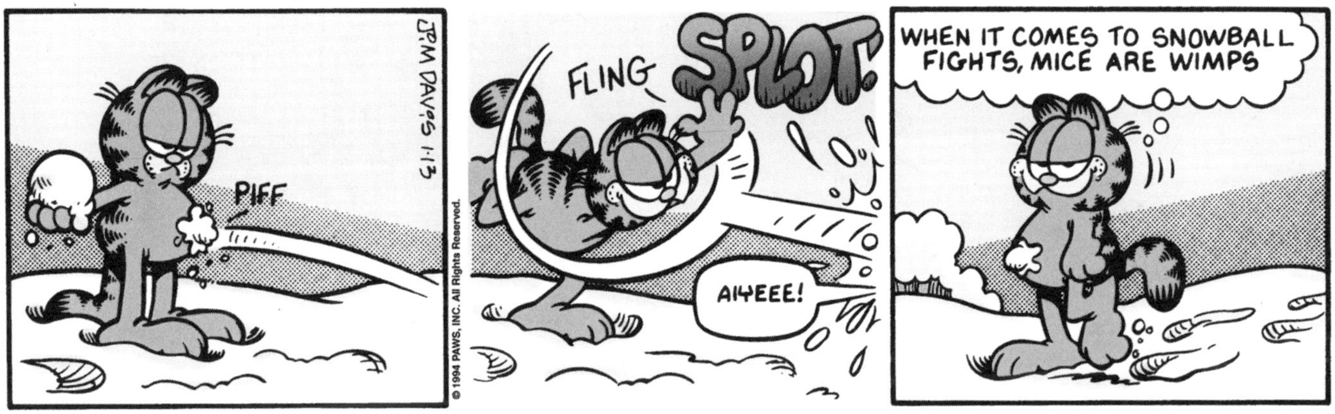
JIM DAVIS 1.13
PIFF
© 1994 PAWS, INC. All Rights Reserved.
FLING
SPLOT!
AIYEEE!
WHEN IT COMES TO SNOWBALL FIGHTS, MICE ARE WIMPS

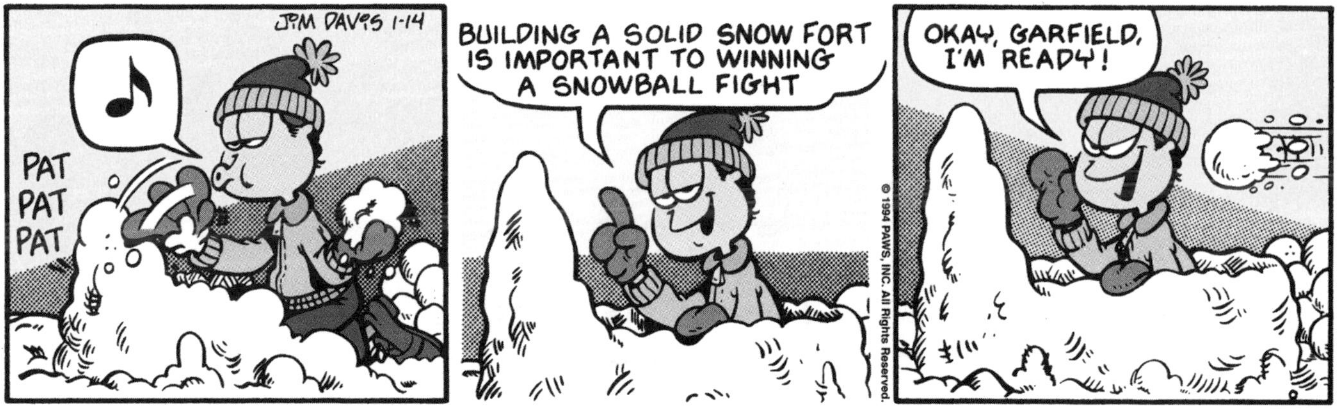
JIM DAVIS 1-14
♪
PAT PAT PAT
BUILDING A SOLID SNOW FORT IS IMPORTANT TO WINNING A SNOWBALL FIGHT
© 1994 PAWS, INC. All Rights Reserved.
OKAY, GARFIELD, I'M READY!

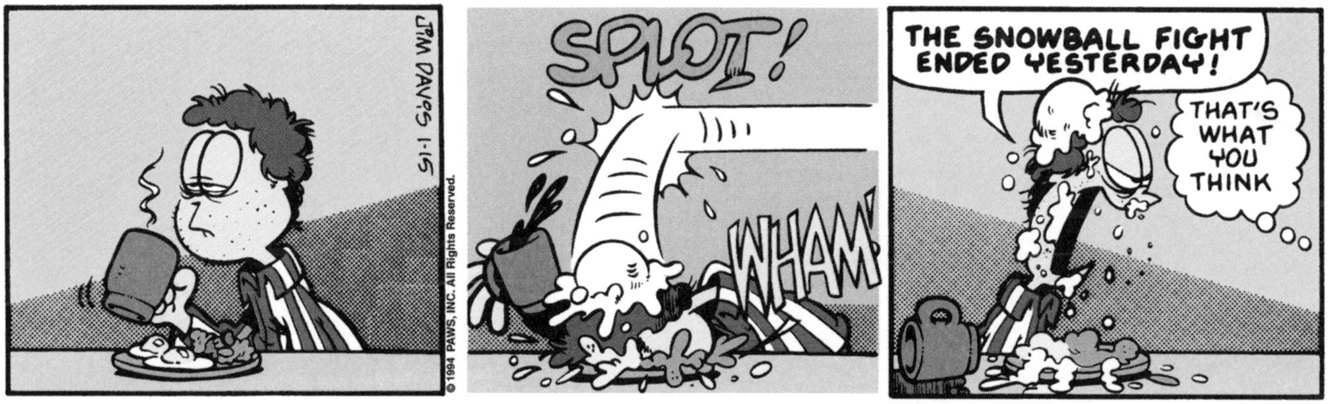
JIM DAVIS 1-15
© 1994 PAWS, INC. All Rights Reserved.
SPLOT!
WHAM!
THE SNOWBALL FIGHT ENDED YESTERDAY!
THAT'S WHAT YOU THINK

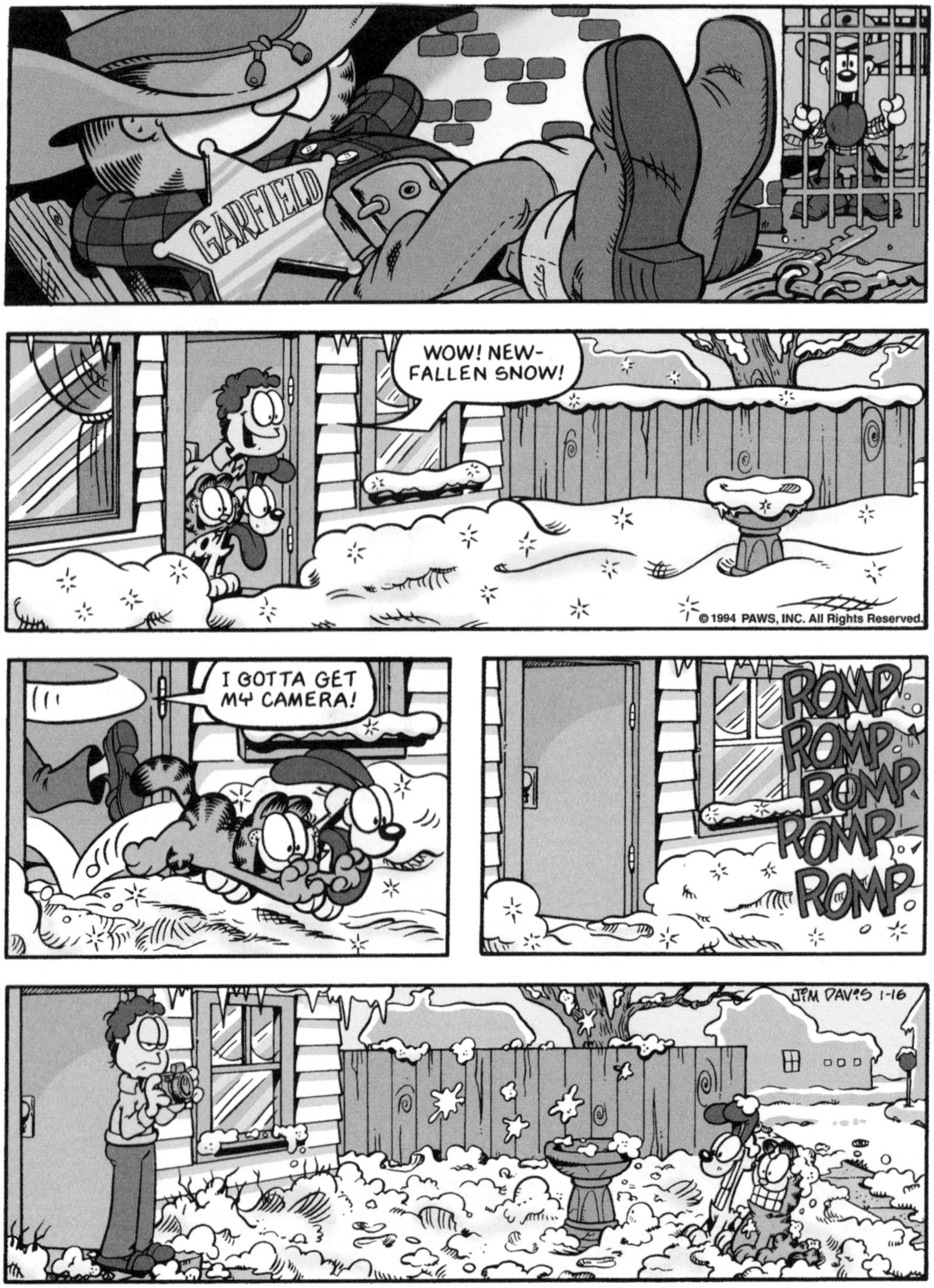
GARFIELD
WOW! NEW-FALLEN SNOW!
© 1994 PAWS, INC. All Rights Reserved.
I GOTTA GET MY CAMERA!
ROMP
ROMP
ROMP
ROMP
ROMP
JIM DAVIS 1-16

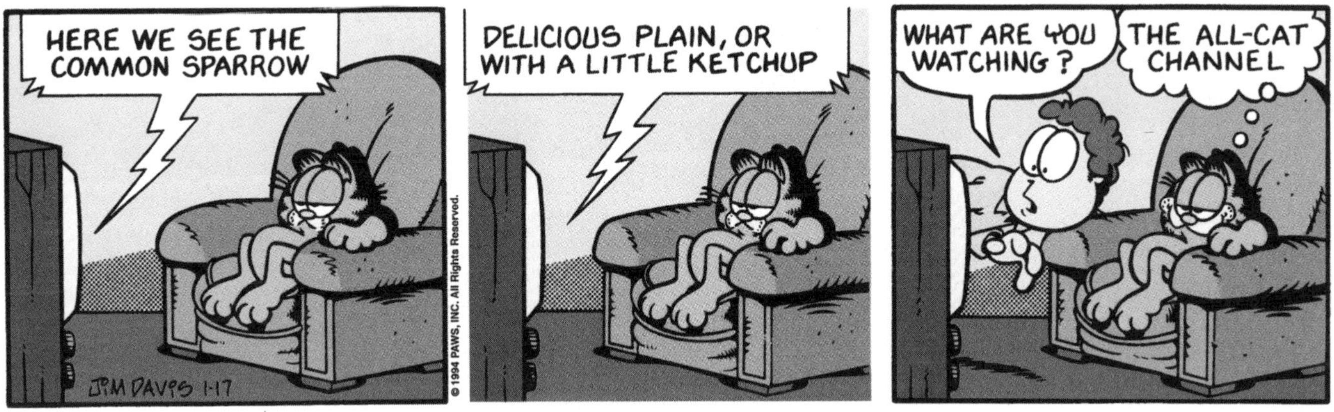
HERE WE SEE THE COMMON SPARROW
JIM DAVIS 1-17
DELICIOUS PLAIN, OR WITH A LITTLE KETCHUP
WHAT ARE YOU WATCHING?
THE ALL-CAT CHANNEL

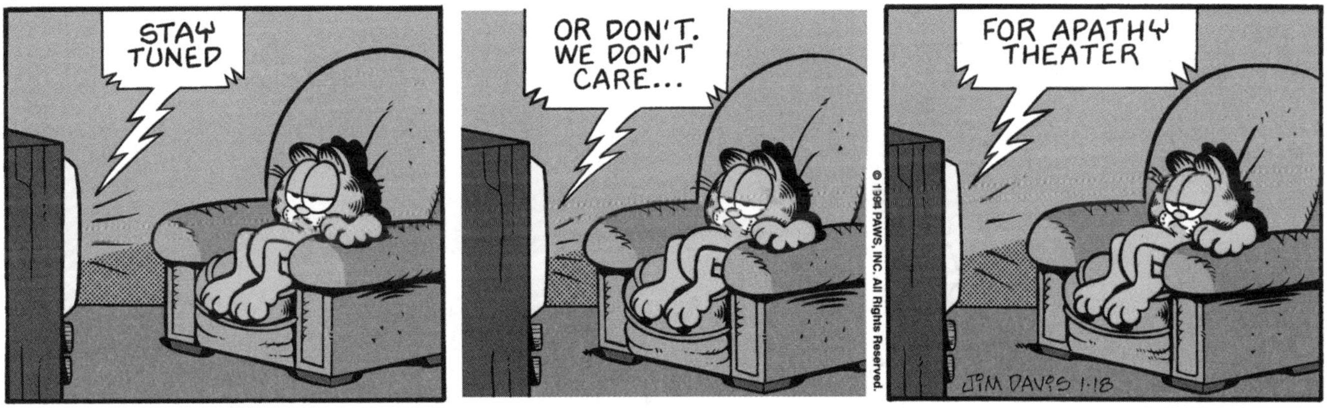
STAY TUNED
OR DON'T. WE DON'T CARE...
FOR APATHY THEATER
JIM DAVIS 1-18

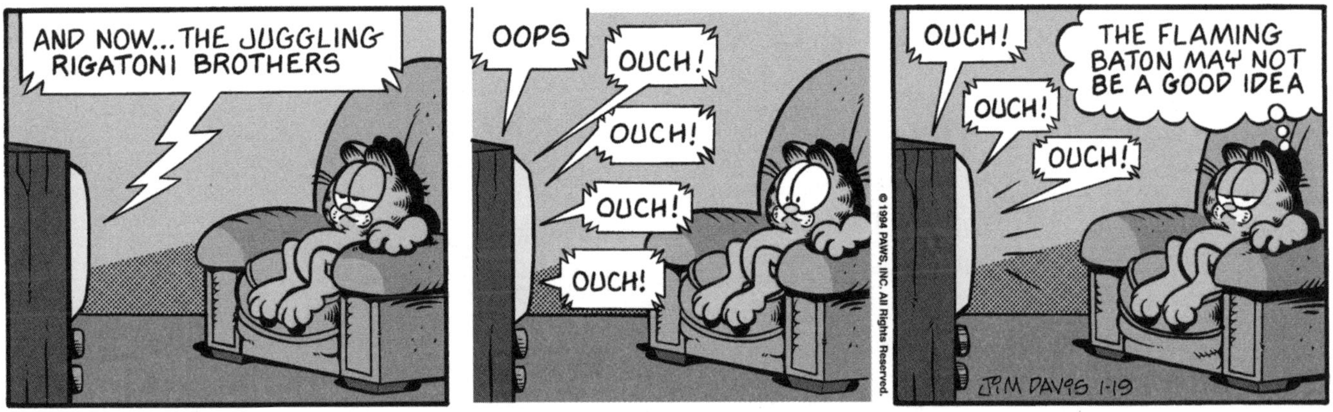
AND NOW... THE JUGGLING RIGATONI BROTHERS
OOPS
OUCH!
OUCH!
OUCH!
OUCH!
OUCH!
OUCH!
OUCH!
THE FLAMING BATON MAY NOT BE A GOOD IDEA
JIM DAVIS 1-19

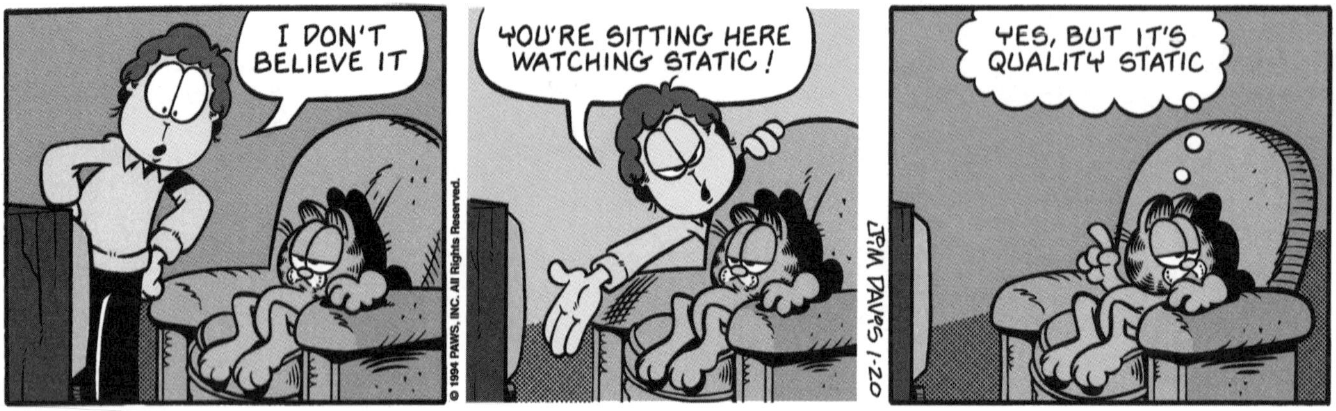
I DON'T BELIEVE IT
YOU'RE SITTING HERE WATCHING STATIC!
YES, BUT IT'S QUALITY STATIC
© 1994 PAWS, INC. All Rights Reserved.
JIM DAVIS 1-20

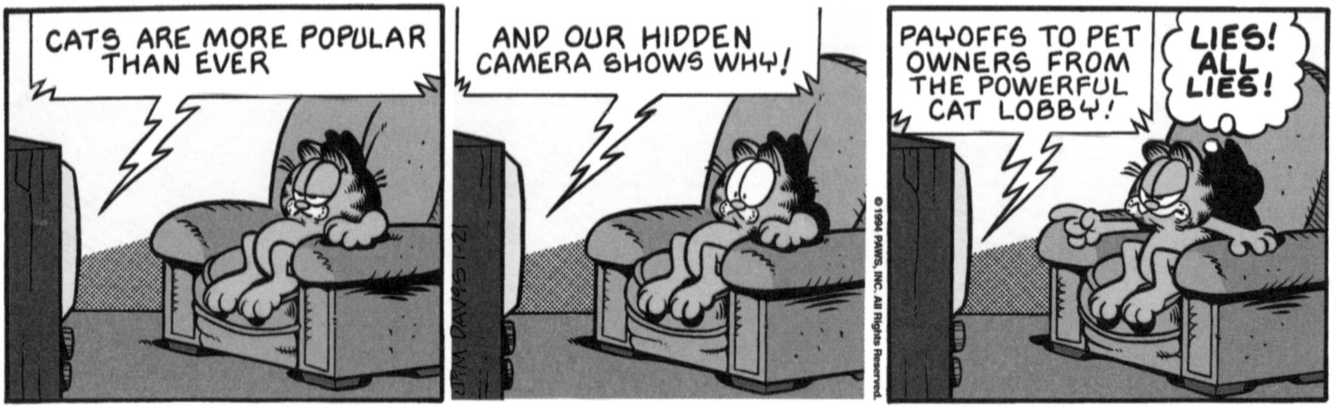
CATS ARE MORE POPULAR THAN EVER
AND OUR HIDDEN CAMERA SHOWS WHY!
PAYOFFS TO PET OWNERS FROM THE POWERFUL CAT LOBBY!
LIES! ALL LIES!
JIM DAVIS 1-21
© 1994 PAWS, INC. All Rights Reserved.

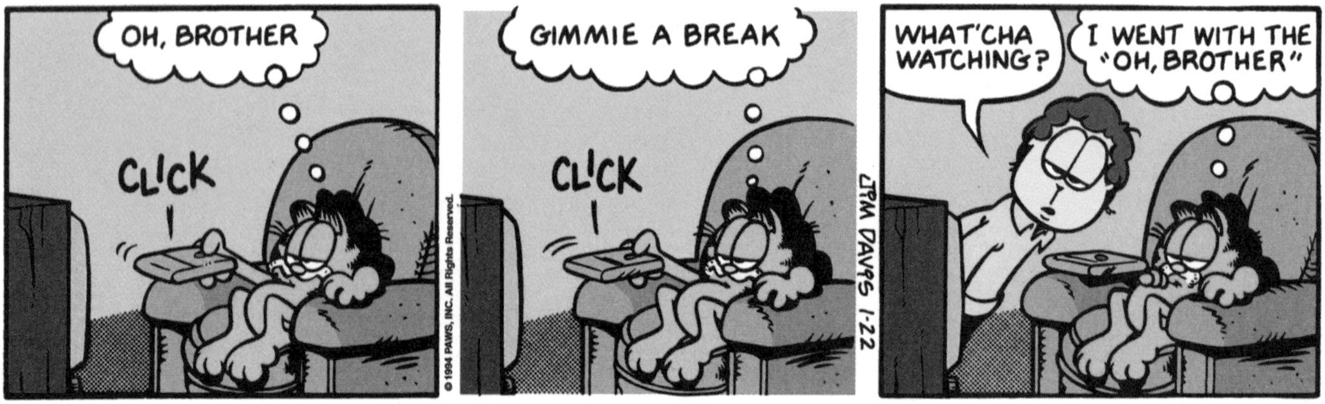
OH, BROTHER
CLICK
GIMMIE A BREAK
CLICK
WHAT'CHA WATCHING?
I WENT WITH THE "OH, BROTHER"
© 1994 PAWS, INC. All Rights Reserved.
JIM DAVIS 1-22

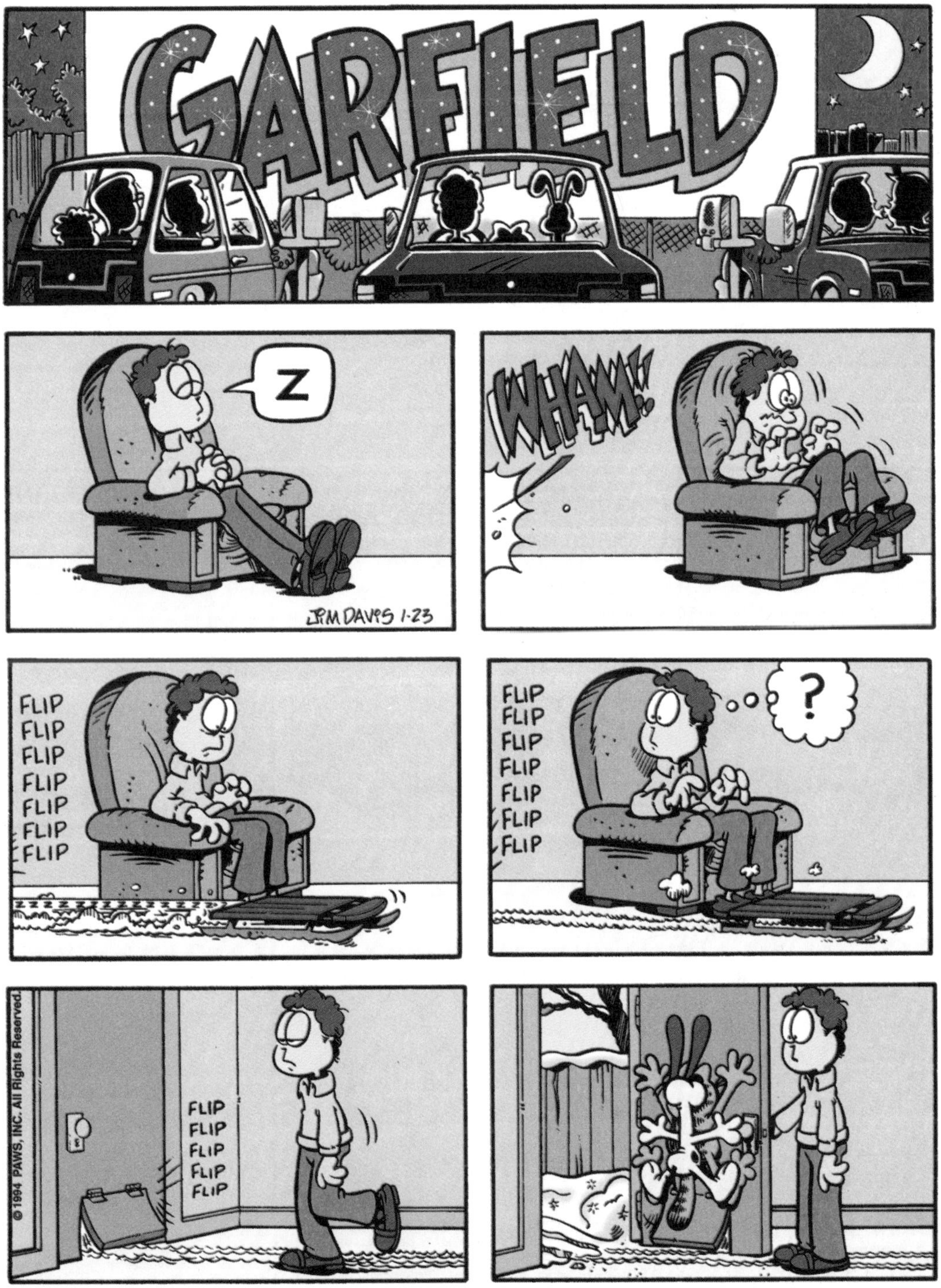
GARFIELD
Z
JIM DAVIS 1-23
WHAM!!
FLIP FLIP FLIP FLIP FLIP FLIP FLIP
FLIP FLIP FLIP FLIP FLIP FLIP FLIP
?
© 1994 PAWS, INC. All Rights Reserved.
FLIP FLIP FLIP FLIP FLIP

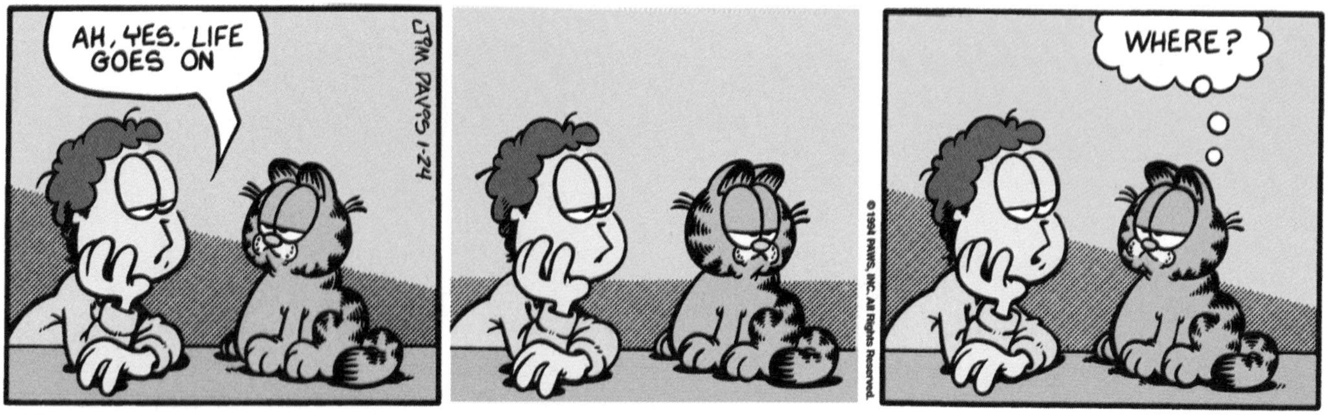
AH, YES. LIFE GOES ON
JIM DAVIS 1-24
© 1994 PAWS, INC. All Rights Reserved.
WHERE?

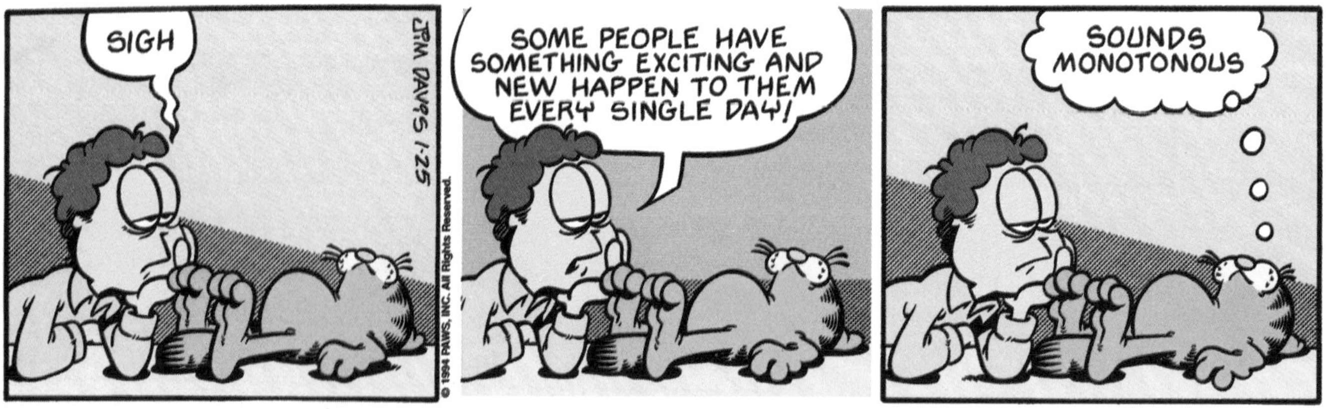
SIGH
JIM DAVIS 1-25
© 1994 PAWS, INC. All Rights Reserved.
SOME PEOPLE HAVE SOMETHING EXCITING AND NEW HAPPEN TO THEM EVERY SINGLE DAY!
SOUNDS MONOTONOUS

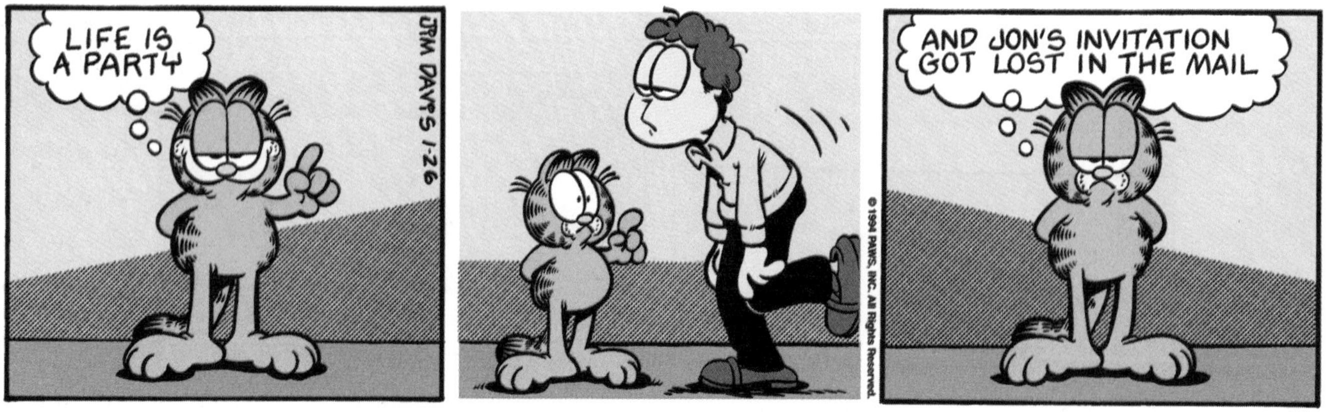
LIFE IS A PARTY
JIM DAVIS 1-26
© 1994 PAWS, INC. All Rights Reserved.
AND JON'S INVITATION GOT LOST IN THE MAIL

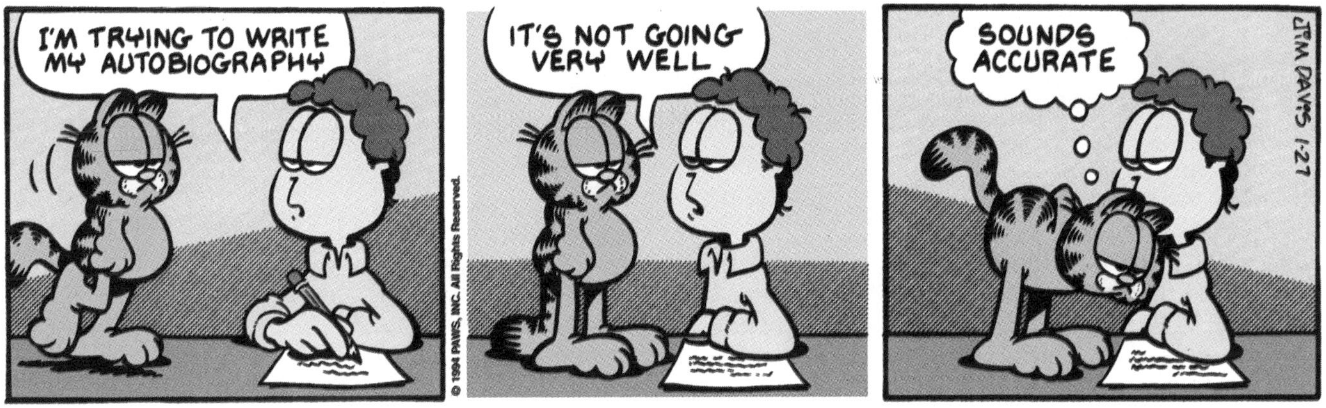
I'M TRYING TO WRITE MY AUTOBIOGRAPHY
IT'S NOT GOING VERY WELL
SOUNDS ACCURATE
© 1994 PAWS, INC. All Rights Reserved.
JIM DAVIS 1-27

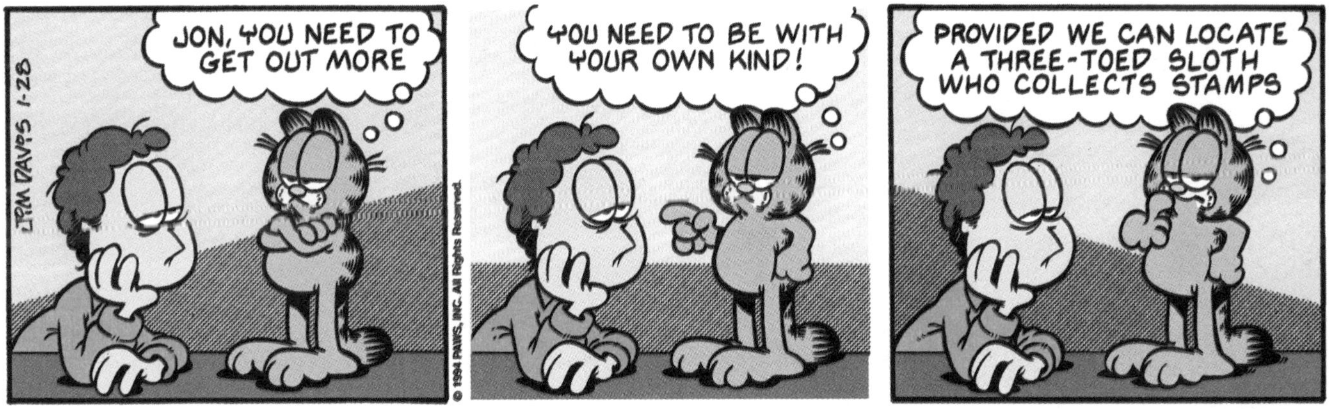
JON, YOU NEED TO GET OUT MORE
YOU NEED TO BE WITH YOUR OWN KIND!
PROVIDED WE CAN LOCATE A THREE-TOED SLOTH WHO COLLECTS STAMPS
JIM DAVIS 1-28
© 1994 PAWS, INC. All Rights Reserved.

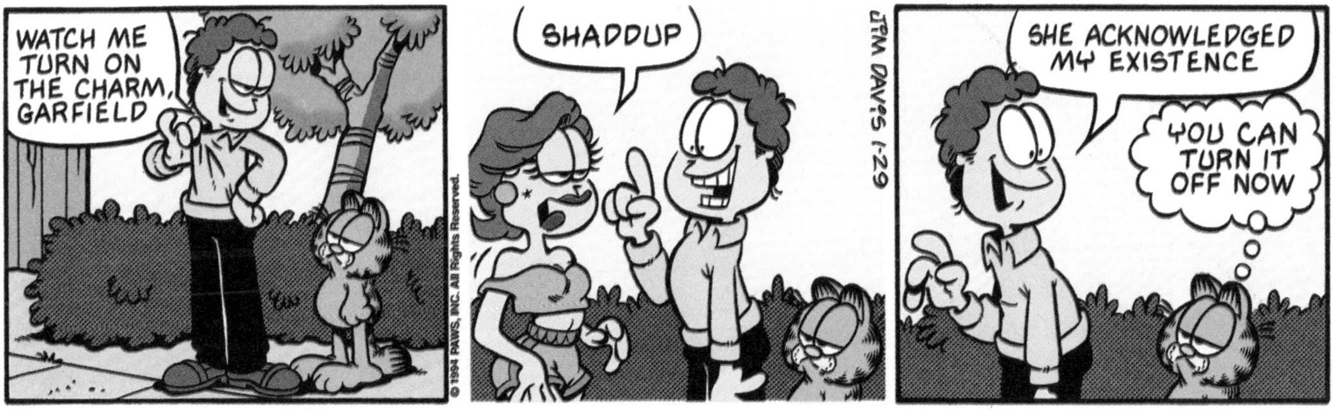
WATCH ME TURN ON THE CHARM, GARFIELD
SHADDUP
SHE ACKNOWLEDGED MY EXISTENCE
YOU CAN TURN IT OFF NOW
© 1994 PAWS, INC. All Rights Reserved.
JIM DAVIS 1-29

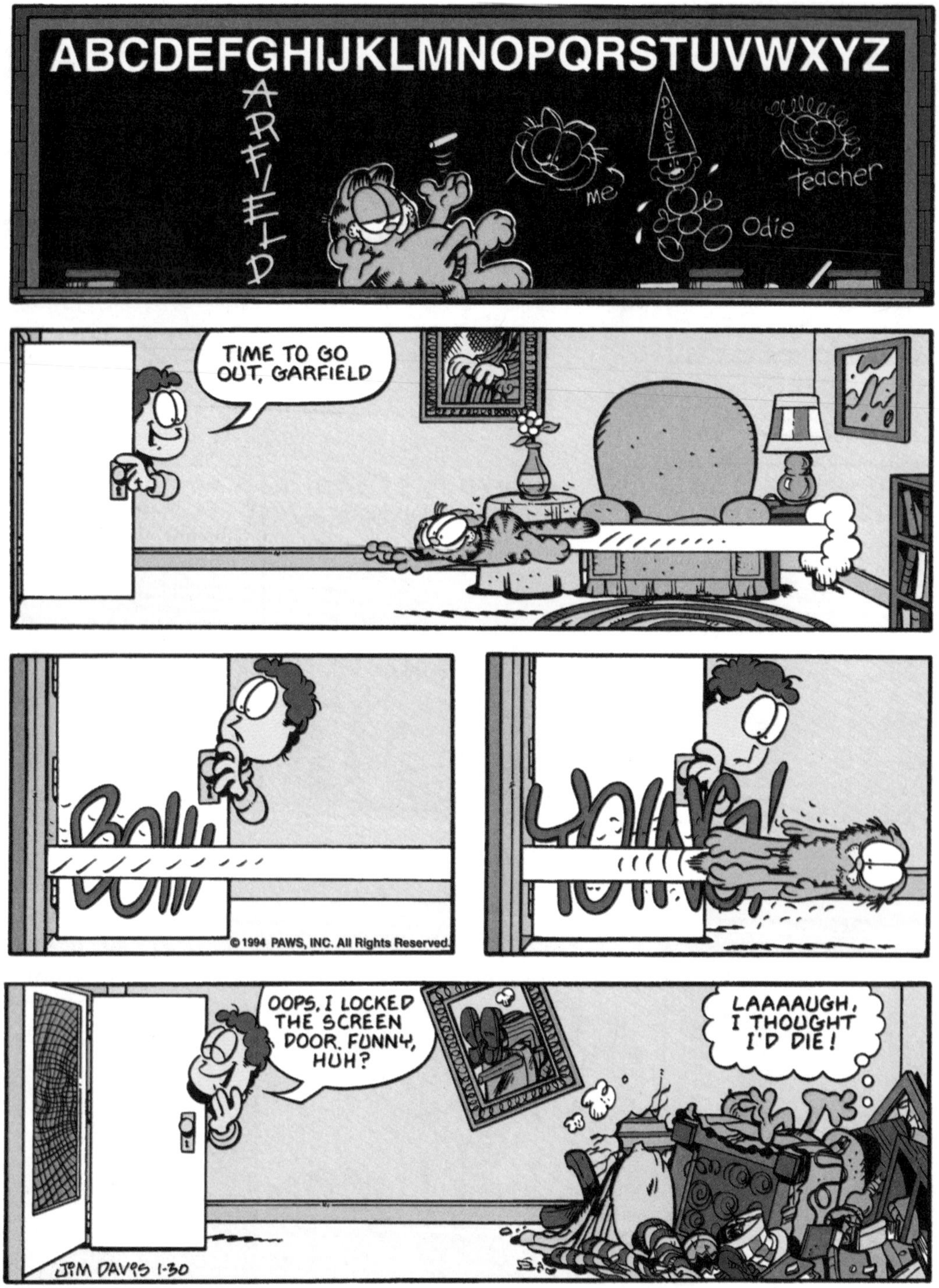

ABCDEFGHIJKLMNOPQRSTUVWXYZ
GARFIELD
DUNCE
me
teacher
Odie
TIME TO GO OUT, GARFIELD
BOW
YOING!
© 1994 PAWS, INC. All Rights Reserved.
OOPS, I LOCKED THE SCREEN DOOR. FUNNY, HUH?
LAAAAUGH, I THOUGHT I'D DIE!
JIM DAVIS 1-30

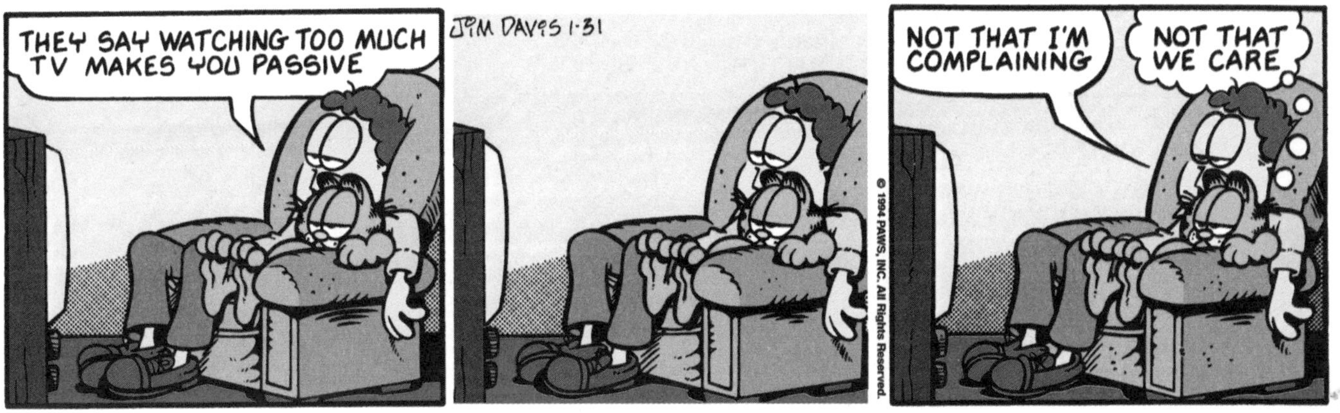
THEY SAY WATCHING TOO MUCH TV MAKES YOU PASSIVE
JIM DAVIS 1-31
© 1994 PAWS, INC. All Rights Reserved.
NOT THAT I'M COMPLAINING
NOT THAT WE CARE

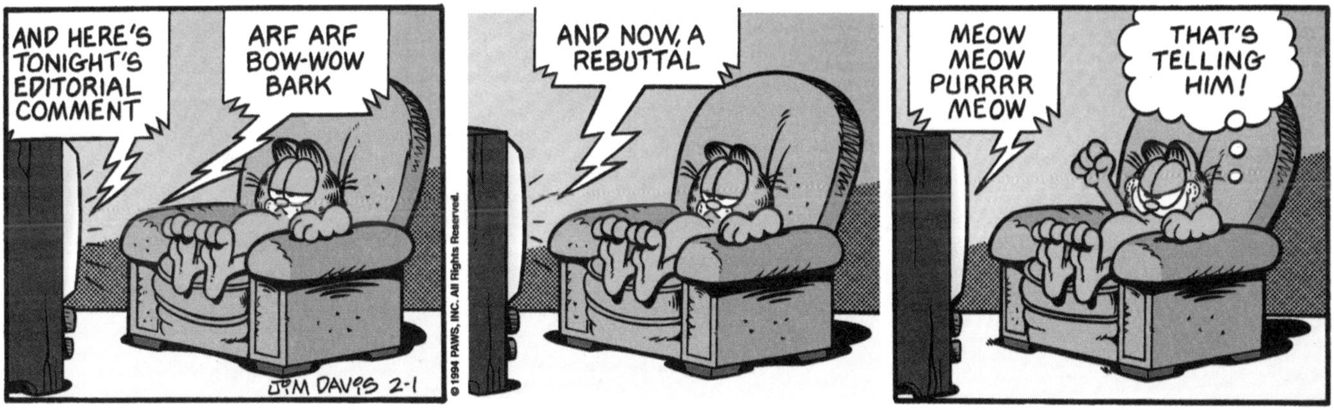
AND HERE'S TONIGHT'S EDITORIAL COMMENT
ARF ARF BOW-WOW BARK
JIM DAVIS 2-1
© 1994 PAWS, INC. All Rights Reserved.
AND NOW, A REBUTTAL
MEOW MEOW PURRRR MEOW
THAT'S TELLING HIM!

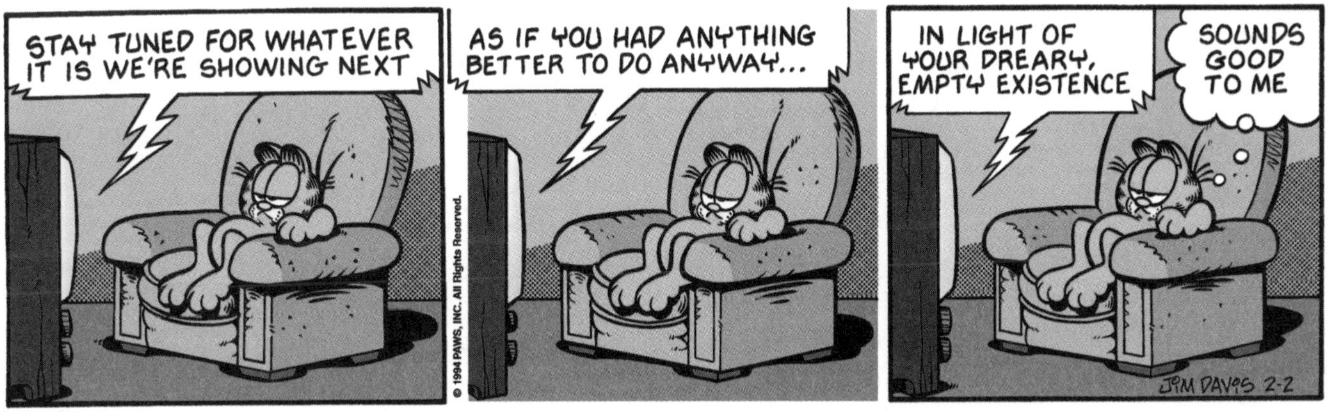
STAY TUNED FOR WHATEVER IT IS WE'RE SHOWING NEXT
© 1994 PAWS, INC. All Rights Reserved.
AS IF YOU HAD ANYTHING BETTER TO DO ANYWAY...
IN LIGHT OF YOUR DREARY, EMPTY EXISTENCE
SOUNDS GOOD TO ME
JIM DAVIS 2-2

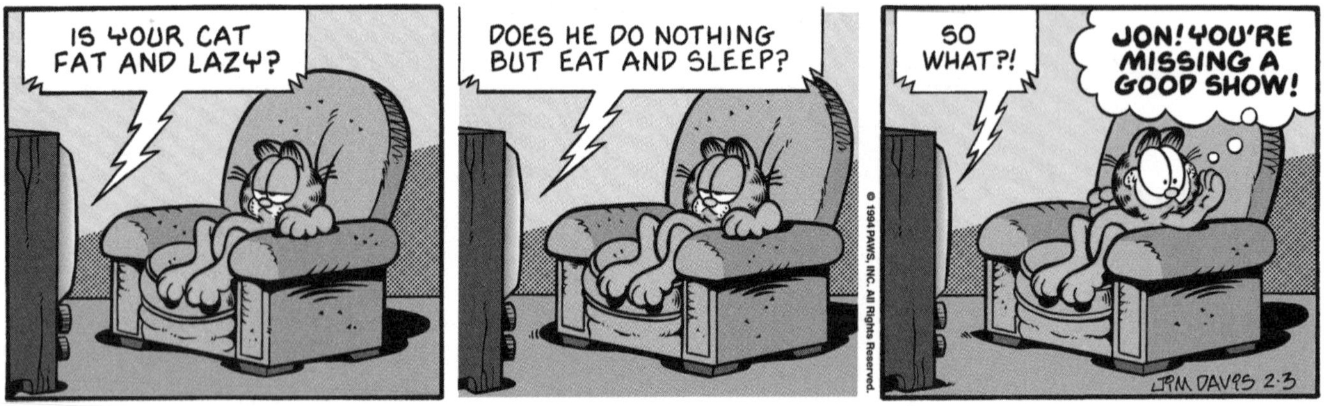
IS YOUR CAT FAT AND LAZY?
DOES HE DO NOTHING BUT EAT AND SLEEP?
© 1994 PAWS, INC. All Rights Reserved.
SO WHAT?!
JON! YOU'RE MISSING A GOOD SHOW!
JIM DAVIS 2-3

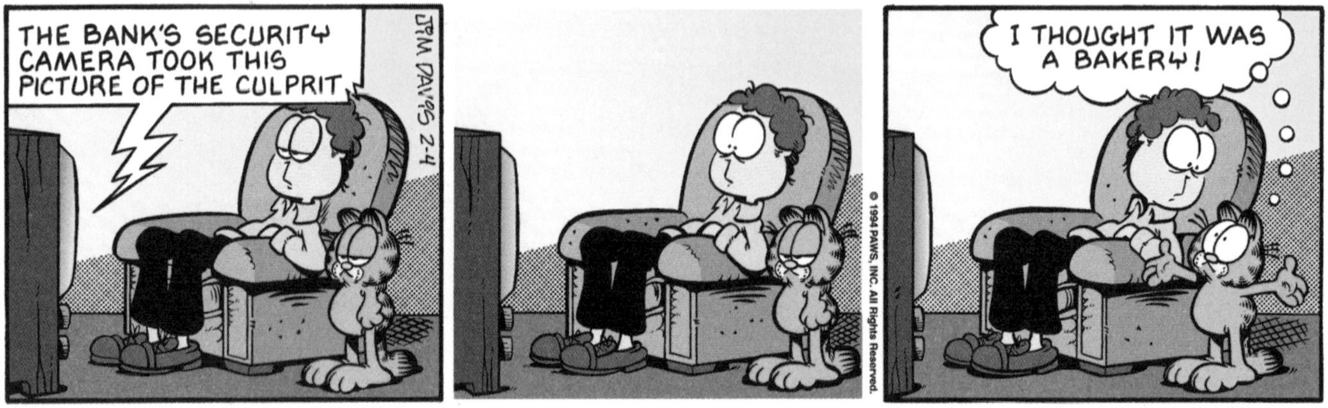
THE BANK'S SECURITY CAMERA TOOK THIS PICTURE OF THE CULPRIT
JIM DAVIS 2-4
© 1994 PAWS, INC. All Rights Reserved.
I THOUGHT IT WAS A BAKERY!

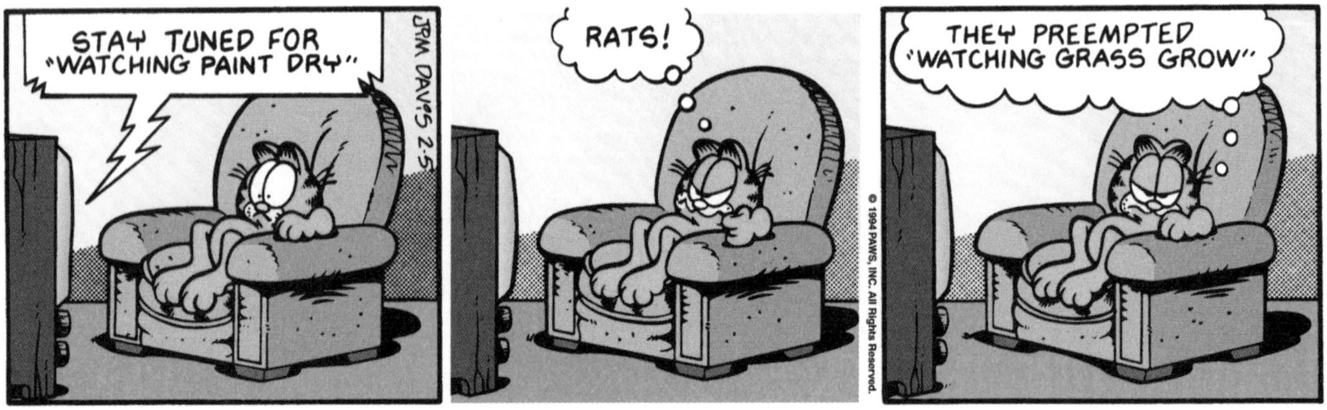
STAY TUNED FOR "WATCHING PAINT DRY"
JIM DAVIS 2-5
RATS!
© 1994 PAWS, INC. All Rights Reserved.
THEY PREEMPTED "WATCHING GRASS GROW"

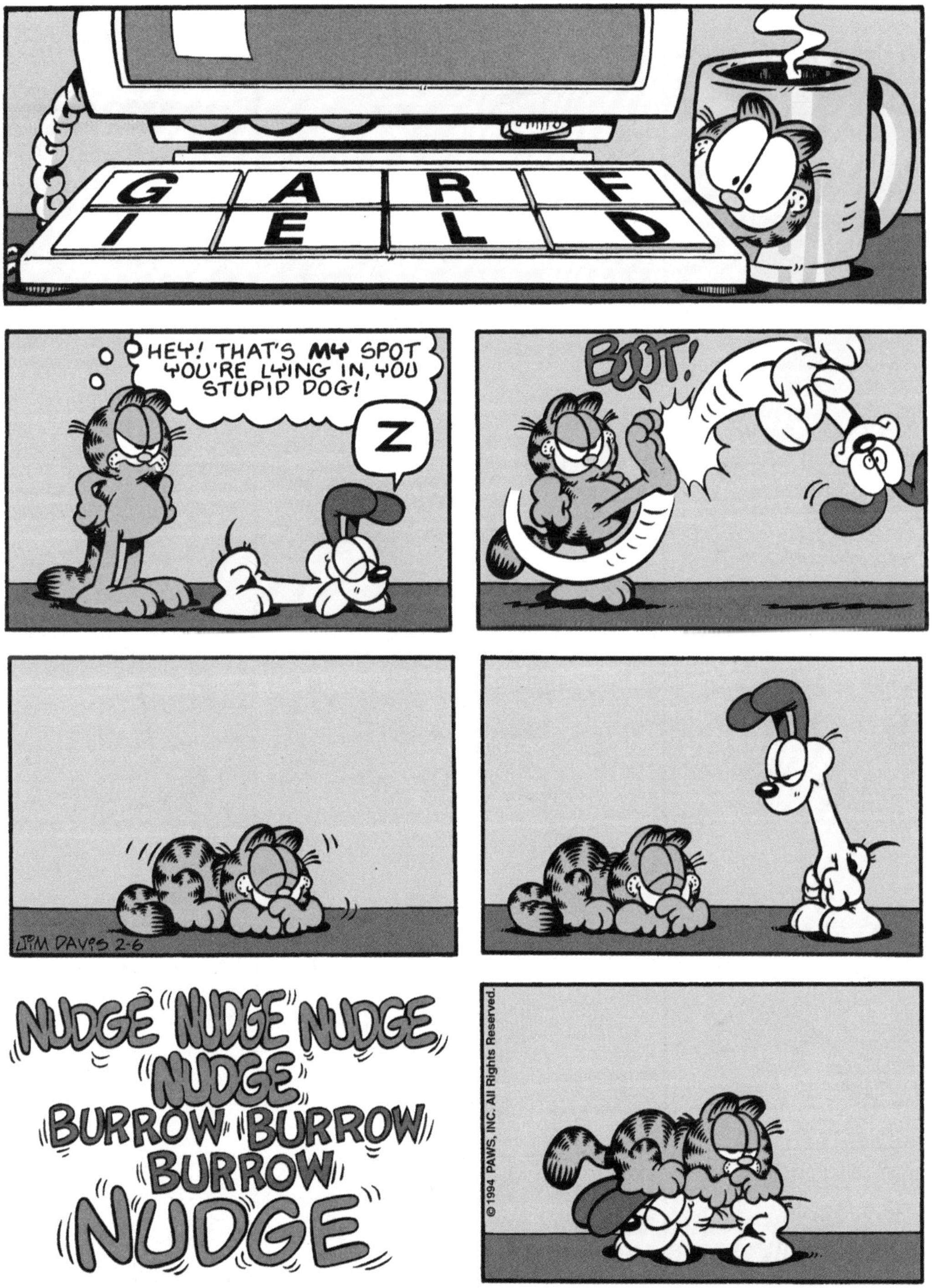
GARFIELD
HEY! THAT'S MY SPOT YOU'RE LYING IN, YOU STUPID DOG!
Z
BOOT!
JIM DAVIS 2-6
NUDGE NUDGE NUDGE
NUDGE
BURROW BURROW
BURROW
NUDGE
© 1994 PAWS, INC. All Rights Reserved.

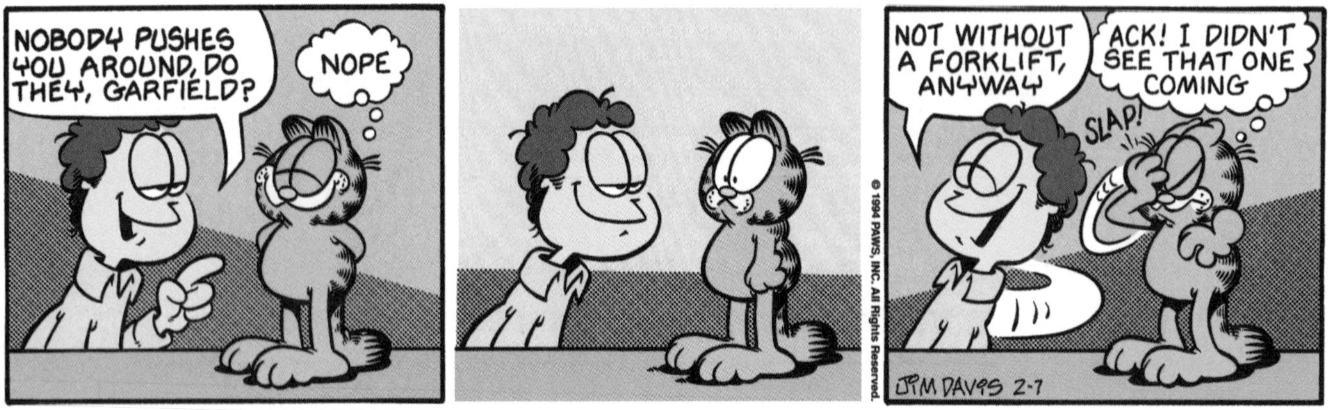
NOBODY PUSHES YOU AROUND, DO THEY, GARFIELD?
NOPE
NOT WITHOUT A FORKLIFT, ANYWAY
ACK! I DIDN'T SEE THAT ONE COMING
SLAP!
© 1994 PAWS, INC. All Rights Reserved.
JIM DAVIS 2-7

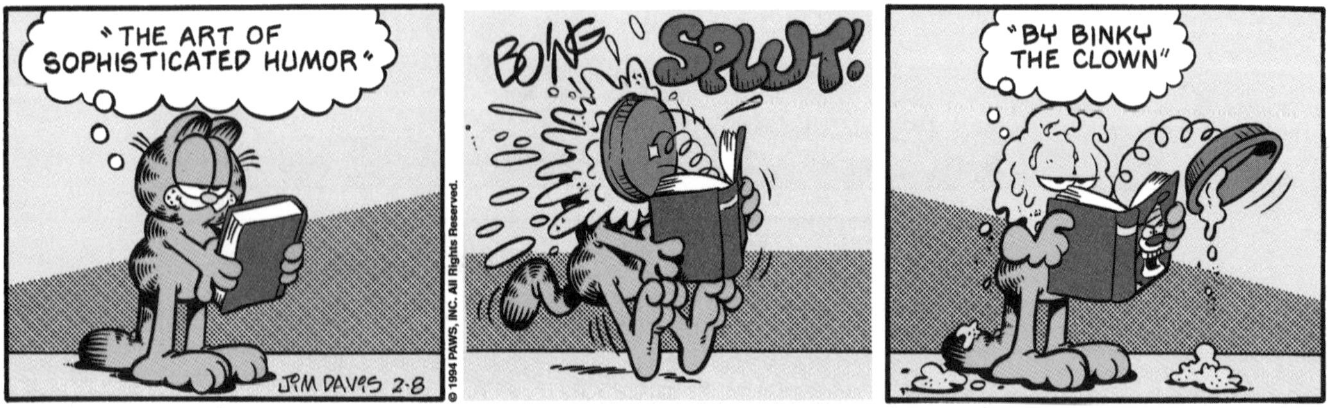
"THE ART OF SOPHISTICATED HUMOR"
JIM DAVIS 2-8
© 1994 PAWS, INC. All Rights Reserved.
BOING
SPLUT!
"BY BINKY THE CLOWN"

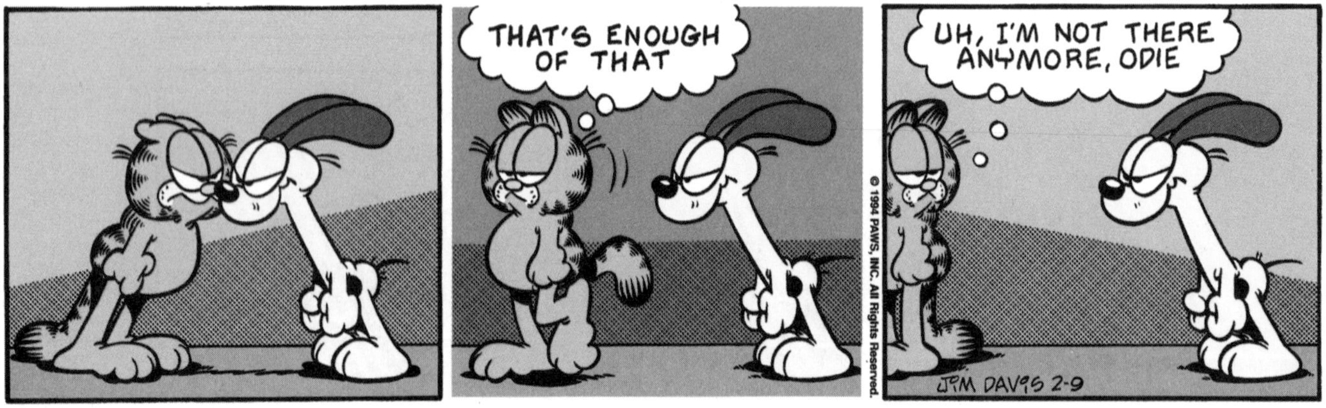
THAT'S ENOUGH OF THAT
UH, I'M NOT THERE ANYMORE, ODIE
© 1994 PAWS, INC. All Rights Reserved.
JIM DAVIS 2-9

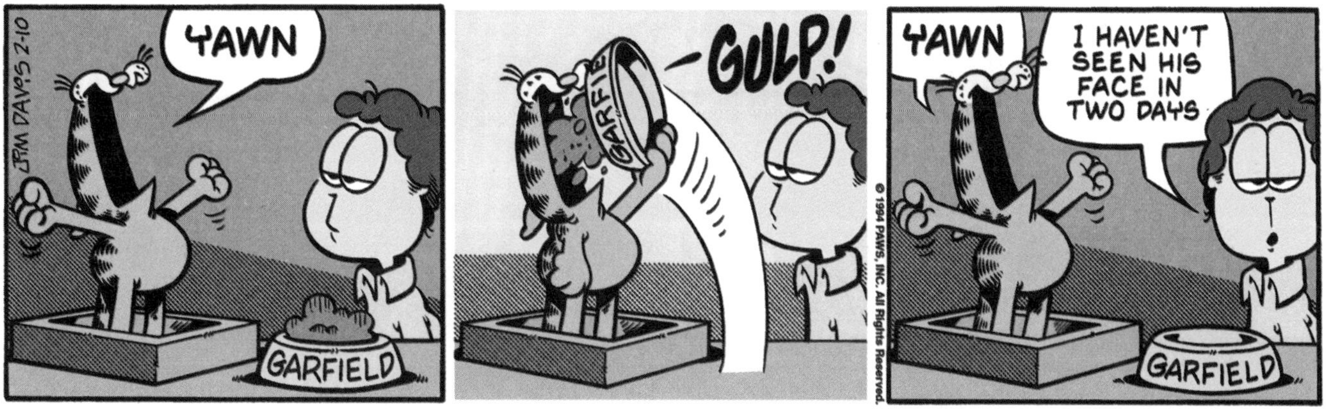
JIM DAVIS 2-10
YAWN
GARFIELD
GARFIE
GULP!
© 1994 PAWS, INC. All Rights Reserved.
YAWN
I HAVEN'T SEEN HIS FACE IN TWO DAYS
GARFIELD

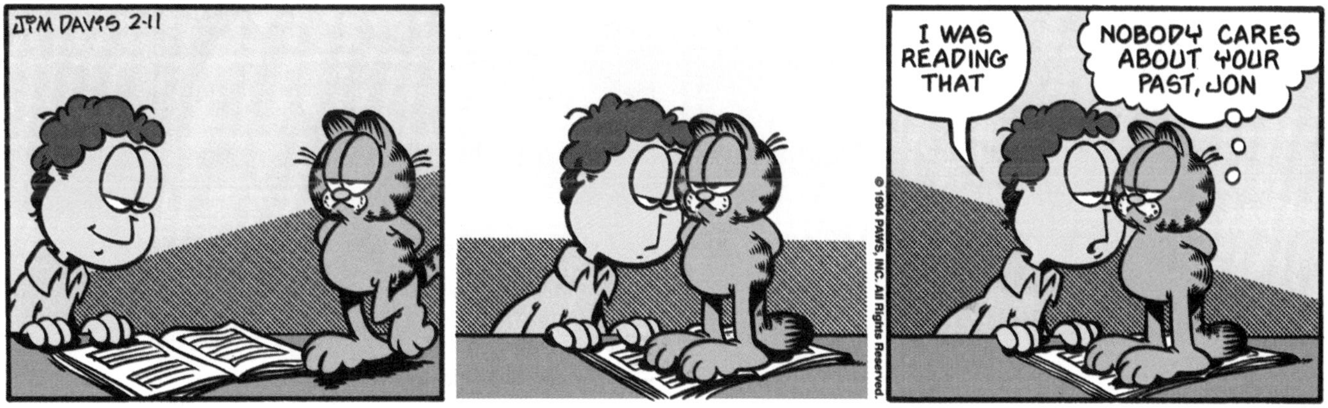
JIM DAVIS 2-11
© 1994 PAWS, INC. All Rights Reserved.
I WAS READING THAT
NOBODY CARES ABOUT YOUR PAST, JON

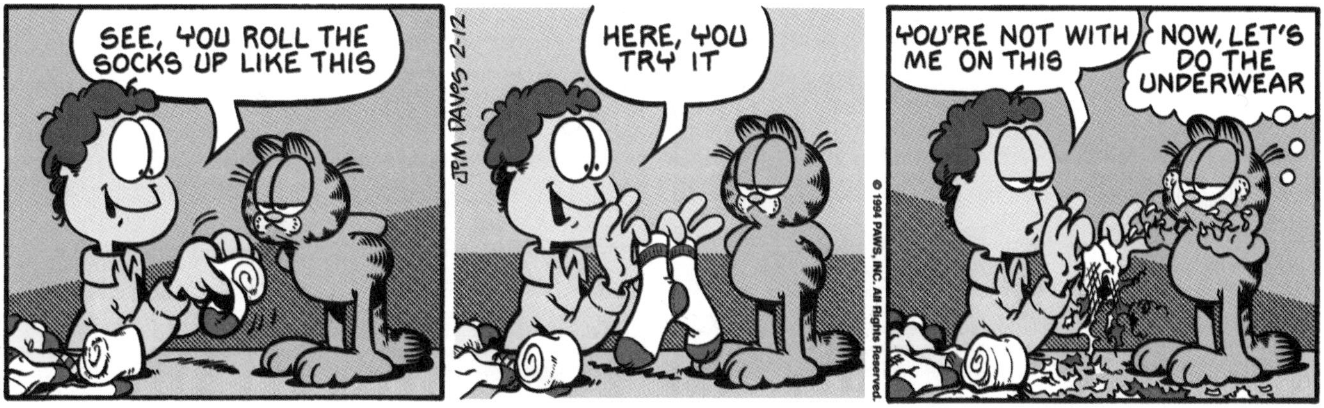
SEE, YOU ROLL THE SOCKS UP LIKE THIS
JIM DAVIS 2-12
HERE, YOU TRY IT
© 1994 PAWS, INC. All Rights Reserved.
YOU'RE NOT WITH ME ON THIS
NOW, LET'S DO THE UNDERWEAR

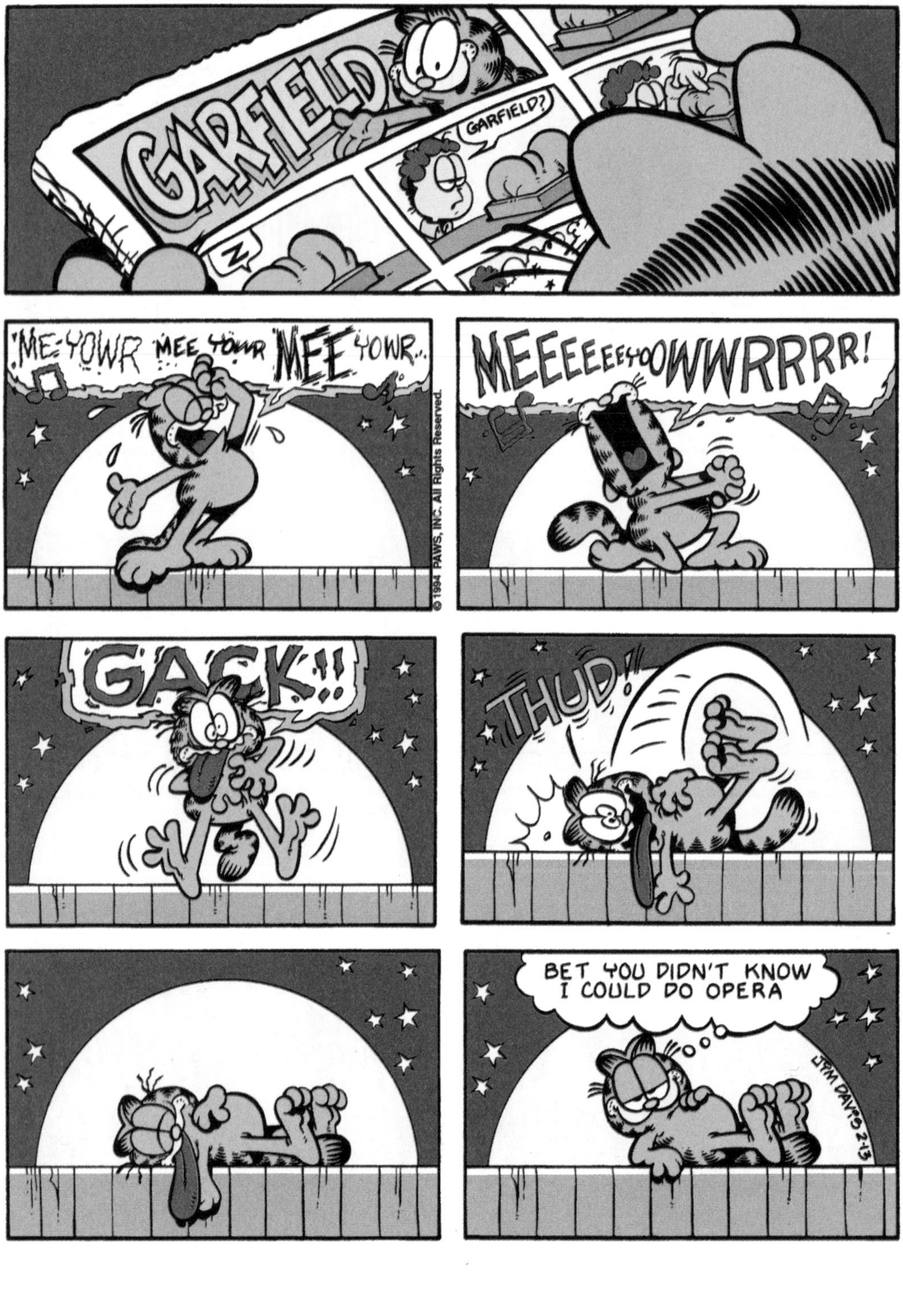
GARFIELD
GARFIELD?
Z
ME-YOWR MEE YOWR MEE YOWR...
MEEEEEEEYOOWWRRRRR!
GACK!!
THUD!
BET YOU DIDN'T KNOW I COULD DO OPERA
JIM DAVIS 2-13

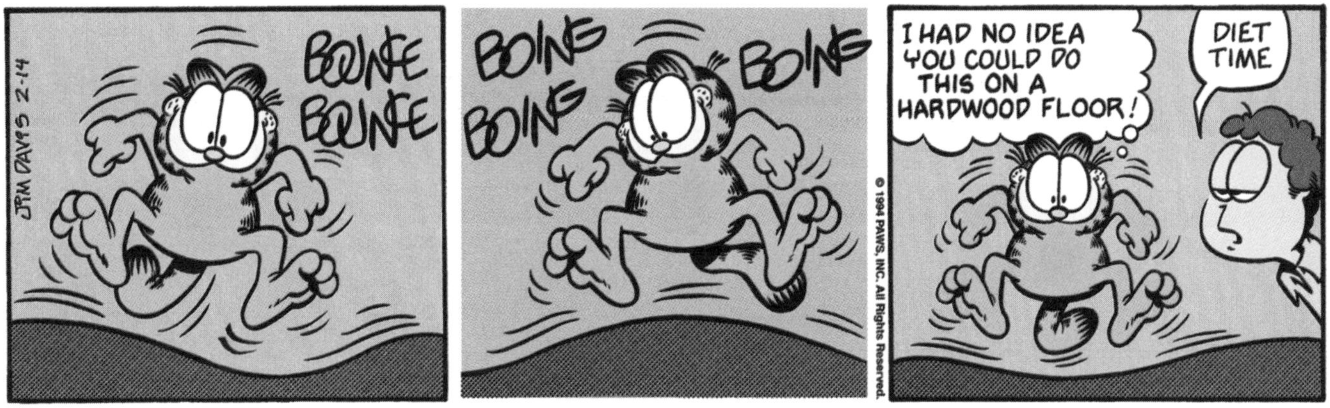
JIM DAVIS 2-14
BOUNCE BOUNCE
BOING BOING BOING
© 1994 PAWS, INC. All Rights Reserved.
I HAD NO IDEA YOU COULD DO THIS ON A HARDWOOD FLOOR!
DIET TIME

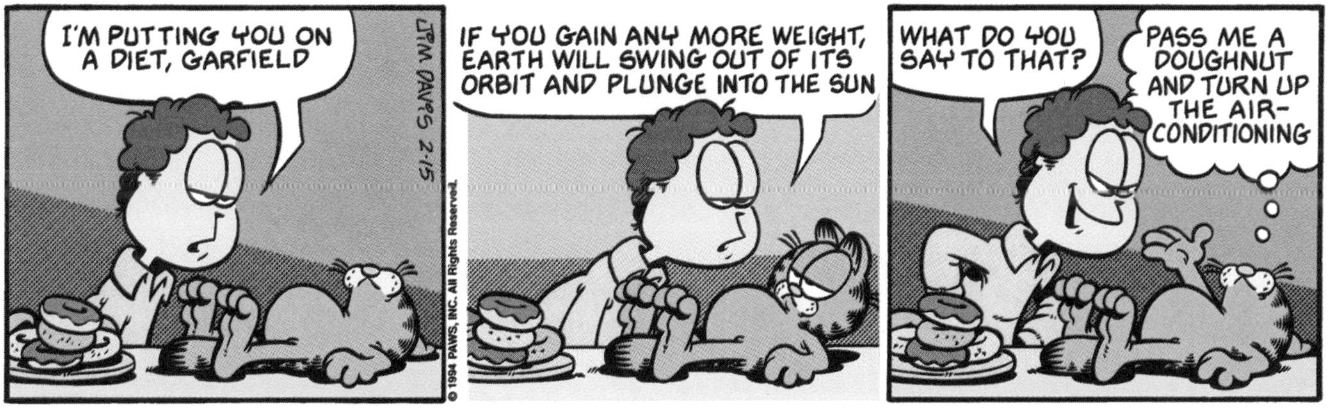
I'M PUTTING YOU ON A DIET, GARFIELD
JIM DAVIS 2-15
© 1994 PAWS, INC. All Rights Reserved.
IF YOU GAIN ANY MORE WEIGHT, EARTH WILL SWING OUT OF ITS ORBIT AND PLUNGE INTO THE SUN
WHAT DO YOU SAY TO THAT?
PASS ME A DOUGHNUT AND TURN UP THE AIR-CONDITIONING

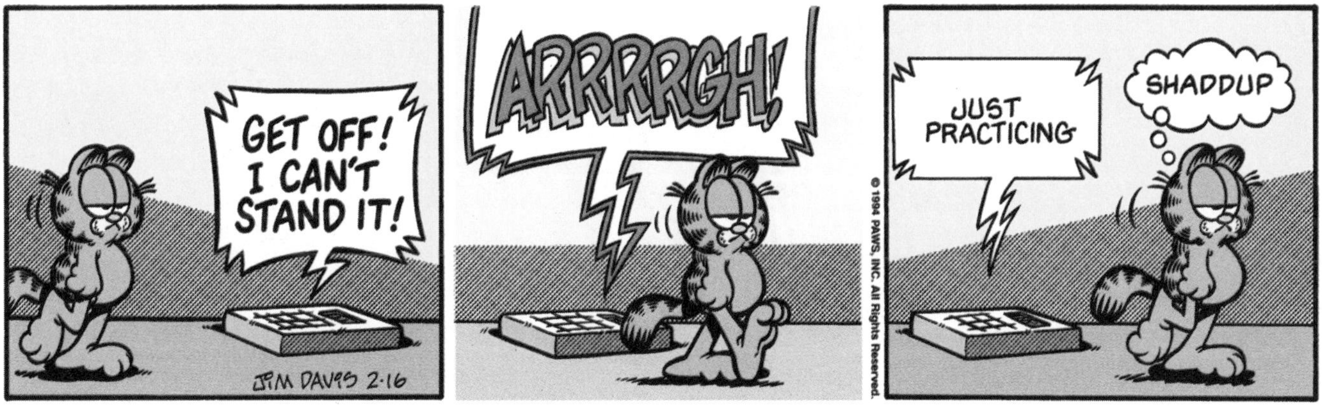
GET OFF! I CAN'T STAND IT!
JIM DAVIS 2-16
ARRRRGH!
© 1994 PAWS, INC. All Rights Reserved.
JUST PRACTICING
SHADDUP

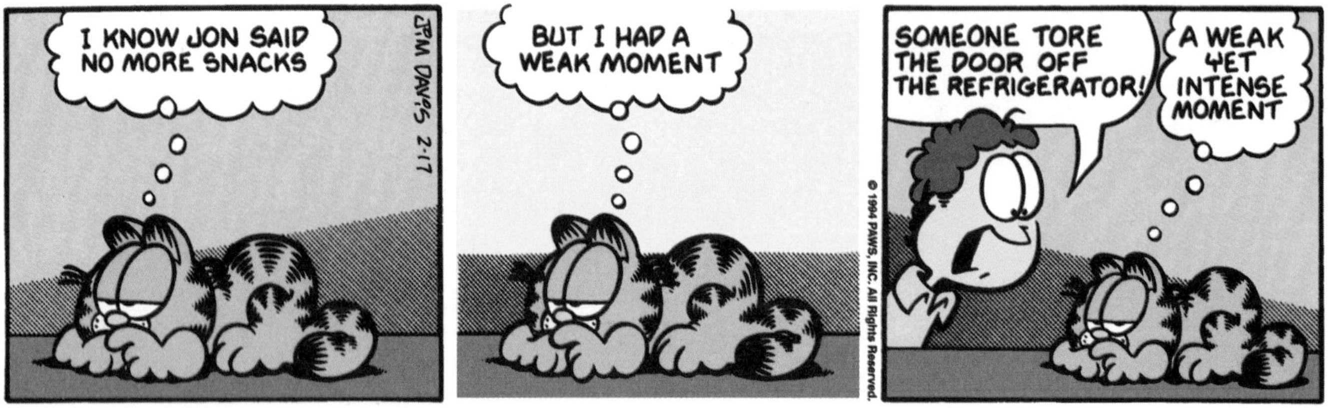
I KNOW JON SAID NO MORE SNACKS
JIM DAVIS 2·17
BUT I HAD A WEAK MOMENT
SOMEONE TORE THE DOOR OFF THE REFRIGERATOR!
A WEAK YET INTENSE MOMENT

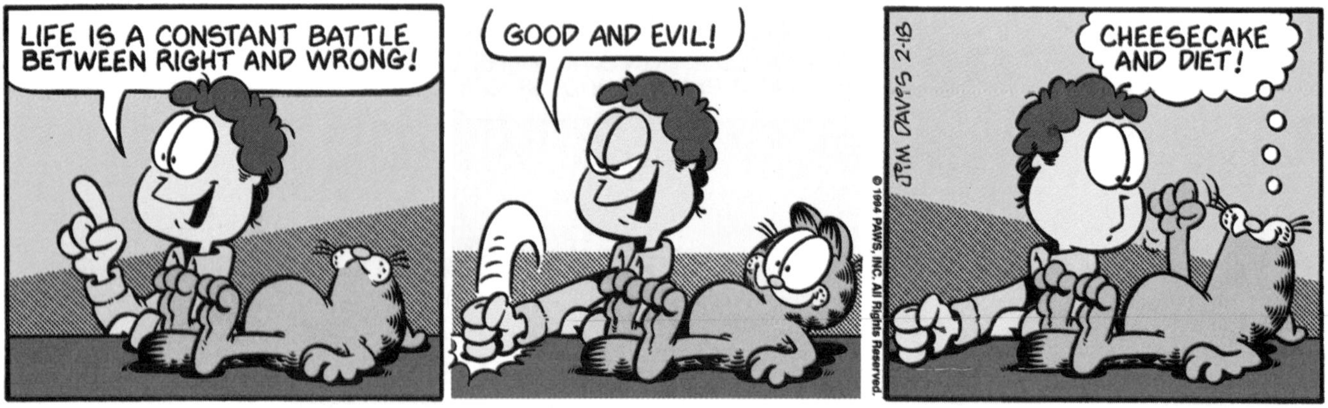
LIFE IS A CONSTANT BATTLE BETWEEN RIGHT AND WRONG!
GOOD AND EVIL!
JIM DAVIS 2·18
CHEESECAKE AND DIET!

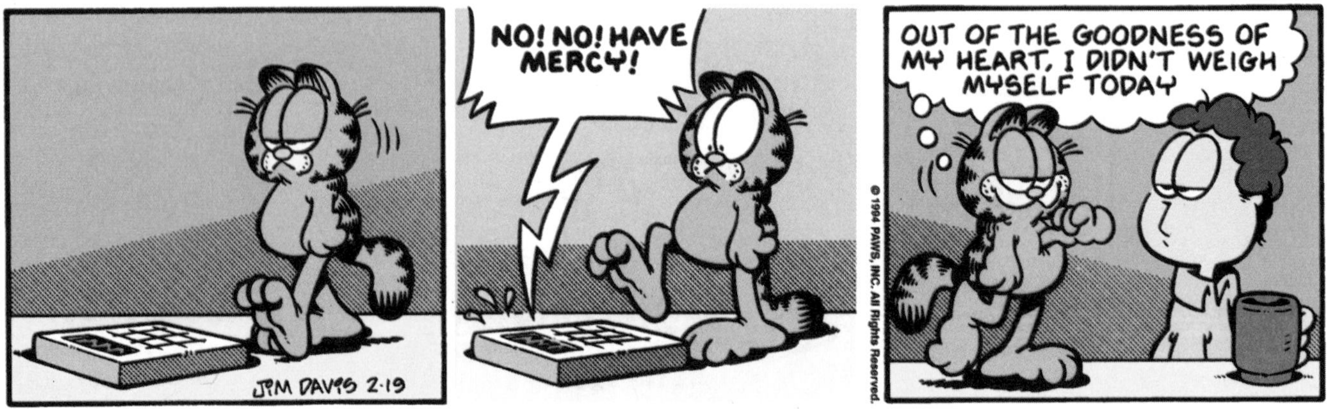
JIM DAVIS 2·19
NO! NO! HAVE MERCY!
OUT OF THE GOODNESS OF MY HEART, I DIDN'T WEIGH MYSELF TODAY

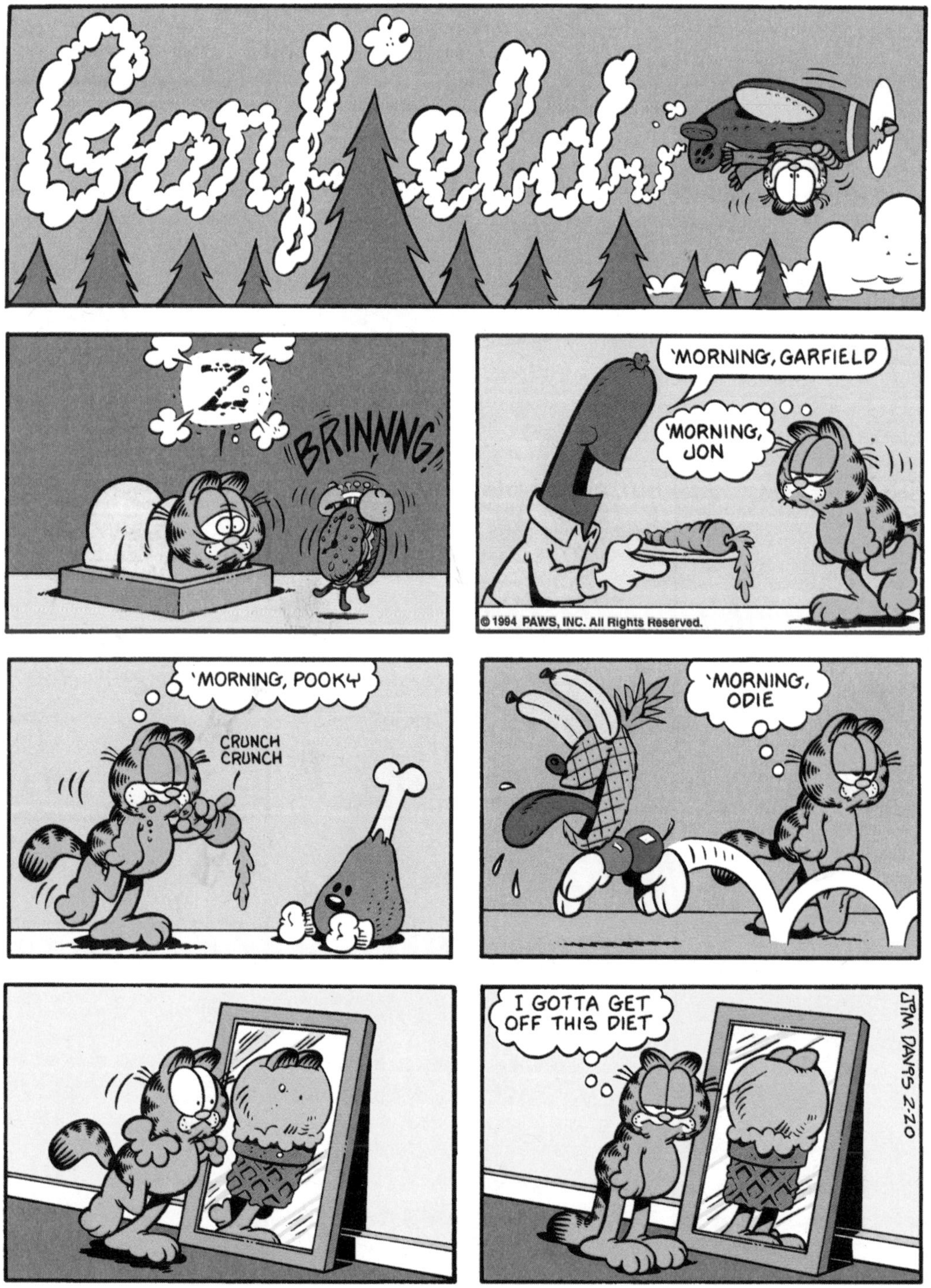
Garfield
Z
BRINNNG!
'MORNING, GARFIELD
'MORNING, JON
© 1994 PAWS, INC. All Rights Reserved.
'MORNING, POOKY
CRUNCH CRUNCH
'MORNING, ODIE
I GOTTA GET OFF THIS DIET
JIM DAVIS 2-20

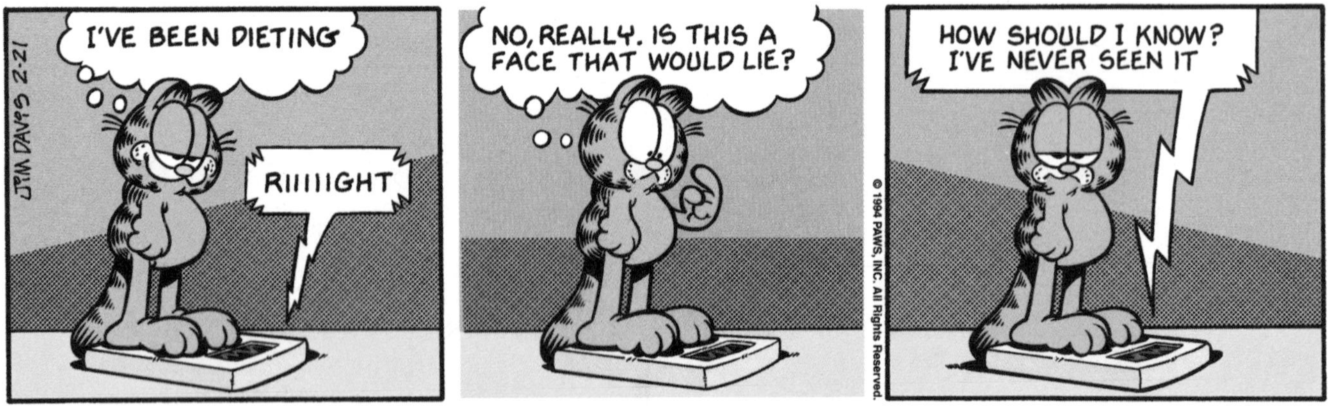
JIM DAVIS 2-21
I'VE BEEN DIETING
RIIIIIGHT
NO, REALLY. IS THIS A FACE THAT WOULD LIE?
© 1994 PAWS, INC. All Rights Reserved.
HOW SHOULD I KNOW? I'VE NEVER SEEN IT

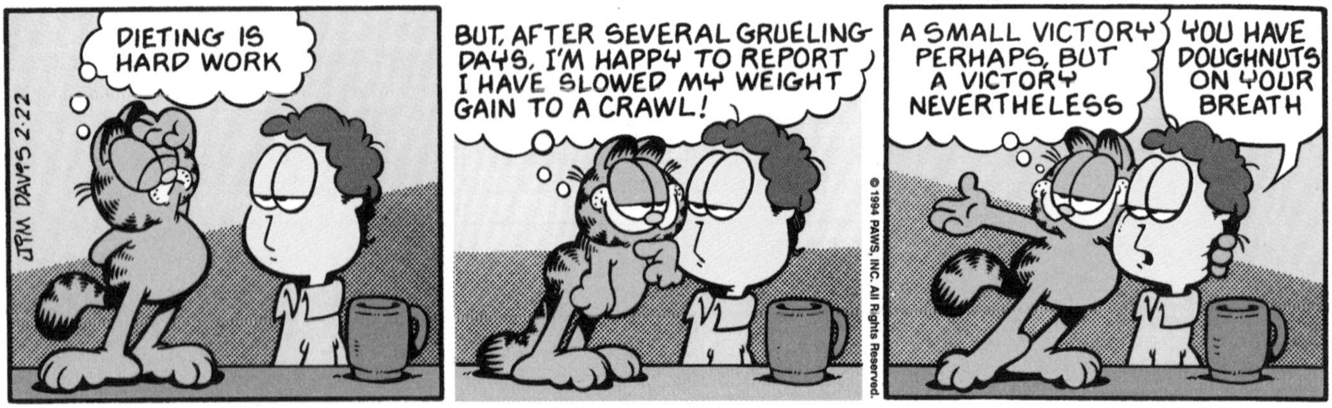
JIM DAVIS 2-22
DIETING IS HARD WORK
BUT, AFTER SEVERAL GRUELING DAYS, I'M HAPPY TO REPORT I HAVE SLOWED MY WEIGHT GAIN TO A CRAWL!
© 1994 PAWS, INC. All Rights Reserved.
A SMALL VICTORY PERHAPS, BUT A VICTORY NEVERTHELESS
YOU HAVE DOUGHNUTS ON YOUR BREATH

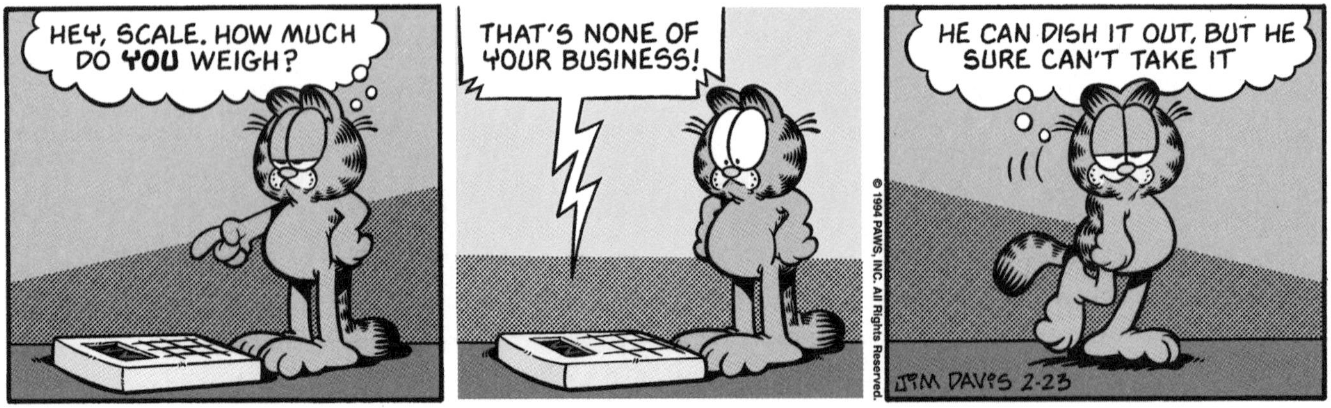
HEY, SCALE. HOW MUCH DO **YOU** WEIGH?
THAT'S NONE OF YOUR BUSINESS!
© 1994 PAWS, INC. All Rights Reserved.
HE CAN DISH IT OUT, BUT HE SURE CAN'T TAKE IT
JIM DAVIS 2-23

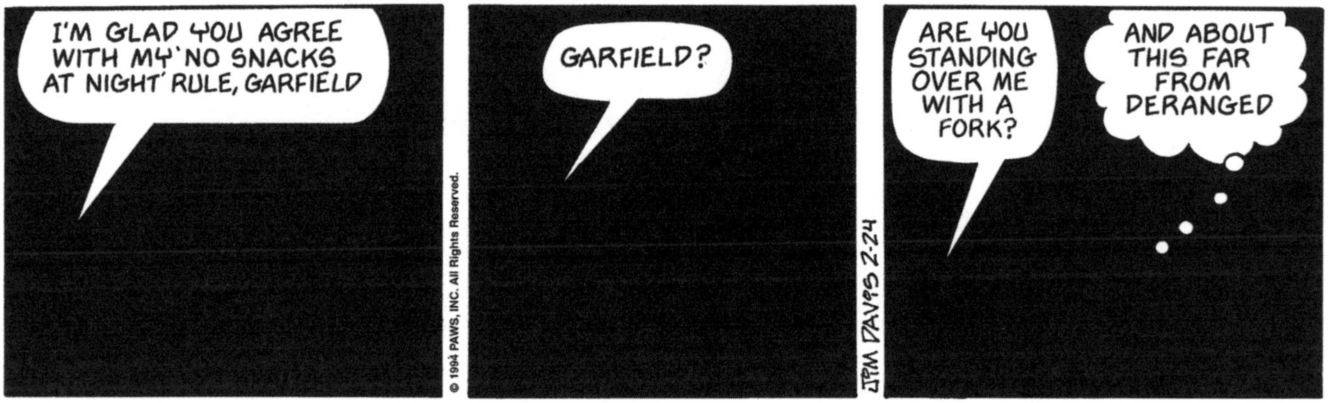
I'M GLAD YOU AGREE WITH MY 'NO SNACKS AT NIGHT' RULE, GARFIELD
© 1994 PAWS, INC. All Rights Reserved.
GARFIELD?
JIM DAVIS 2-24
ARE YOU STANDING OVER ME WITH A FORK?
AND ABOUT THIS FAR FROM DERANGED

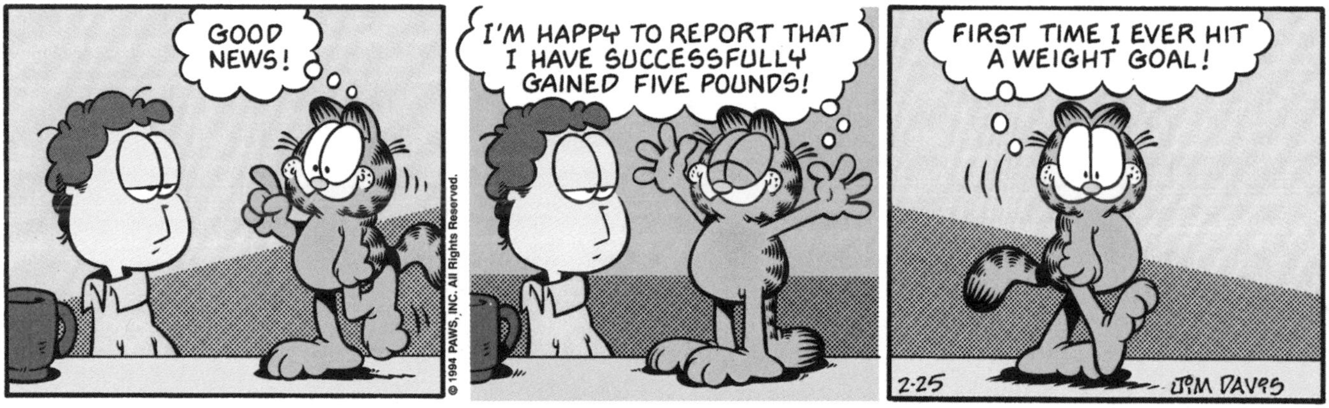
GOOD NEWS!
© 1994 PAWS, INC. All Rights Reserved.
I'M HAPPY TO REPORT THAT I HAVE SUCCESSFULLY GAINED FIVE POUNDS!
FIRST TIME I EVER HIT A WEIGHT GOAL!
2-25
JIM DAVIS

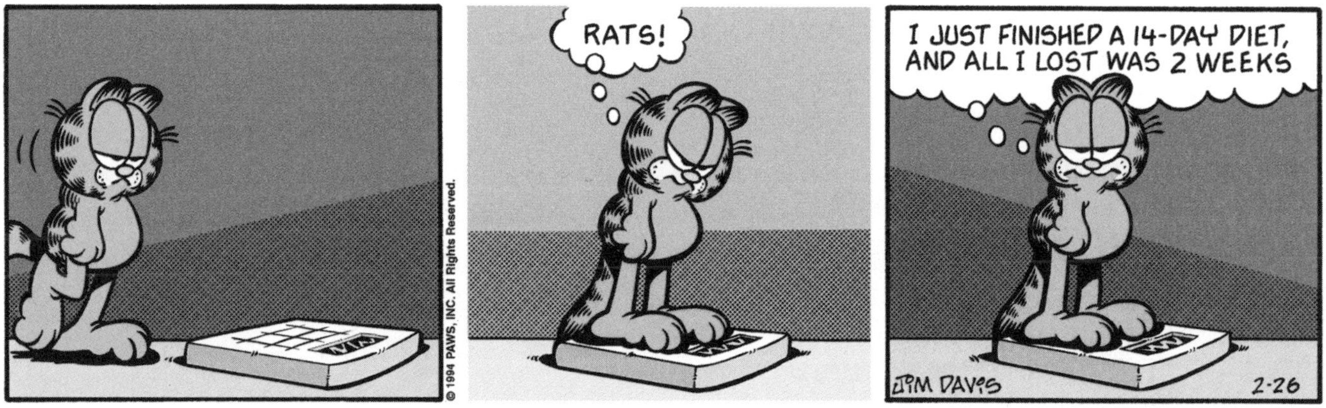
© 1994 PAWS, INC. All Rights Reserved.
RATS!
I JUST FINISHED A 14-DAY DIET, AND ALL I LOST WAS 2 WEEKS
JIM DAVIS
2-26

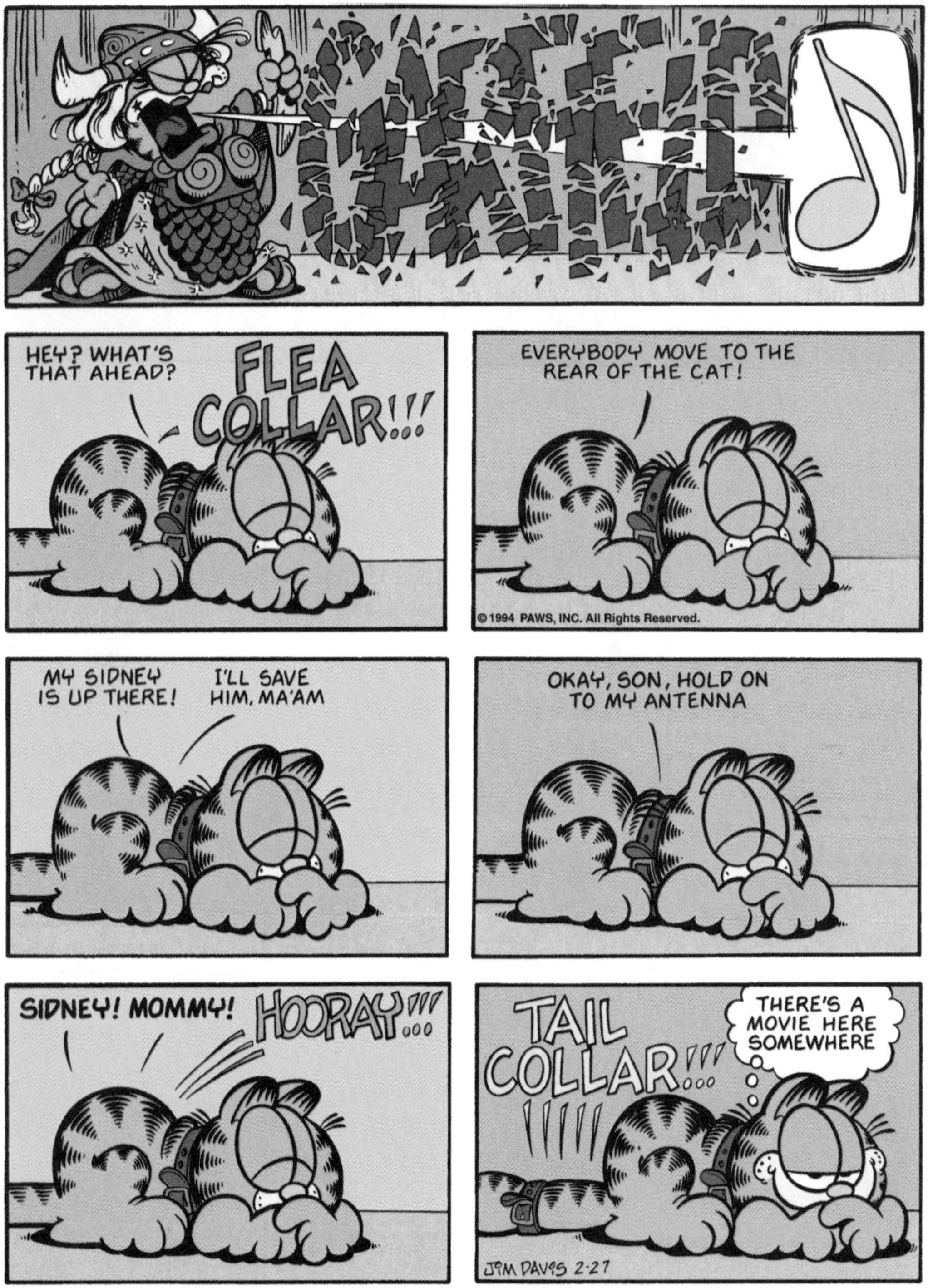
HEY? WHAT'S THAT AHEAD?
FLEA COLLAR!!!
EVERYBODY MOVE TO THE REAR OF THE CAT!
© 1994 PAWS, INC. All Rights Reserved.
MY SIDNEY IS UP THERE!
I'LL SAVE HIM, MA'AM
OKAY, SON, HOLD ON TO MY ANTENNA
SIDNEY!
MOMMY!
HOORAY!!!
TAIL COLLAR!!!
THERE'S A MOVIE HERE SOMEWHERE
JIM DAVIS 2-27

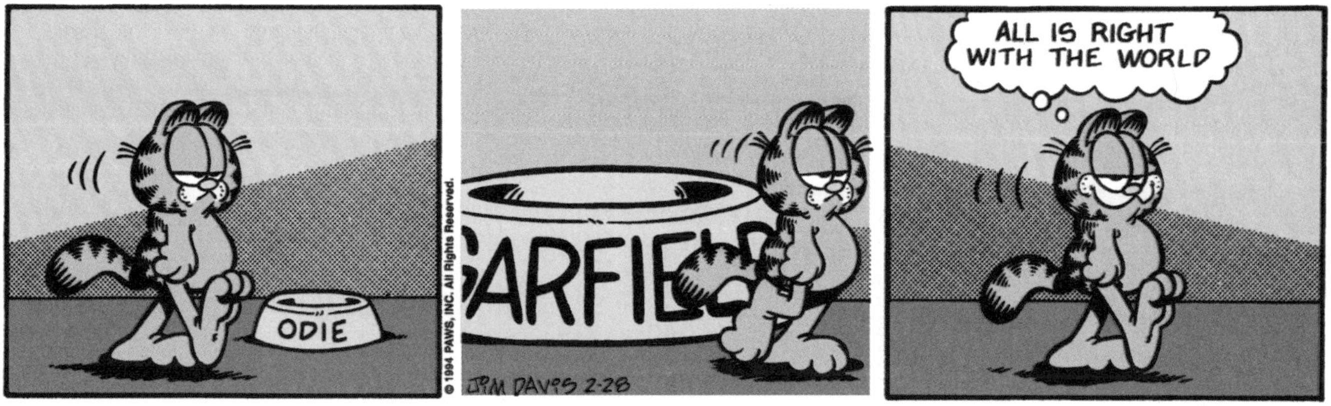
ODIE
GARFIE
© 1994 PAWS, INC. All Rights Reserved.
JIM DAVIS 2-28
ALL IS RIGHT WITH THE WORLD

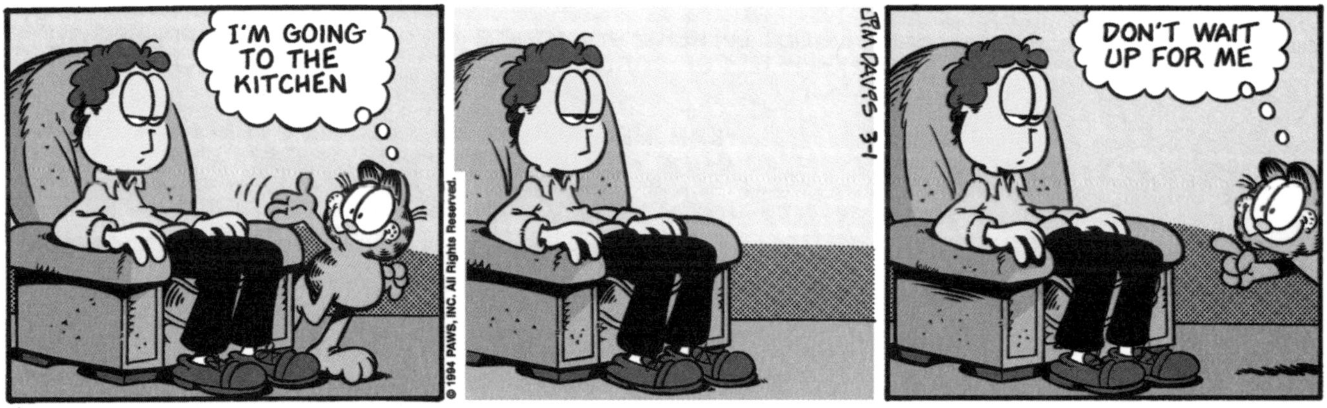
I'M GOING TO THE KITCHEN
© 1994 PAWS, INC. All Rights Reserved.
JIM DAVIS 3-1
DON'T WAIT UP FOR ME

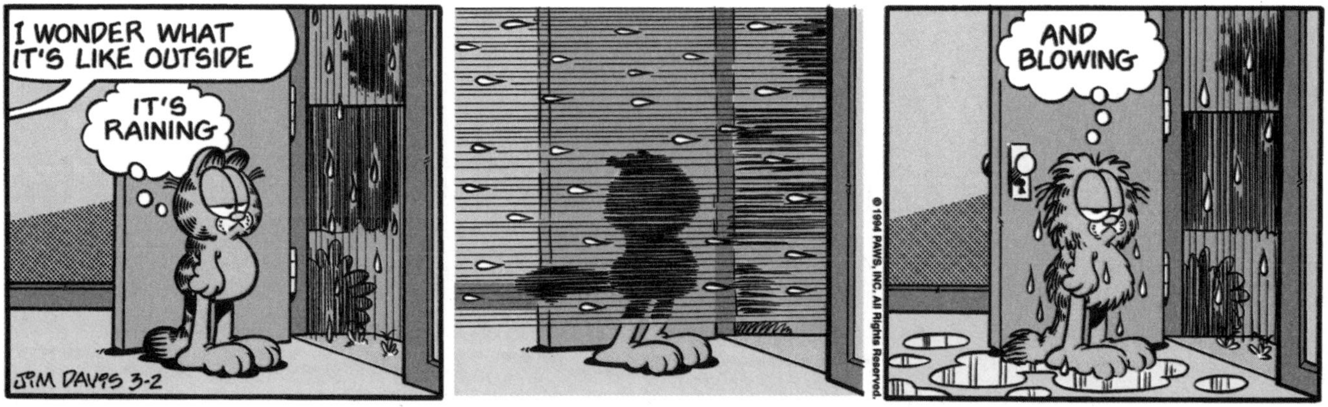
I WONDER WHAT IT'S LIKE OUTSIDE
IT'S RAINING
JIM DAVIS 3-2
© 1994 PAWS, INC. All Rights Reserved.
AND BLOWING

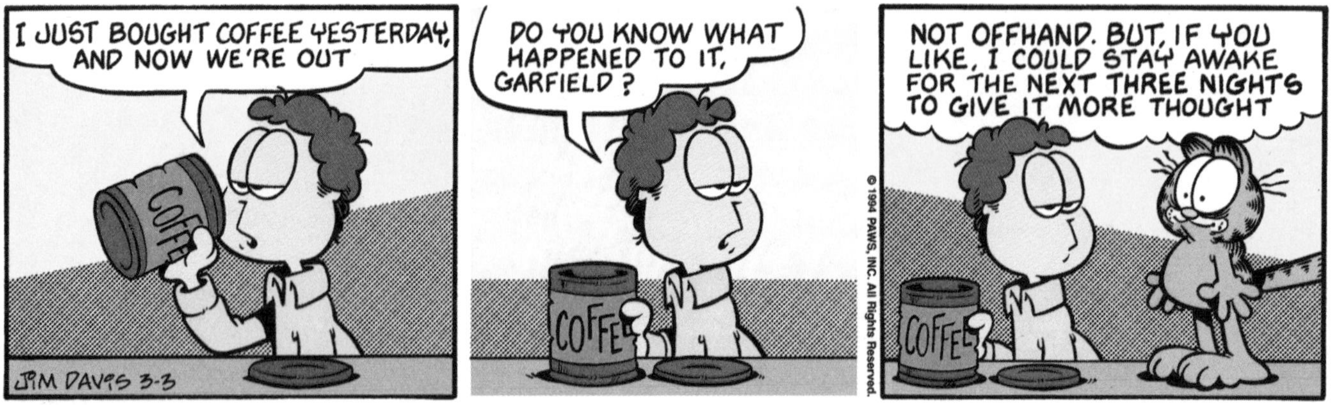
I JUST BOUGHT COFFEE YESTERDAY, AND NOW WE'RE OUT
COFFEE
DO YOU KNOW WHAT HAPPENED TO IT, GARFIELD?
NOT OFFHAND. BUT, IF YOU LIKE, I COULD STAY AWAKE FOR THE NEXT THREE NIGHTS TO GIVE IT MORE THOUGHT
JIM DAVIS 3-3

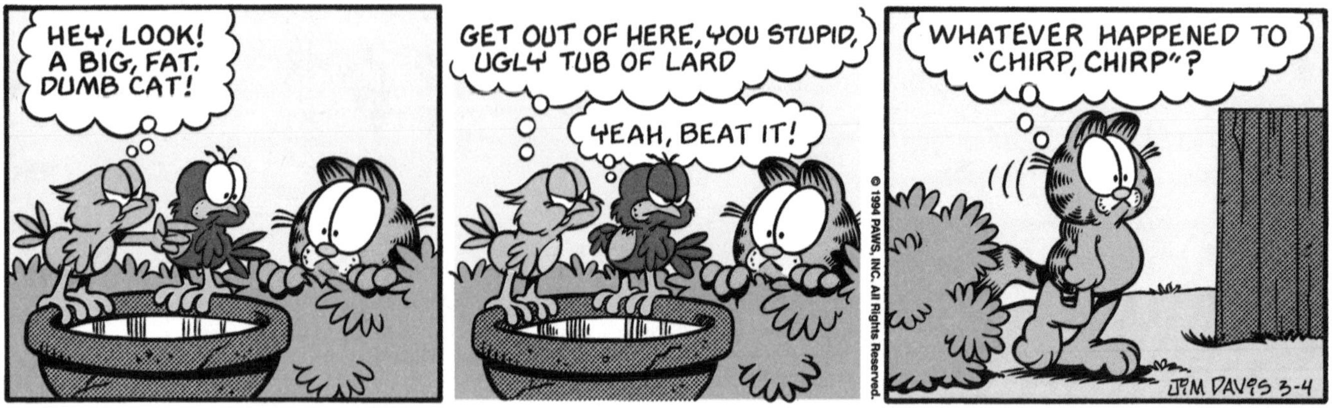
HEY, LOOK! A BIG, FAT, DUMB CAT!
GET OUT OF HERE, YOU STUPID, UGLY TUB OF LARD
YEAH, BEAT IT!
WHATEVER HAPPENED TO "CHIRP, CHIRP"?
JIM DAVIS 3-4

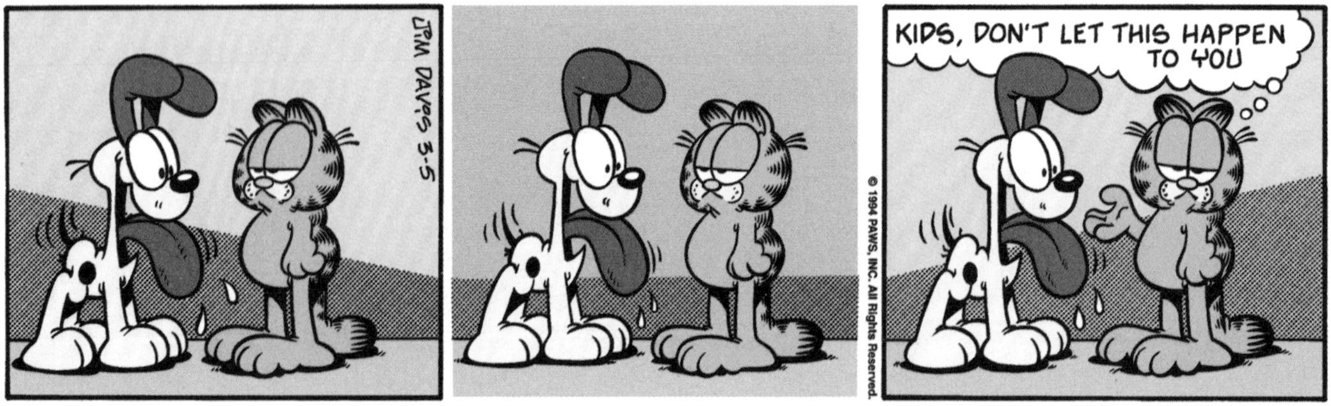
JIM DAVIS 3-5
KIDS, DON'T LET THIS HAPPEN TO YOU

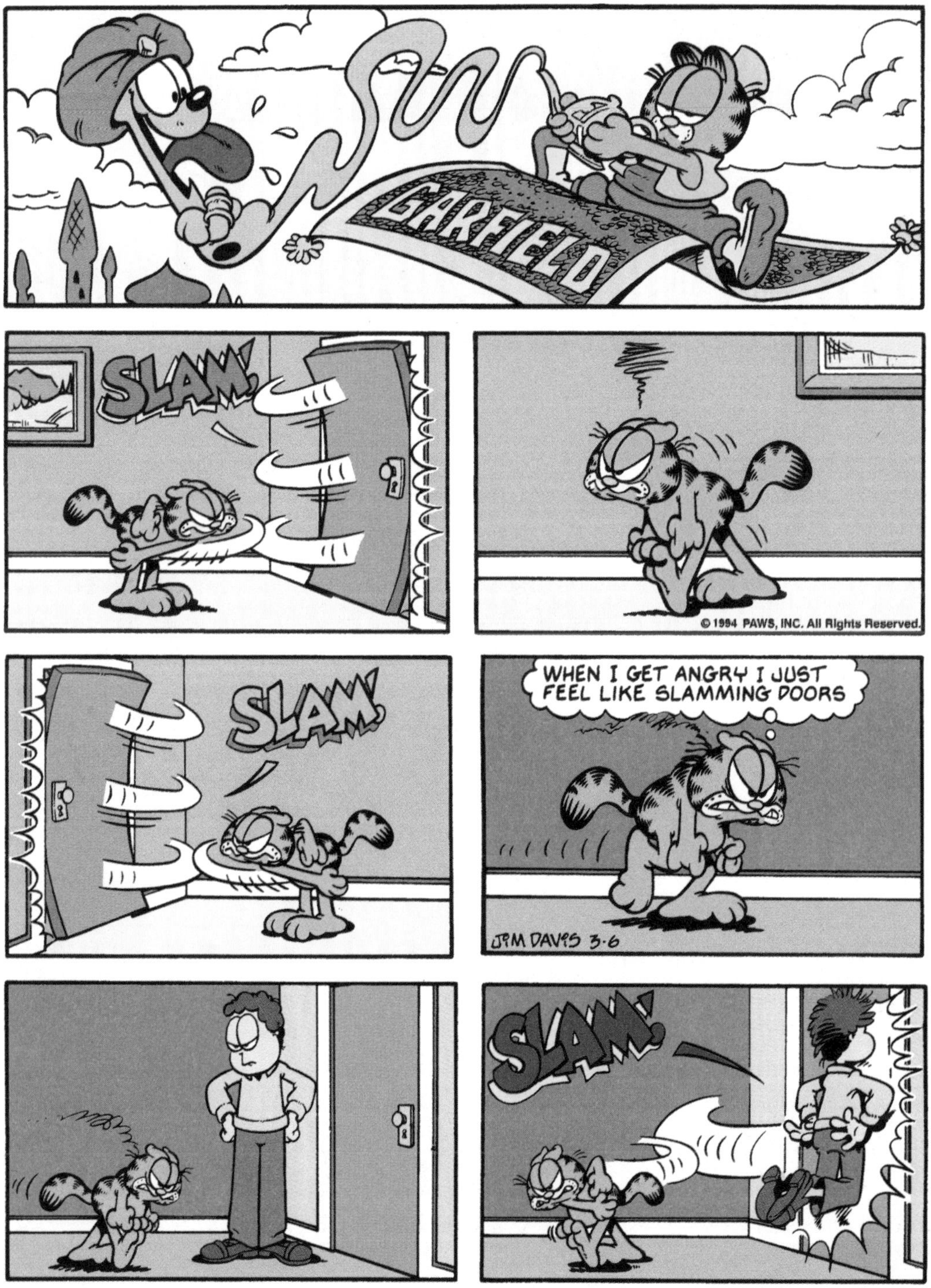
GARFIELD
SLAM!
© 1994 PAWS, INC. All Rights Reserved.
SLAM!
WHEN I GET ANGRY I JUST FEEL LIKE SLAMMING DOORS
JIM DAVIS 3-6
SLAM!

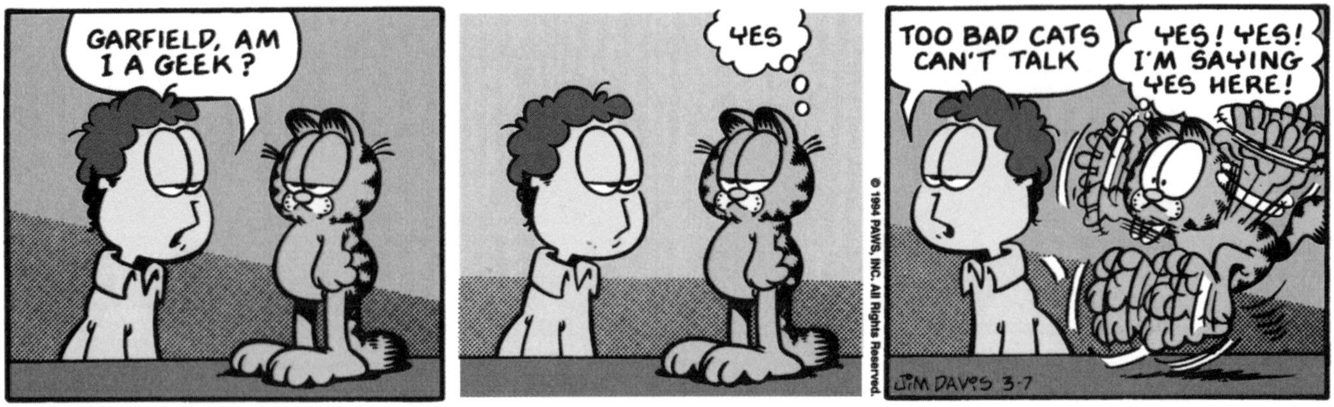
GARFIELD, AM I A GEEK?
YES
© 1994 PAWS, INC. All Rights Reserved.
TOO BAD CATS CAN'T TALK
YES! YES! I'M SAYING YES HERE!
JIM DAVIS 3-7

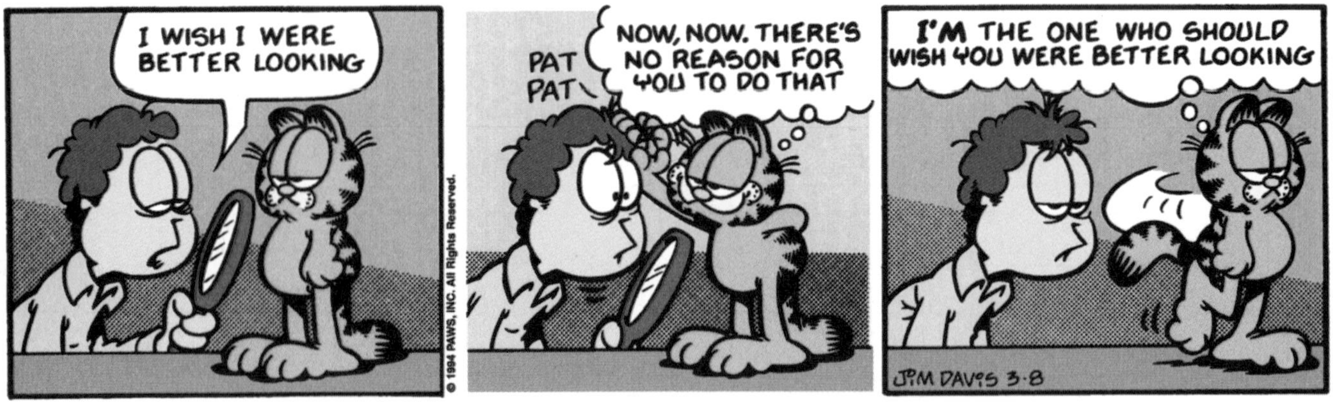
I WISH I WERE BETTER LOOKING
© 1994 PAWS, INC. All Rights Reserved.
PAT PAT
NOW, NOW. THERE'S NO REASON FOR YOU TO DO THAT
I'M THE ONE WHO SHOULD WISH YOU WERE BETTER LOOKING
JIM DAVIS 3-8

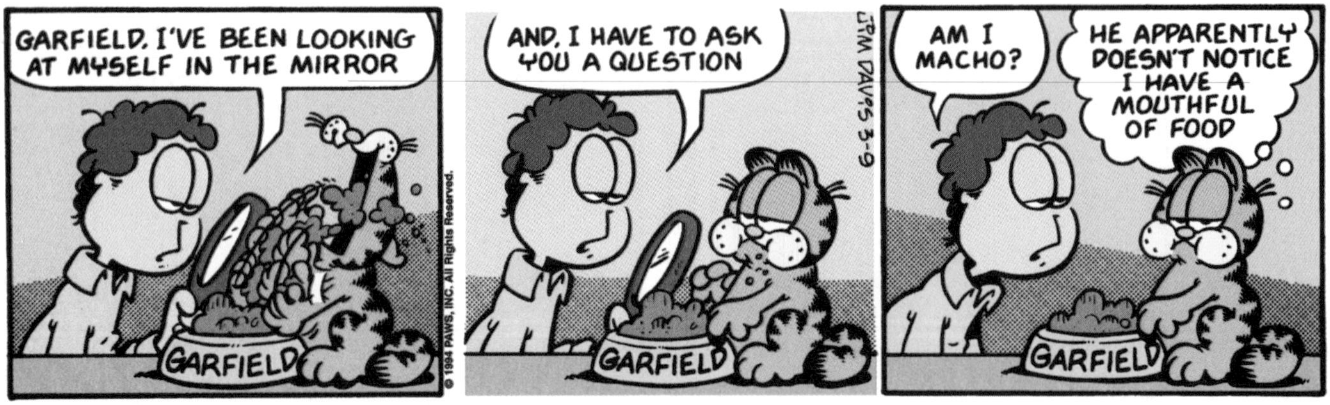
GARFIELD, I'VE BEEN LOOKING AT MYSELF IN THE MIRROR
GARFIELD
© 1994 PAWS, INC. All Rights Reserved.
AND, I HAVE TO ASK YOU A QUESTION
GARFIELD
JIM DAVIS 3-9
AM I MACHO?
HE APPARENTLY DOESN'T NOTICE I HAVE A MOUTHFUL OF FOOD
GARFIELD

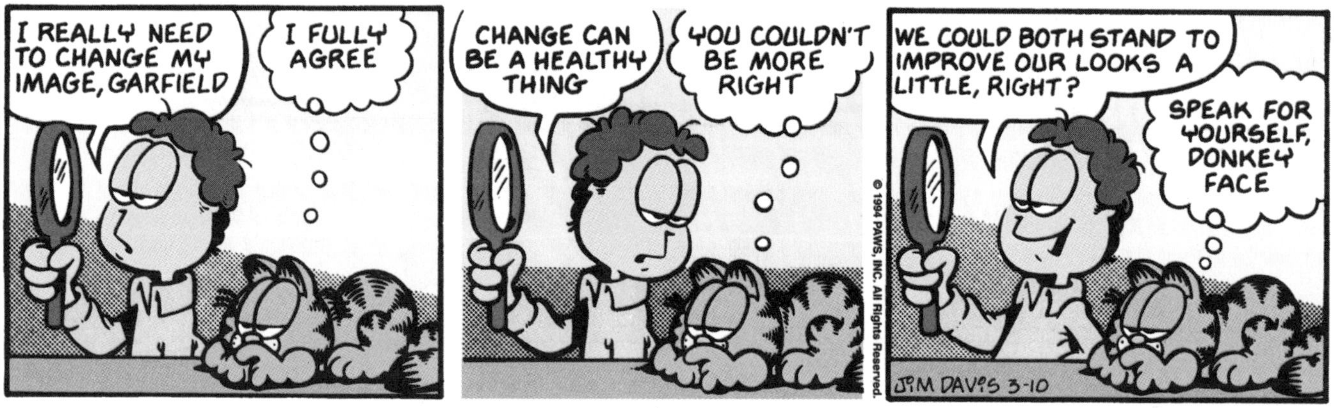
I REALLY NEED TO CHANGE MY IMAGE, GARFIELD
I FULLY AGREE
CHANGE CAN BE A HEALTHY THING
YOU COULDN'T BE MORE RIGHT
© 1994 PAWS, INC. All Rights Reserved.
WE COULD BOTH STAND TO IMPROVE OUR LOOKS A LITTLE, RIGHT?
SPEAK FOR YOURSELF, DONKEY FACE
JIM DAVIS 3-10

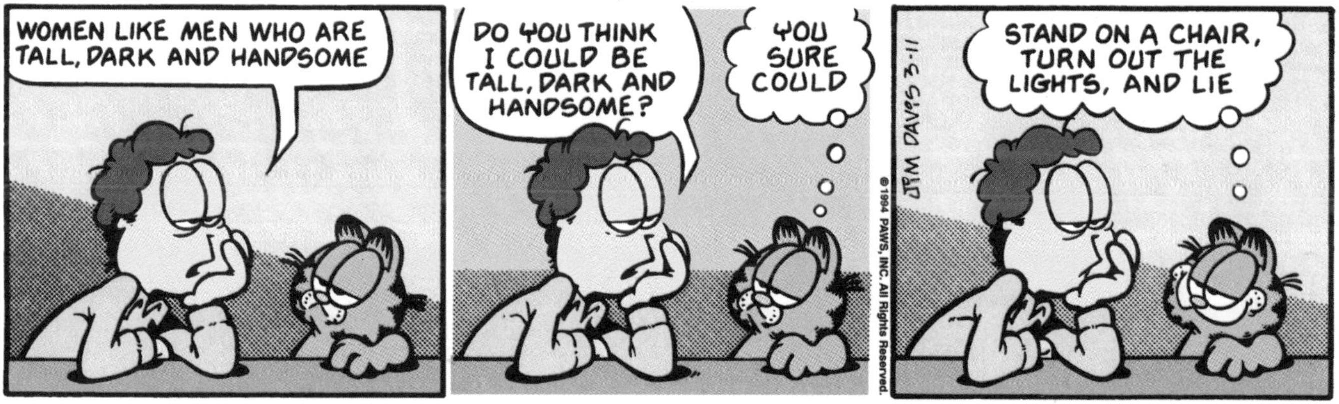
WOMEN LIKE MEN WHO ARE TALL, DARK AND HANDSOME
DO YOU THINK I COULD BE TALL, DARK AND HANDSOME?
YOU SURE COULD
© 1994 PAWS, INC. All Rights Reserved.
JIM DAVIS 3-11
STAND ON A CHAIR, TURN OUT THE LIGHTS, AND LIE

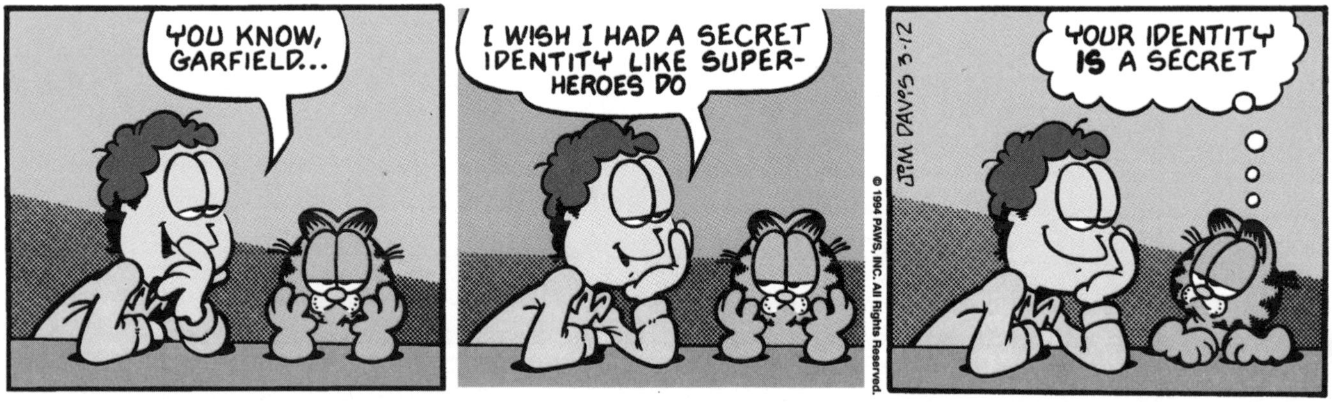
YOU KNOW, GARFIELD...
I WISH I HAD A SECRET IDENTITY LIKE SUPER-HEROES DO
© 1994 PAWS, INC. All Rights Reserved.
JIM DAVIS 3-12
YOUR IDENTITY **IS** A SECRET

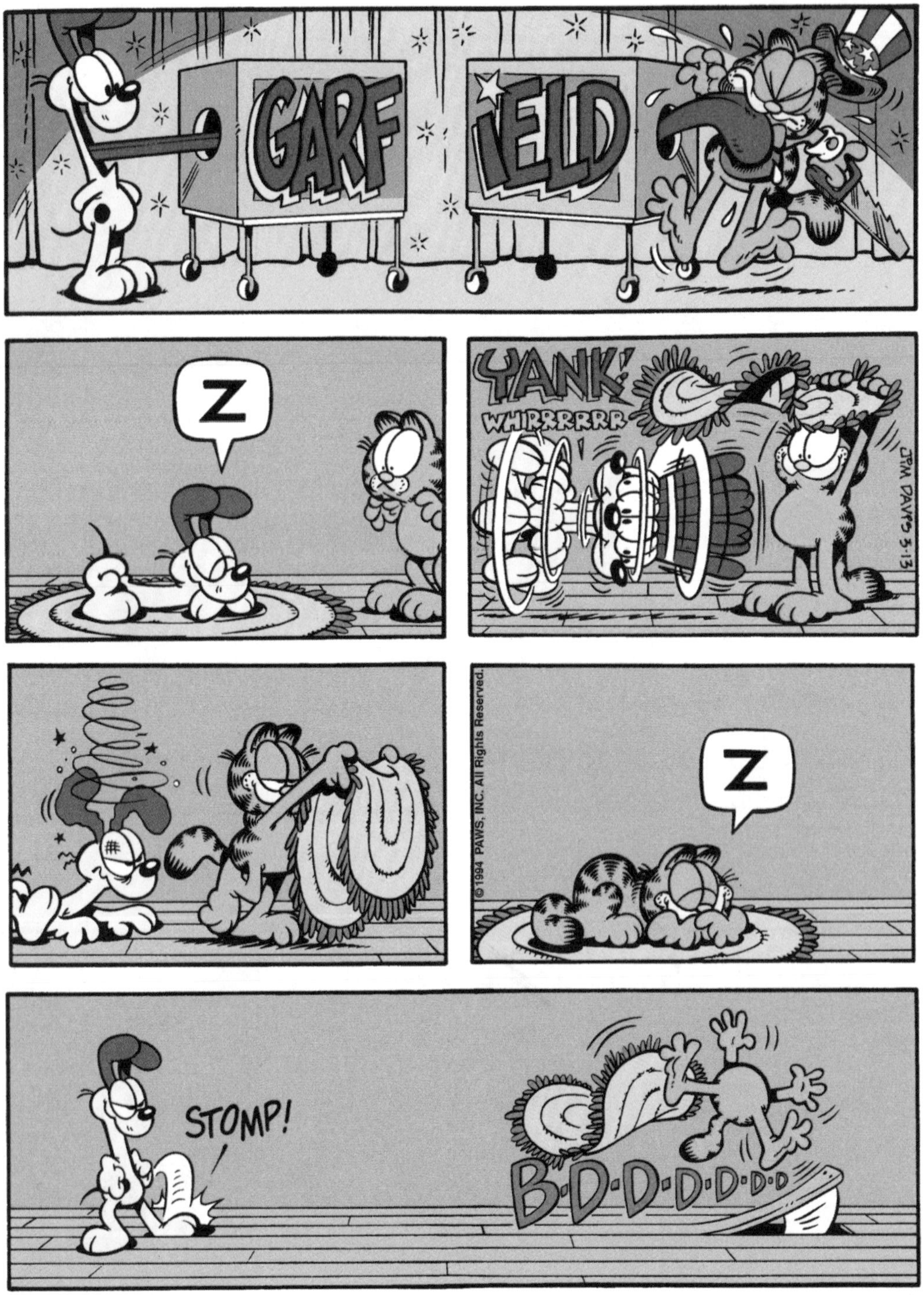
GARF
IELD
Z
YANK!
WHIRRRRRR
JIM DAVIS 3-13
© 1994 PAWS, INC. All Rights Reserved.
Z
STOMP!
B-D-D-D-D-D-D

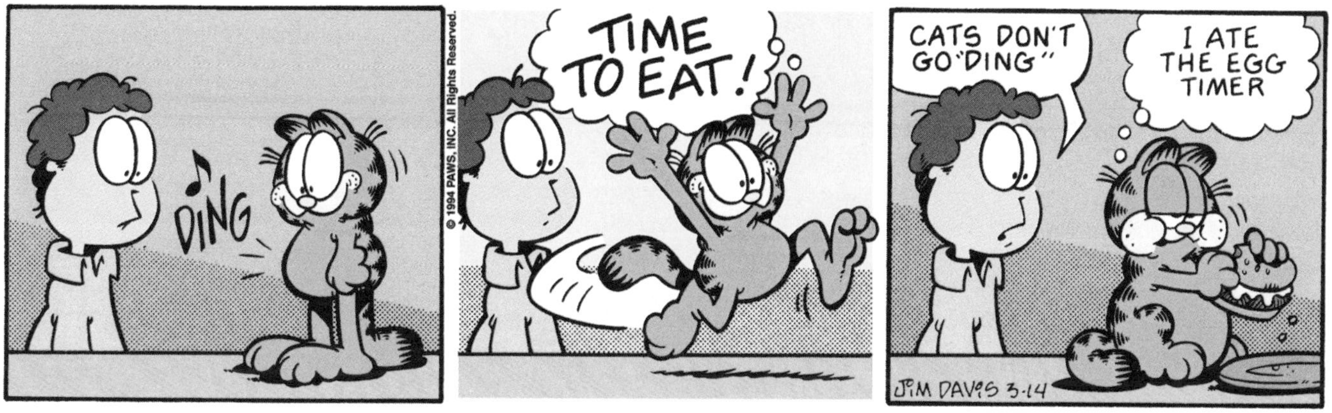
DING
© 1994 PAWS, INC. All Rights Reserved.
TIME TO EAT!
CATS DON'T GO "DING"
I ATE THE EGG TIMER
JIM DAVIS 3-14

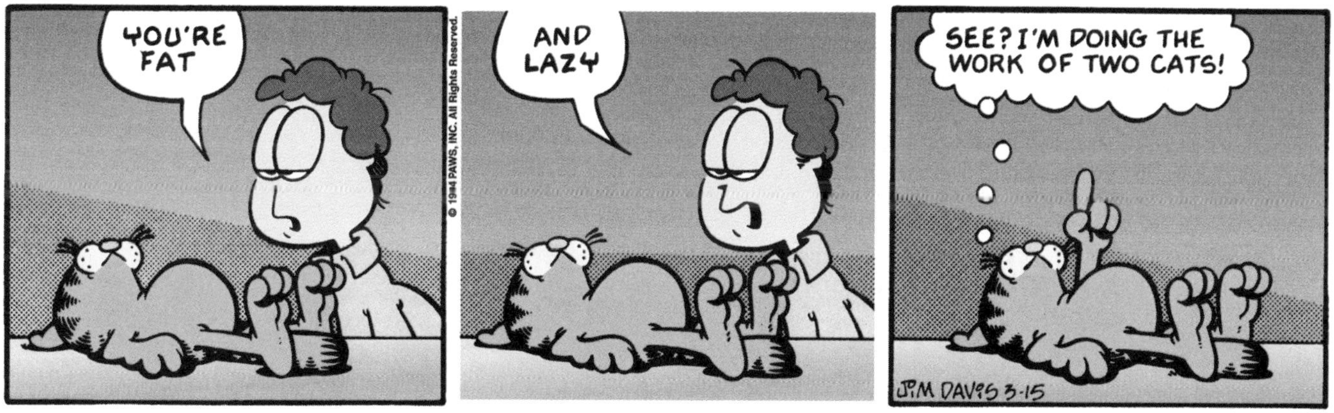
YOU'RE FAT
© 1994 PAWS, INC. All Rights Reserved.
AND LAZY
SEE? I'M DOING THE WORK OF TWO CATS!
JIM DAVIS 3-15

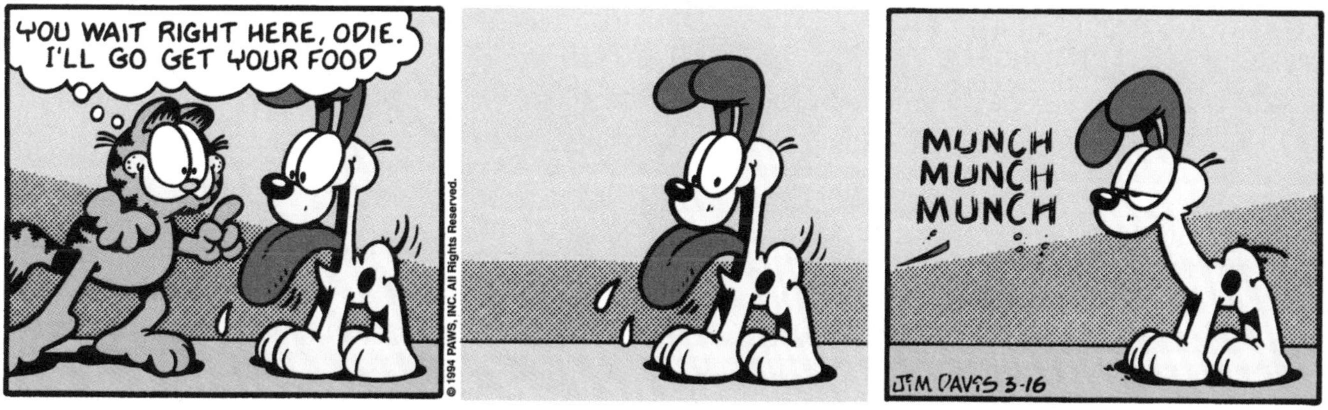
YOU WAIT RIGHT HERE, ODIE. I'LL GO GET YOUR FOOD
© 1994 PAWS, INC. All Rights Reserved.
MUNCH MUNCH MUNCH
JIM DAVIS 3-16

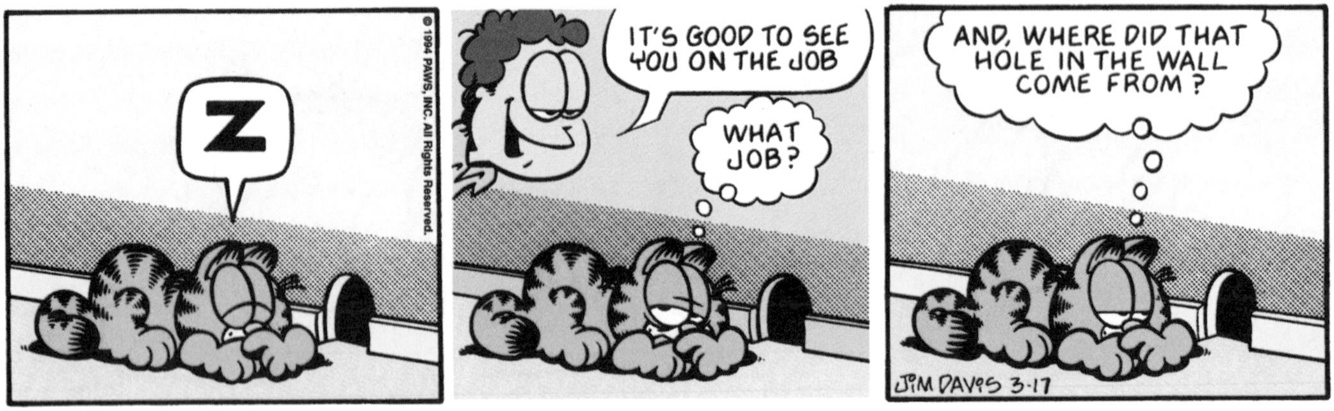
Z
IT'S GOOD TO SEE YOU ON THE JOB
WHAT JOB?
AND, WHERE DID THAT HOLE IN THE WALL COME FROM?
© 1994 PAWS, INC. All Rights Reserved.
JIM DAVIS 3-17

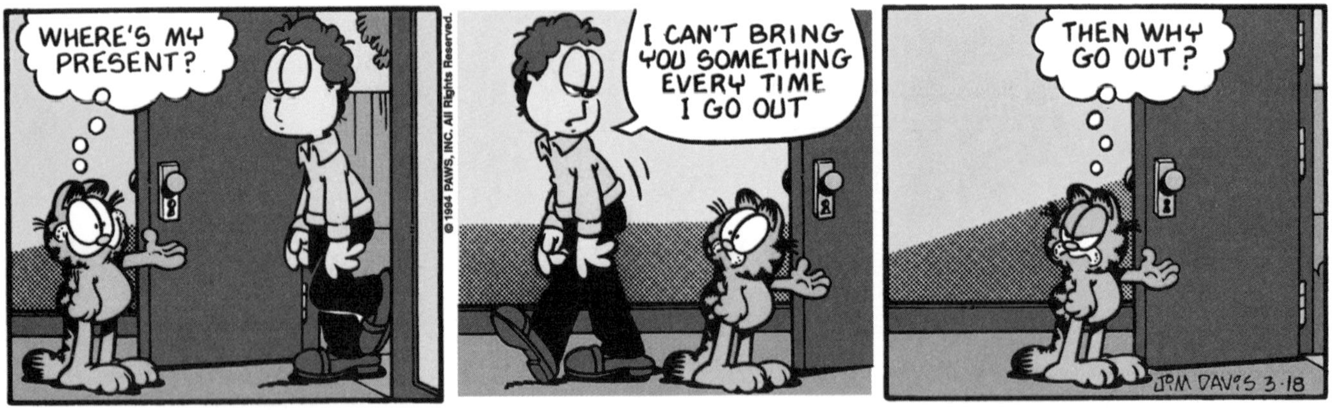
WHERE'S MY PRESENT?
I CAN'T BRING YOU SOMETHING EVERY TIME I GO OUT
THEN WHY GO OUT?
© 1994 PAWS, INC. All Rights Reserved.
JIM DAVIS 3-18

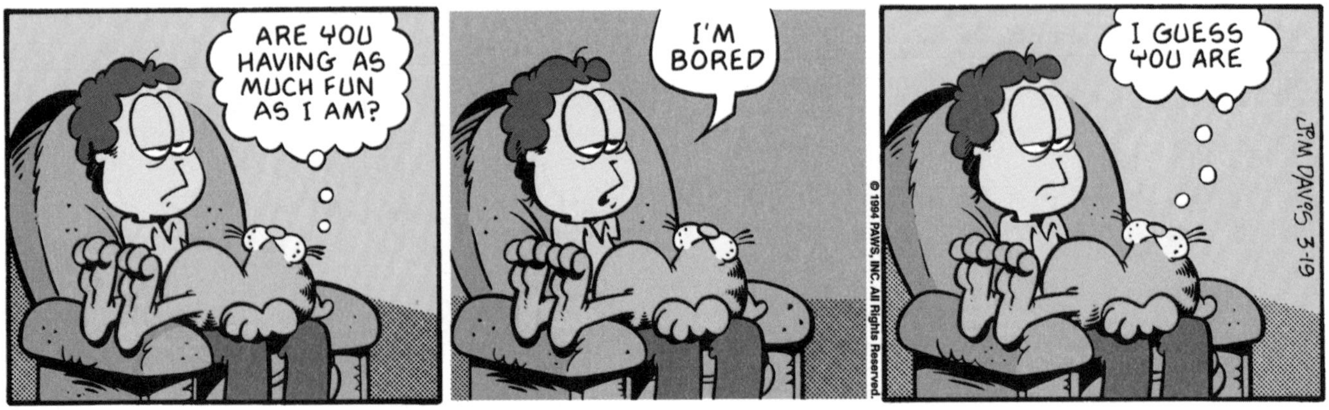
ARE YOU HAVING AS MUCH FUN AS I AM?
I'M BORED
I GUESS YOU ARE
© 1994 PAWS, INC. All Rights Reserved.
JIM DAVIS 3-19

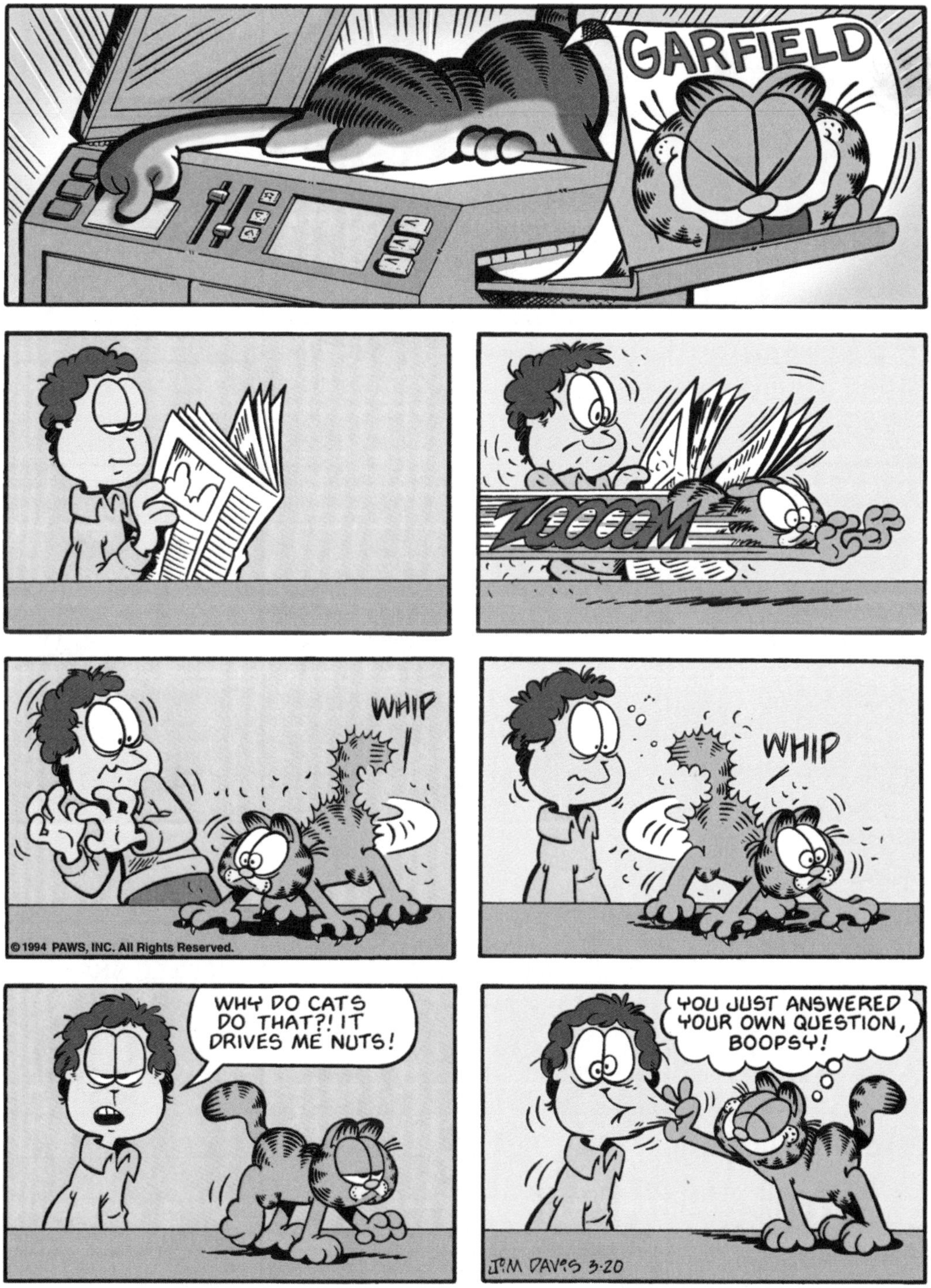
GARFIELD
ZOOOOM
WHIP
WHIP
WHY DO CATS DO THAT?! IT DRIVES ME NUTS!
YOU JUST ANSWERED YOUR OWN QUESTION, BOOPSY!
JIM DAVIS 3-20

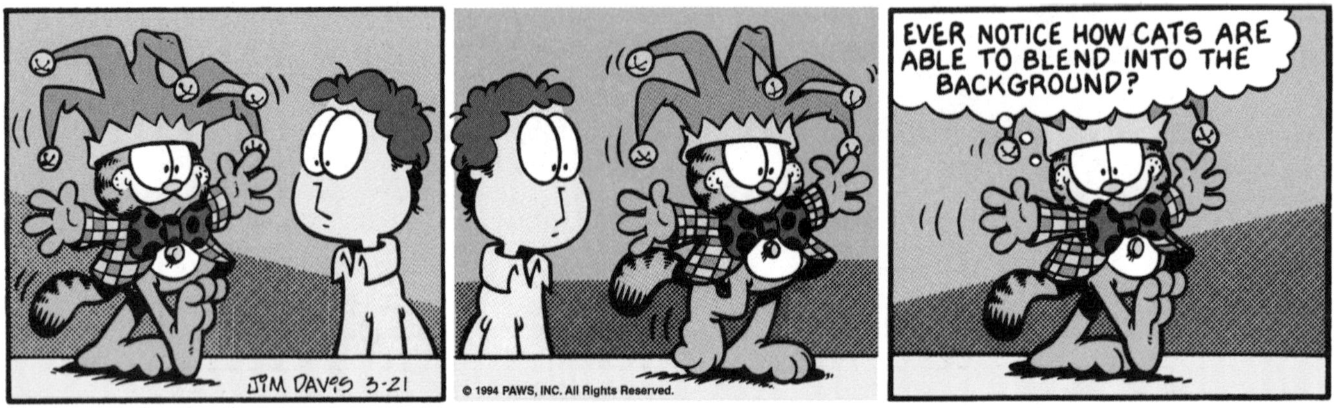
JIM DAVIS 3-21
© 1994 PAWS, INC. All Rights Reserved.
EVER NOTICE HOW CATS ARE ABLE TO BLEND INTO THE BACKGROUND?

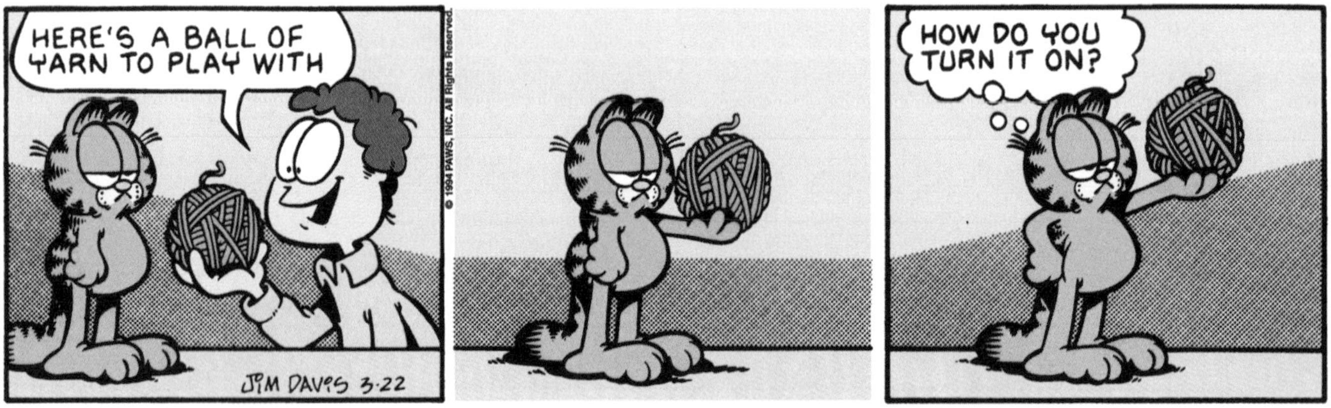
HERE'S A BALL OF YARN TO PLAY WITH
JIM DAVIS 3-22
© 1994 PAWS, INC. All Rights Reserved.
HOW DO YOU TURN IT ON?

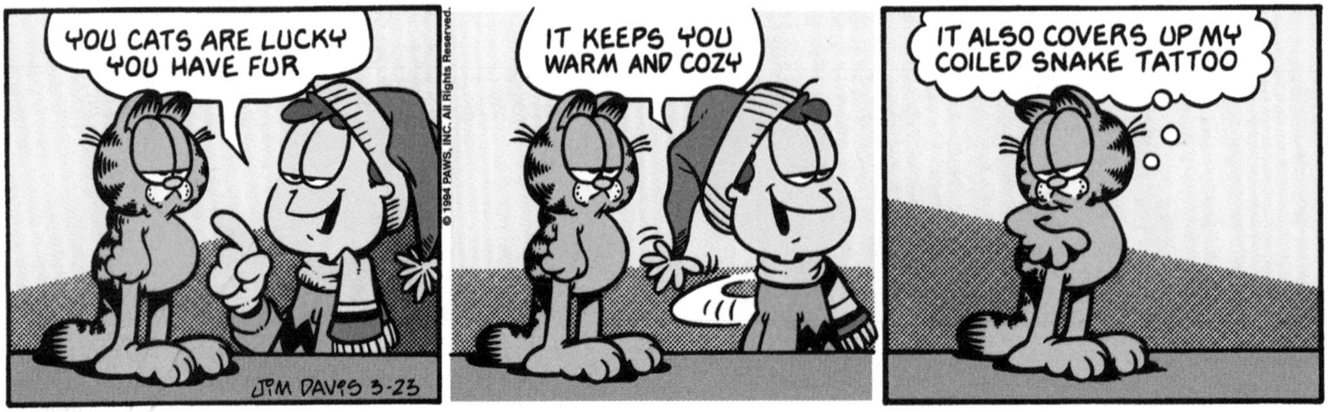
YOU CATS ARE LUCKY YOU HAVE FUR
JIM DAVIS 3-23
© 1994 PAWS, INC. All Rights Reserved.
IT KEEPS YOU WARM AND COZY
IT ALSO COVERS UP MY COILED SNAKE TATTOO

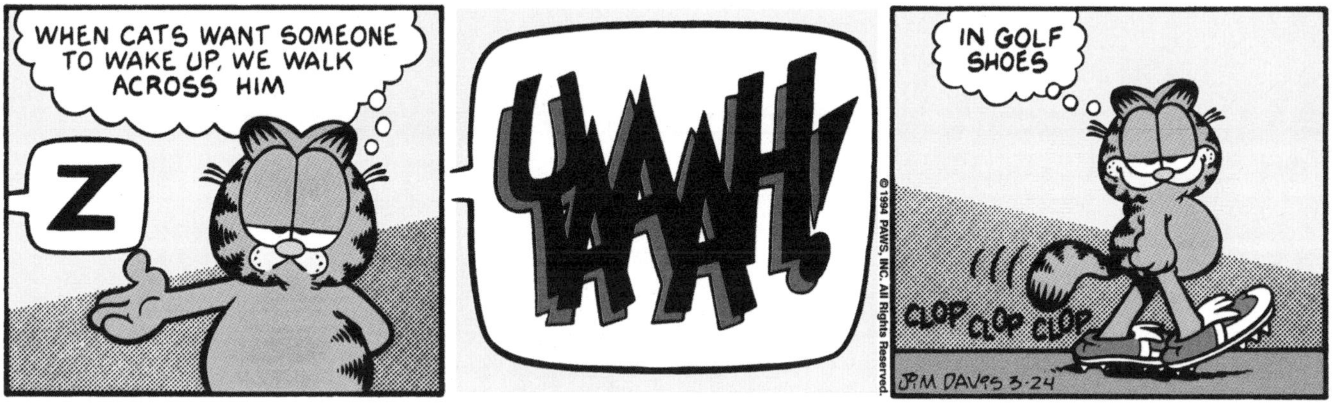
WHEN CATS WANT SOMEONE TO WAKE UP, WE WALK ACROSS HIM
Z
YAAAH!
IN GOLF SHOES
CLOP CLOP CLOP
© 1994 PAWS, INC. All Rights Reserved.
JIM DAVIS 3-24

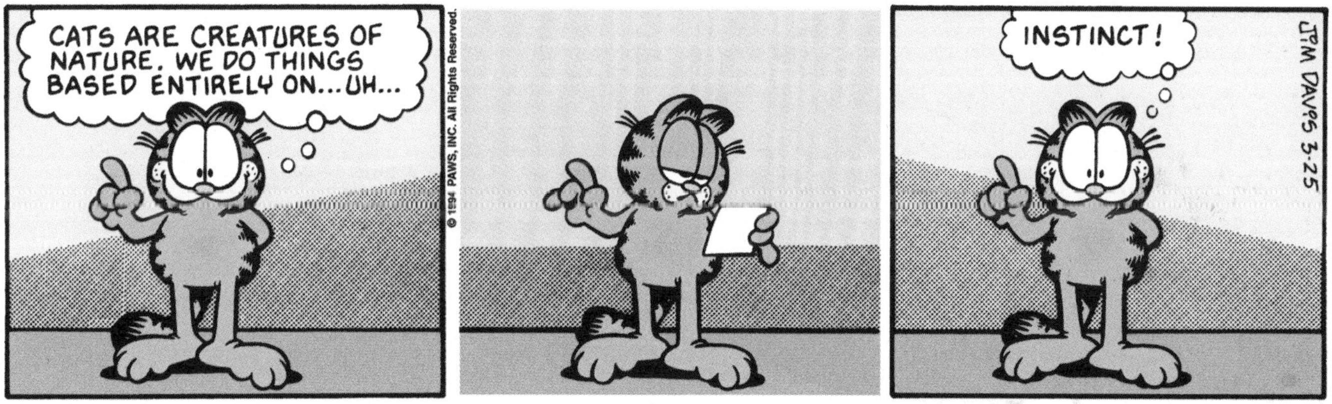
CATS ARE CREATURES OF NATURE. WE DO THINGS BASED ENTIRELY ON...UH...
© 1994 PAWS, INC. All Rights Reserved.
INSTINCT!
JIM DAVIS 3-25

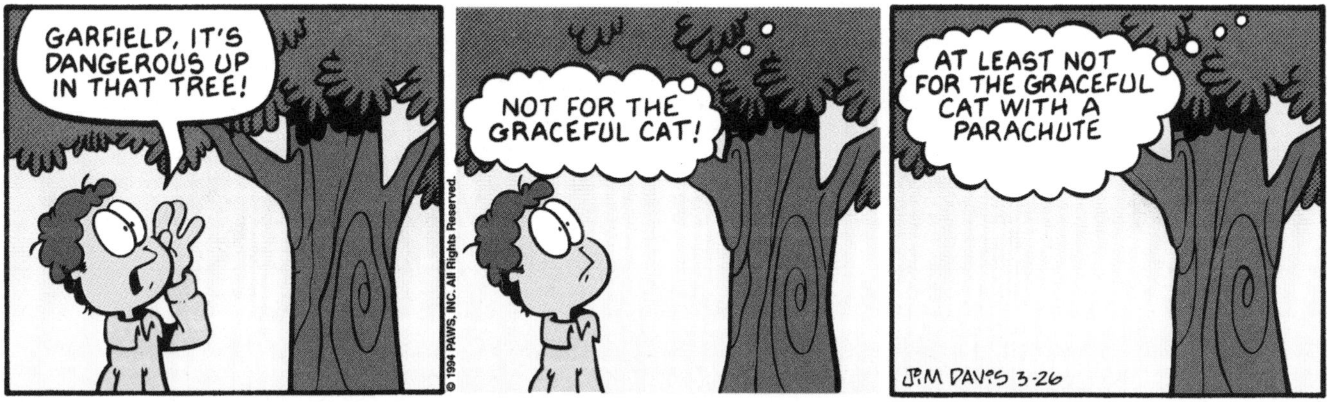
GARFIELD, IT'S DANGEROUS UP IN THAT TREE!
© 1994 PAWS, INC. All Rights Reserved.
NOT FOR THE GRACEFUL CAT!
AT LEAST NOT FOR THE GRACEFUL CAT WITH A PARACHUTE
JIM DAVIS 3-26

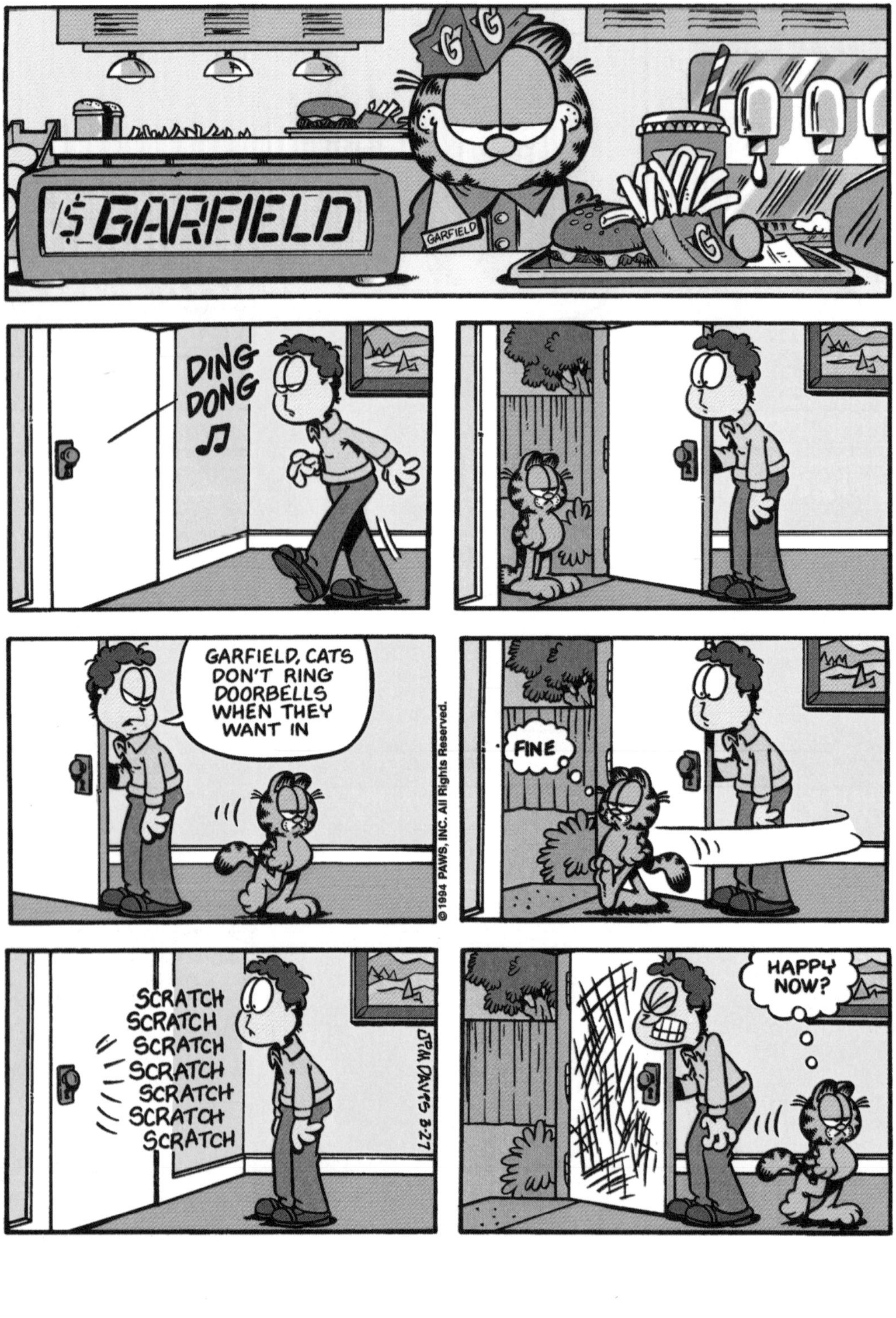
$GARFIELD
GARFIELD
DING DONG
GARFIELD, CATS DON'T RING DOORBELLS WHEN THEY WANT IN
FINE
SCRATCH SCRATCH SCRATCH SCRATCH SCRATCH SCRATCH SCRATCH SCRATCH
JPM DAVIS 3-27
HAPPY NOW?

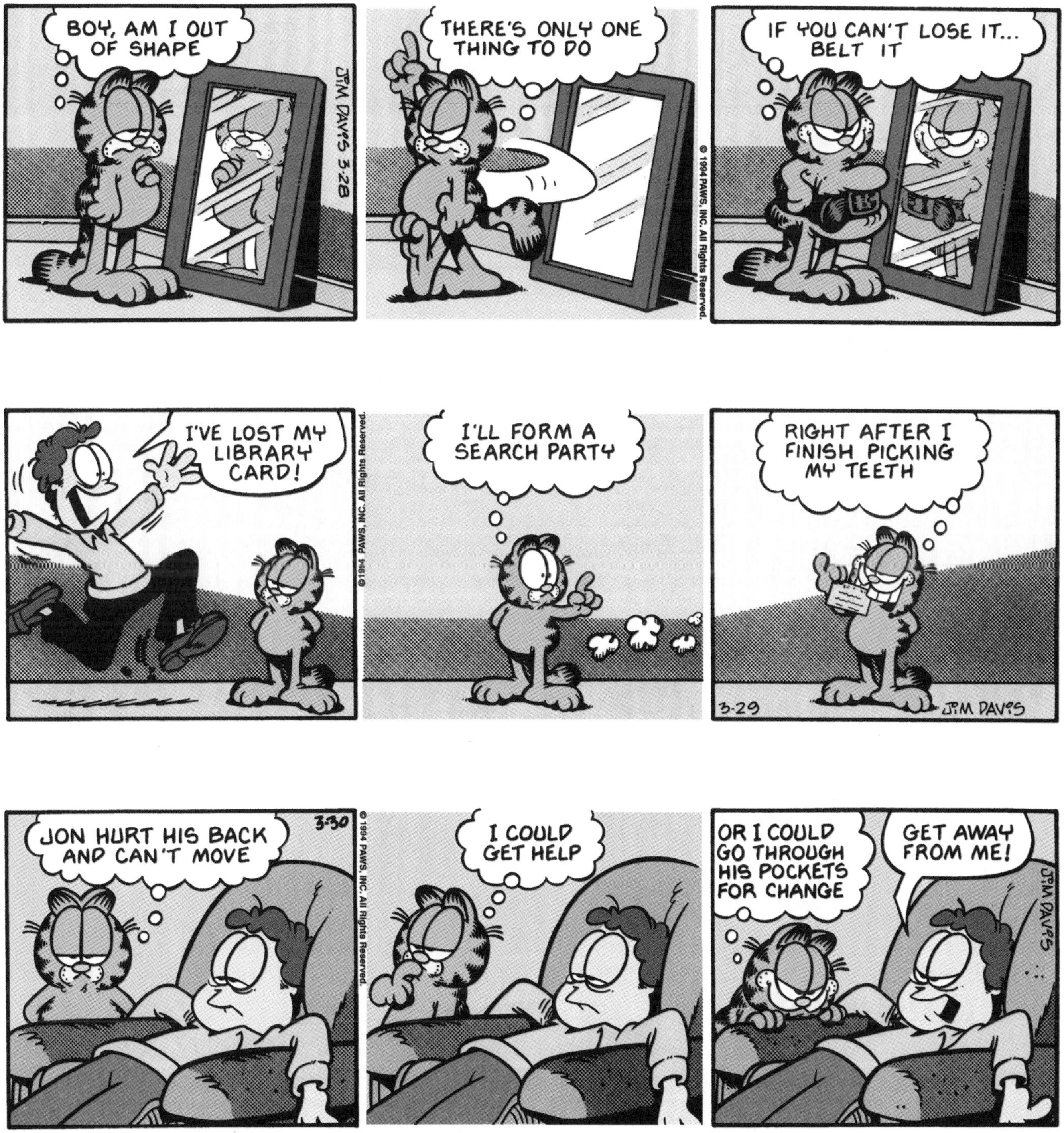
BOY, AM I OUT OF SHAPE
JIM DAVIS 3-28
THERE'S ONLY ONE THING TO DO
© 1994 PAWS, INC. All Rights Reserved.
IF YOU CAN'T LOSE IT... BELT IT
I'VE LOST MY LIBRARY CARD!
© 1994 PAWS, INC. All Rights Reserved.
I'LL FORM A SEARCH PARTY
RIGHT AFTER I FINISH PICKING MY TEETH
3-29
JIM DAVIS
JON HURT HIS BACK AND CAN'T MOVE
3-30
© 1994 PAWS, INC. All Rights Reserved.
I COULD GET HELP
OR I COULD GO THROUGH HIS POCKETS FOR CHANGE
GET AWAY FROM ME!
JIM DAVIS

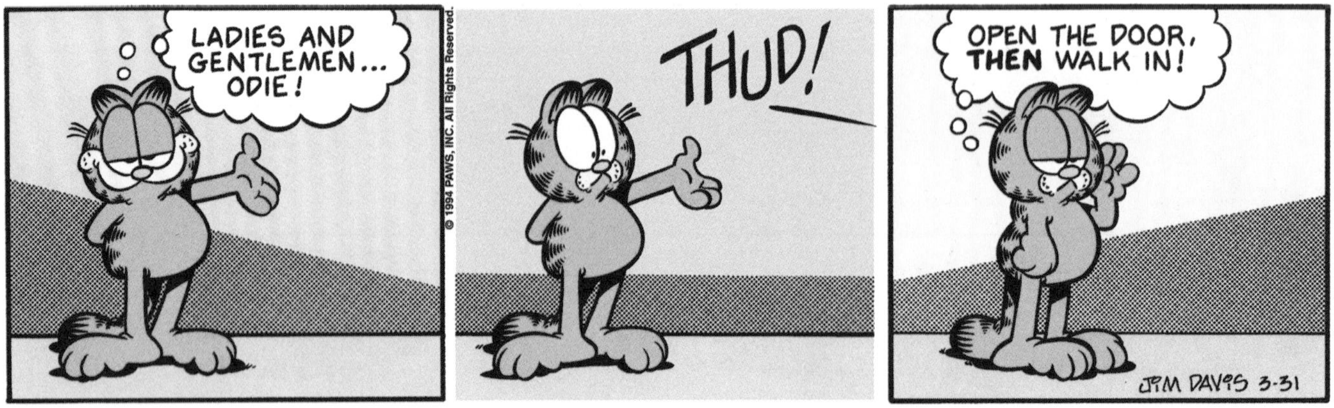
LADIES AND GENTLEMEN... ODIE!
© 1994 PAWS, INC. All Rights Reserved.
THUD!
OPEN THE DOOR, **THEN** WALK IN!
JIM DAVIS 3-31

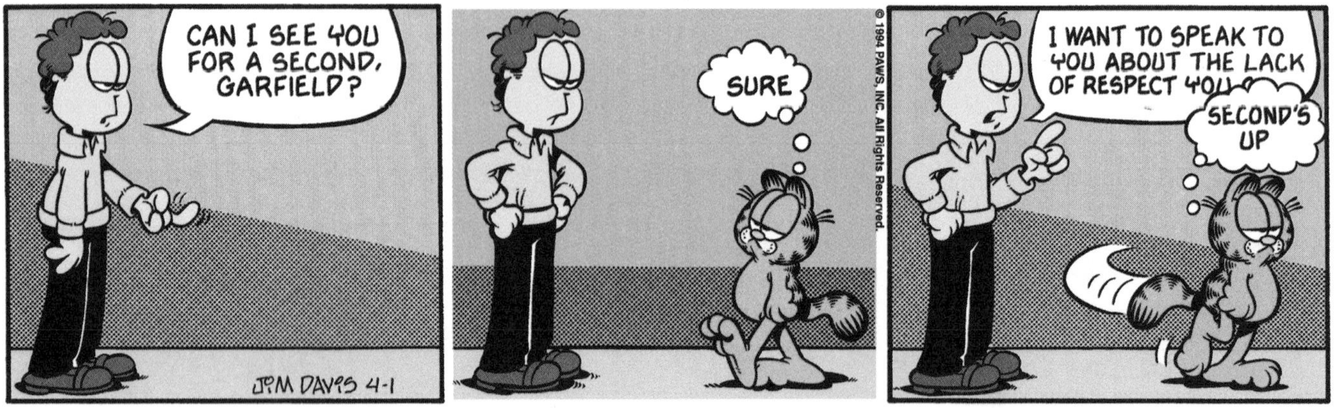
CAN I SEE YOU FOR A SECOND, GARFIELD?
JIM DAVIS 4-1
SURE
© 1994 PAWS, INC. All Rights Reserved.
I WANT TO SPEAK TO YOU ABOUT THE LACK OF RESPECT YOU
SECOND'S UP

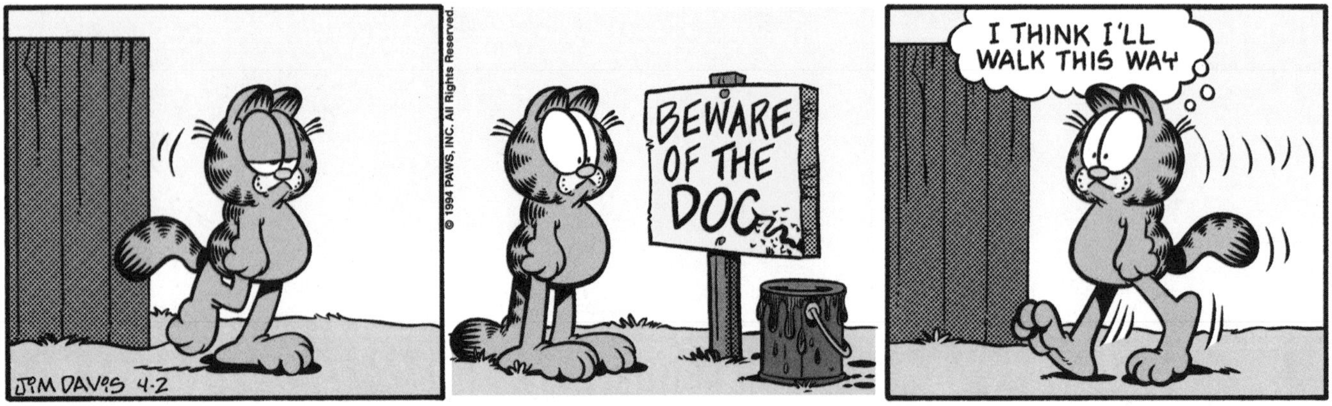
JIM DAVIS 4-2
© 1994 PAWS, INC. All Rights Reserved.
BEWARE OF THE DOG
I THINK I'LL WALK THIS WAY

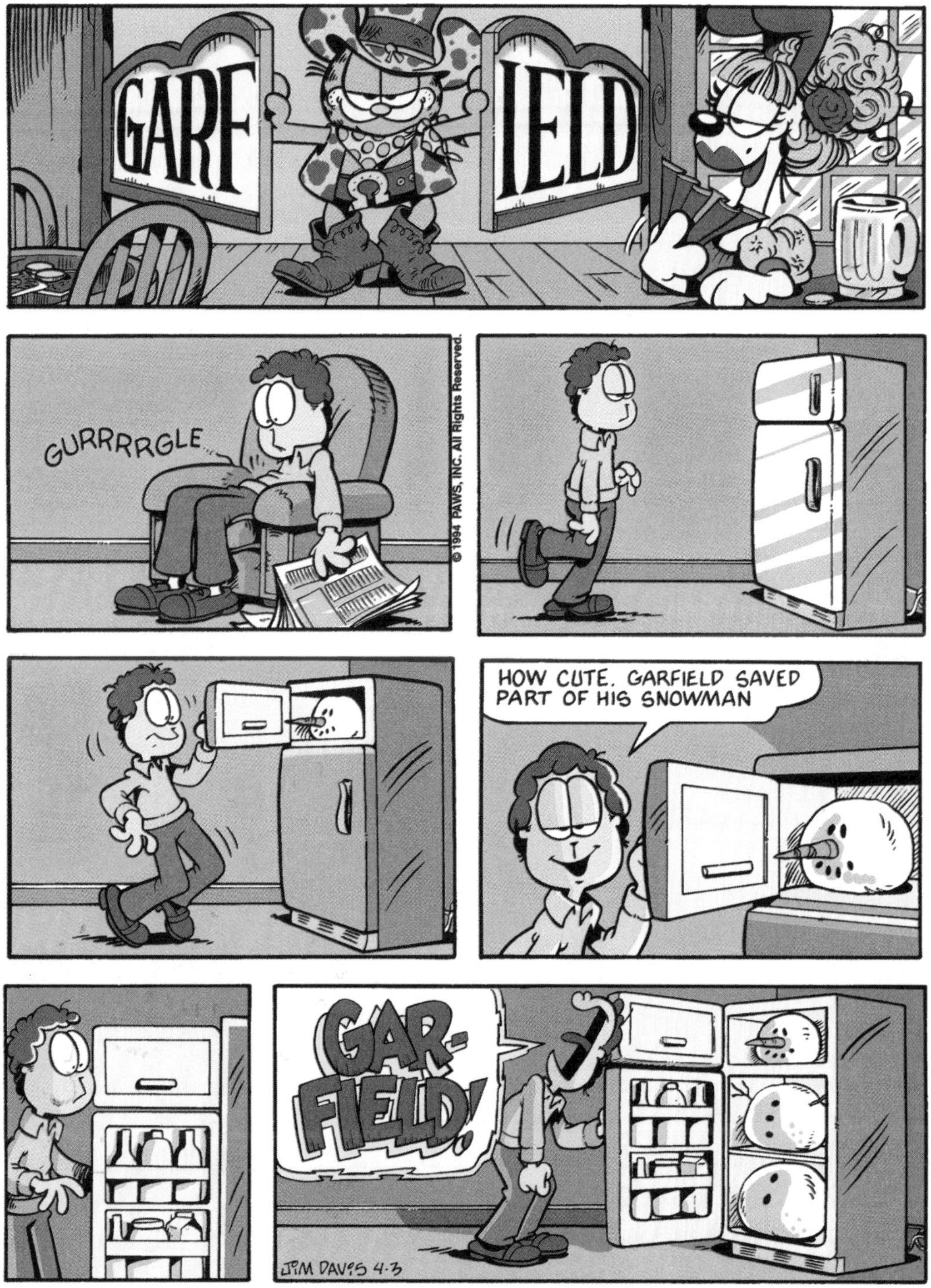
GARF
IELD
© 1994 PAWS, INC. All Rights Reserved.
GURRRRGLE...
HOW CUTE. GARFIELD SAVED PART OF HIS SNOWMAN
GAR-FIELD!
JIM DAVIS 4-3

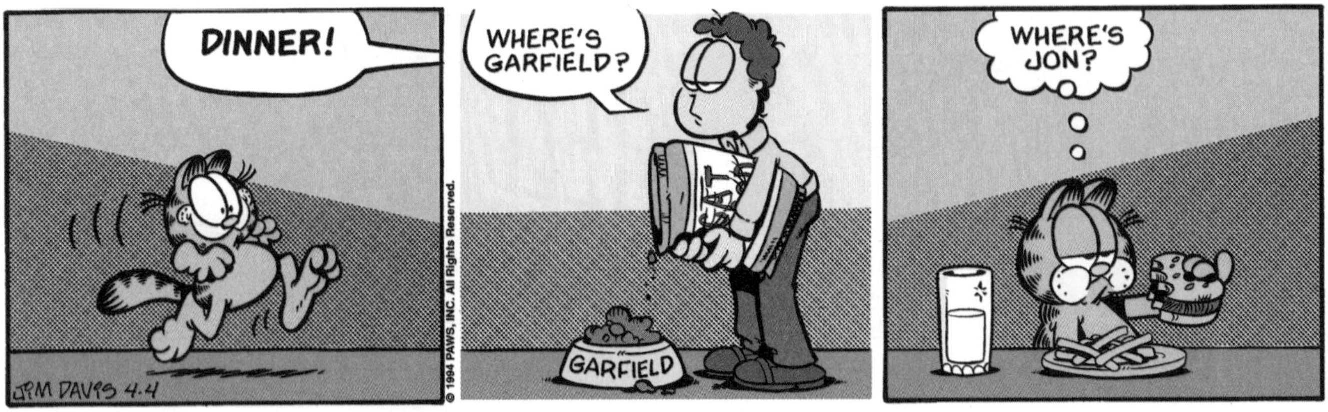
DINNER!
WHERE'S GARFIELD?
WHERE'S JON?
GARFIELD
JIM DAVIS 4-4
© 1994 PAWS, INC. All Rights Reserved.

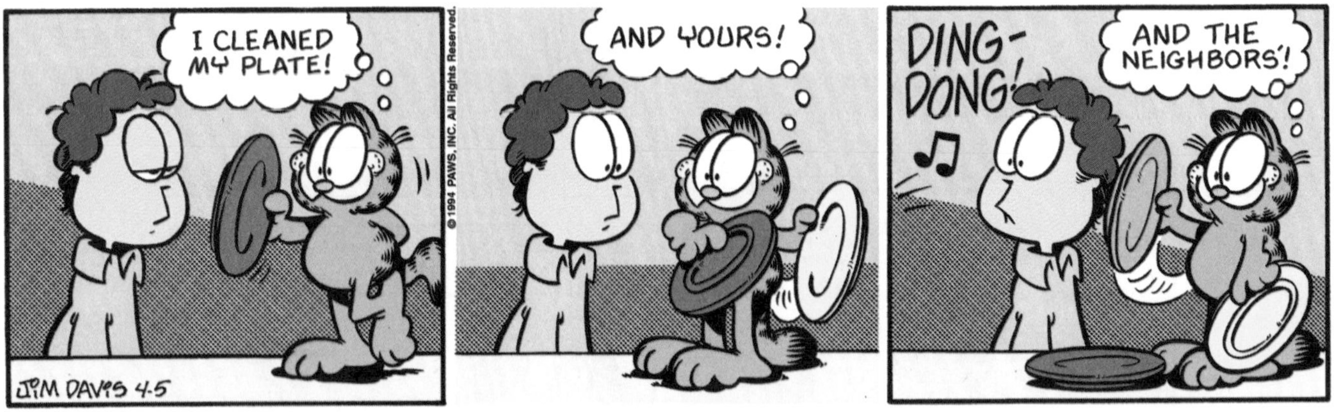
I CLEANED MY PLATE!
AND YOURS!
DING-DONG!
AND THE NEIGHBORS'!
JIM DAVIS 4-5
© 1994 PAWS, INC. All Rights Reserved.

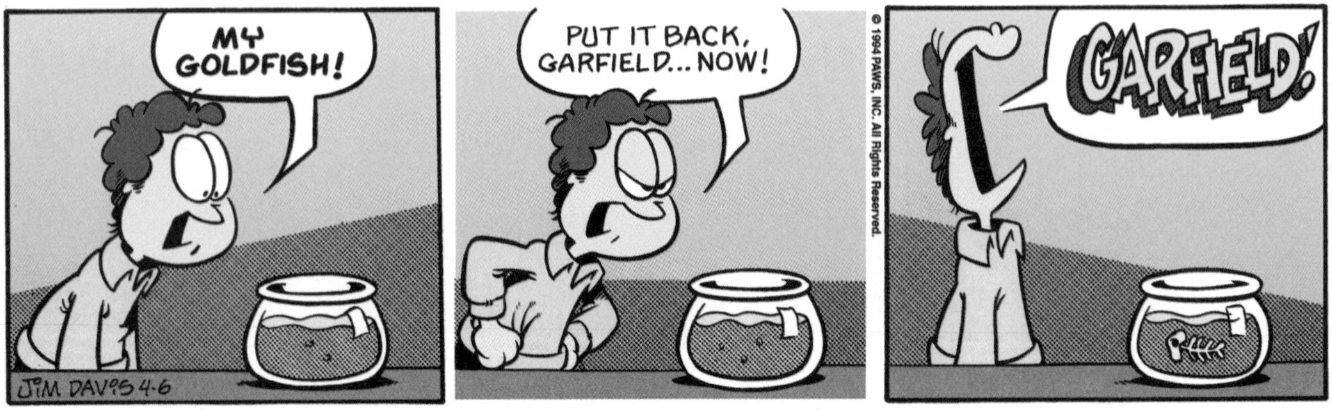
MY GOLDFISH!
PUT IT BACK, GARFIELD... NOW!
GARFIELD!
JIM DAVIS 4-6
© 1994 PAWS, INC. All Rights Reserved.

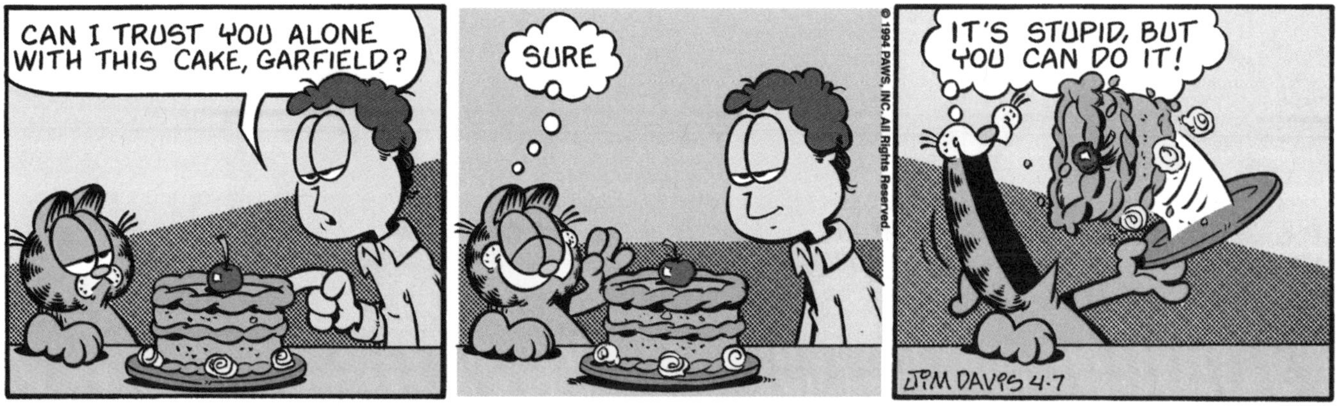
CAN I TRUST YOU ALONE WITH THIS CAKE, GARFIELD?
SURE
© 1994 PAWS, INC. All Rights Reserved.
IT'S STUPID, BUT YOU CAN DO IT!
JIM DAVIS 4-7

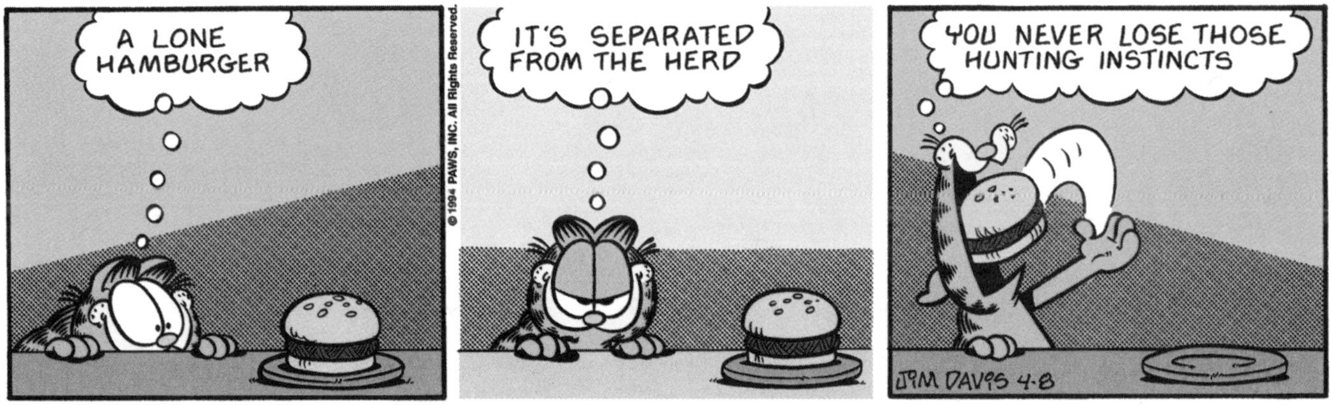
A LONE HAMBURGER
© 1994 PAWS, INC. All Rights Reserved.
IT'S SEPARATED FROM THE HERD
YOU NEVER LOSE THOSE HUNTING INSTINCTS
JIM DAVIS 4-8

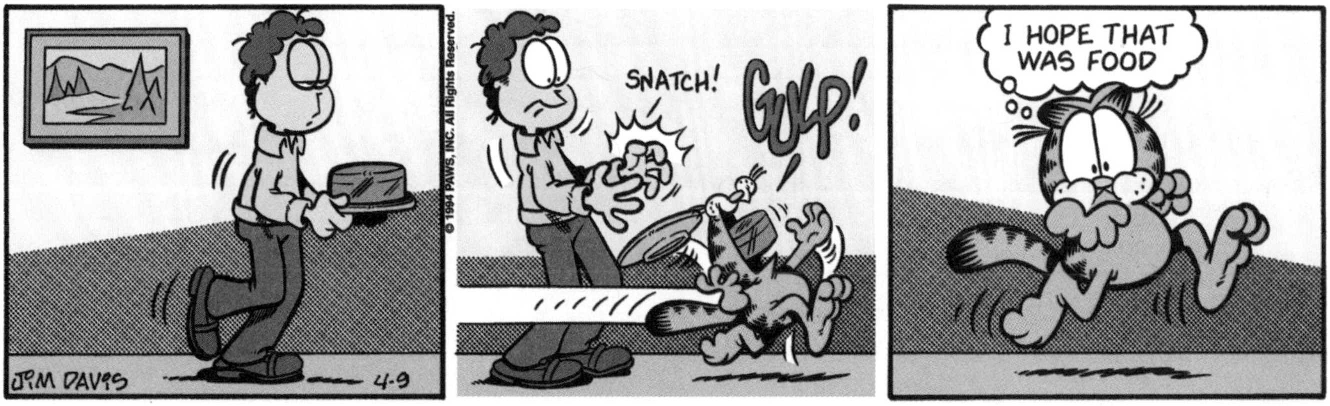
JIM DAVIS 4-9
© 1994 PAWS, INC. All Rights Reserved.
SNATCH!
GULP!
I HOPE THAT WAS FOOD

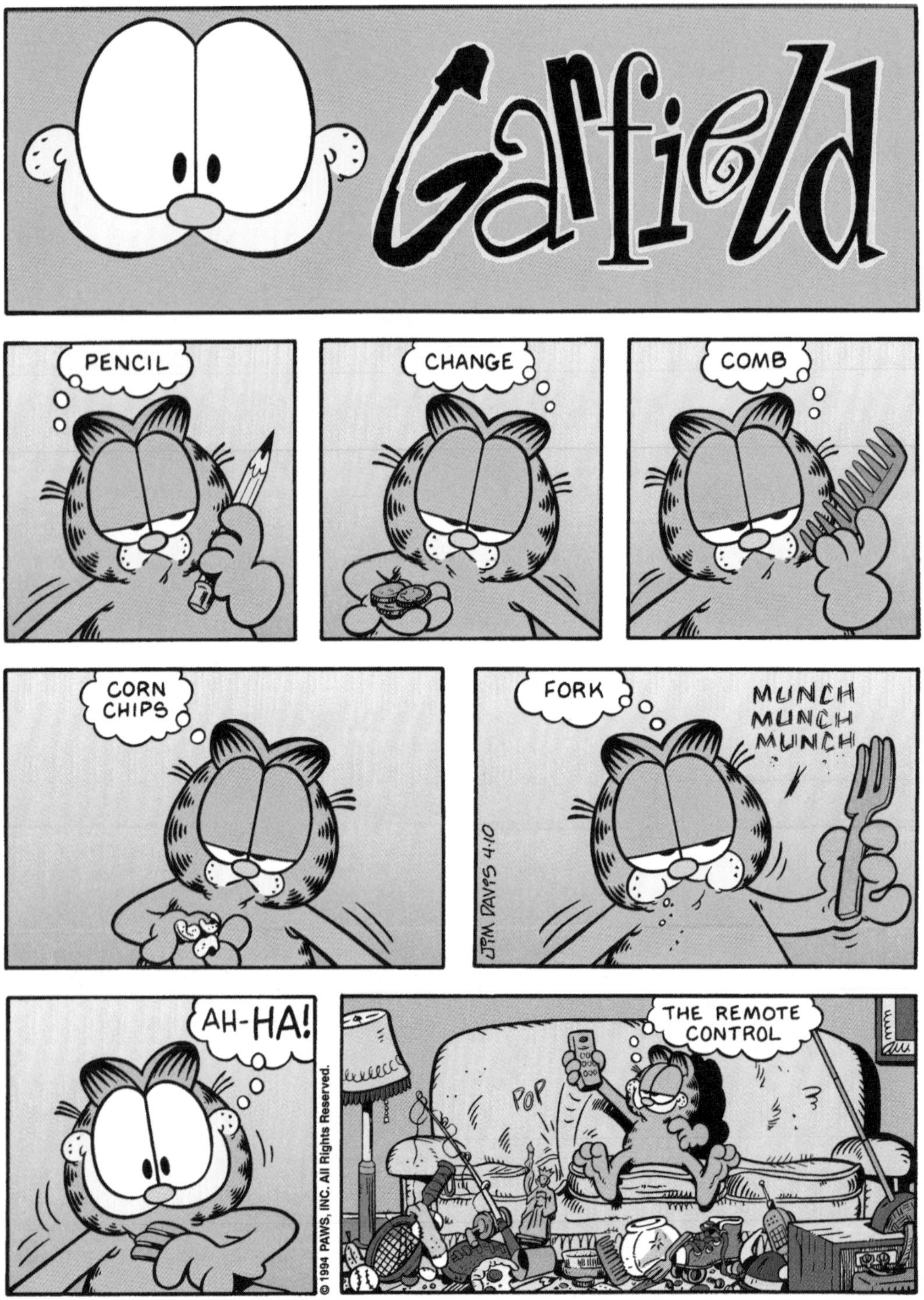
Garfield
PENCIL
CHANGE
COMB
CORN CHIPS
FORK
MUNCH
MUNCH
MUNCH
JIM DAVIS 4-10
AH-HA!
© 1994 PAWS, INC. All Rights Reserved.
THE REMOTE CONTROL
POP

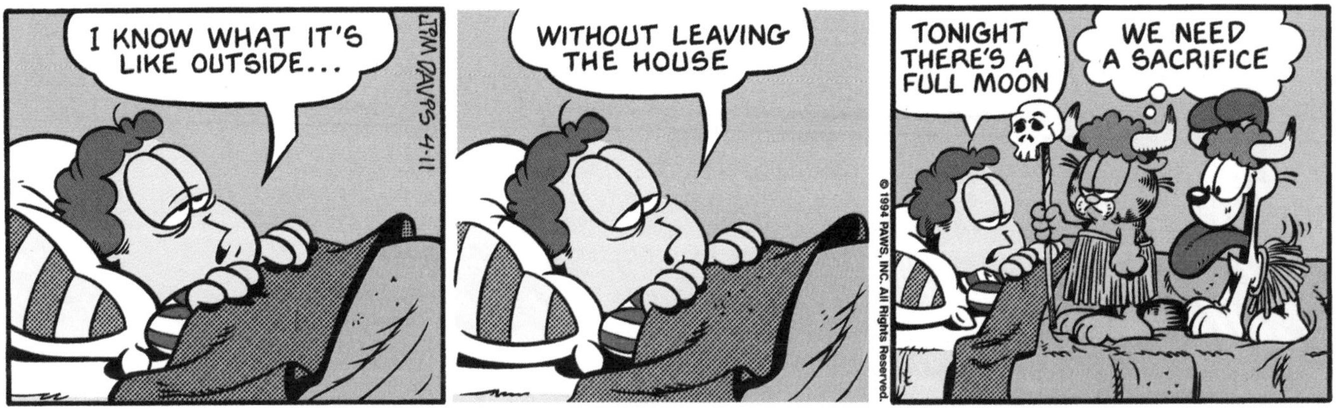
I KNOW WHAT IT'S LIKE OUTSIDE...
JIM DAVIS 4-11
WITHOUT LEAVING THE HOUSE
© 1994 PAWS, INC. All Rights Reserved.
TONIGHT THERE'S A FULL MOON
WE NEED A SACRIFICE

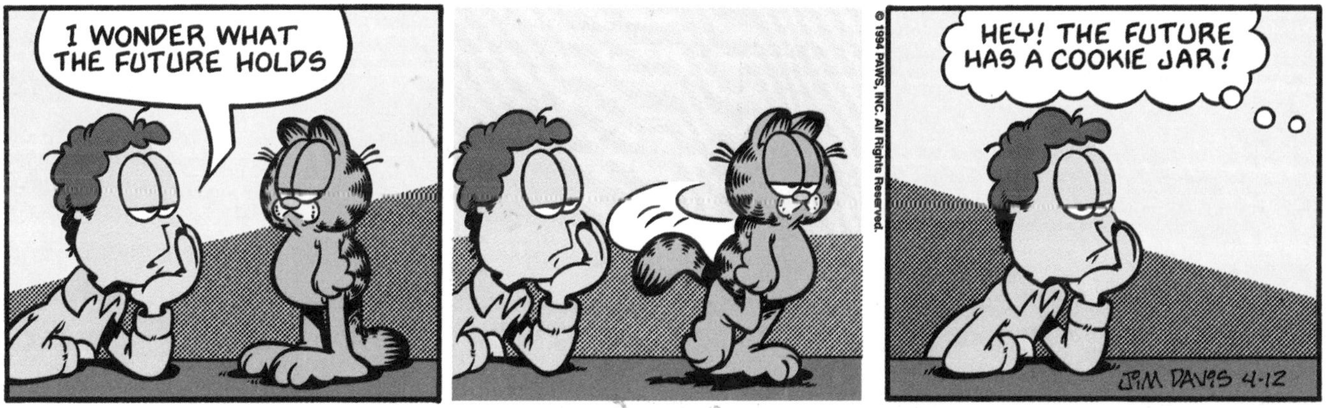
I WONDER WHAT THE FUTURE HOLDS
© 1994 PAWS, INC. All Rights Reserved.
HEY! THE FUTURE HAS A COOKIE JAR!
JIM DAVIS 4-12

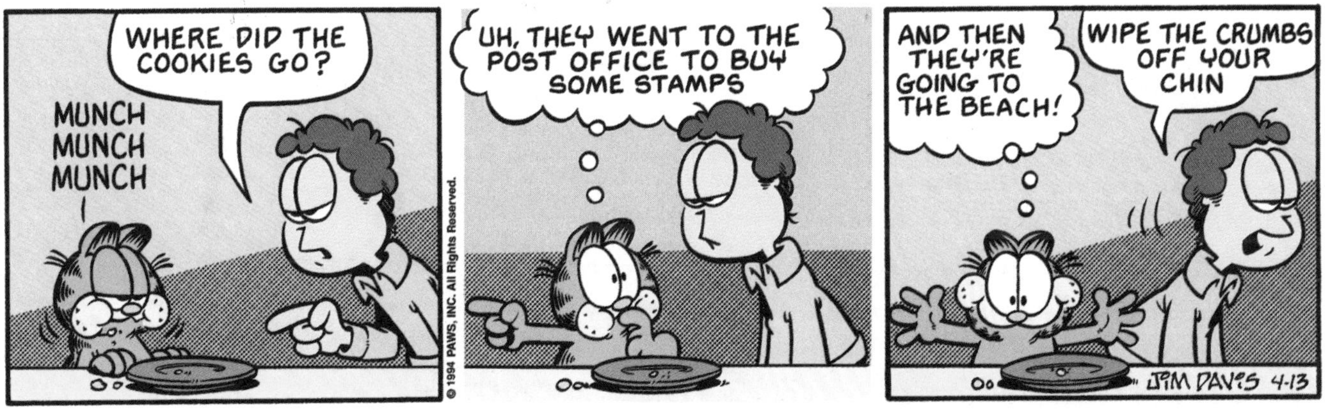
WHERE DID THE COOKIES GO?
MUNCH MUNCH MUNCH
© 1994 PAWS, INC. All Rights Reserved.
UH, THEY WENT TO THE POST OFFICE TO BUY SOME STAMPS
AND THEN THEY'RE GOING TO THE BEACH!
WIPE THE CRUMBS OFF YOUR CHIN
JIM DAVIS 4-13

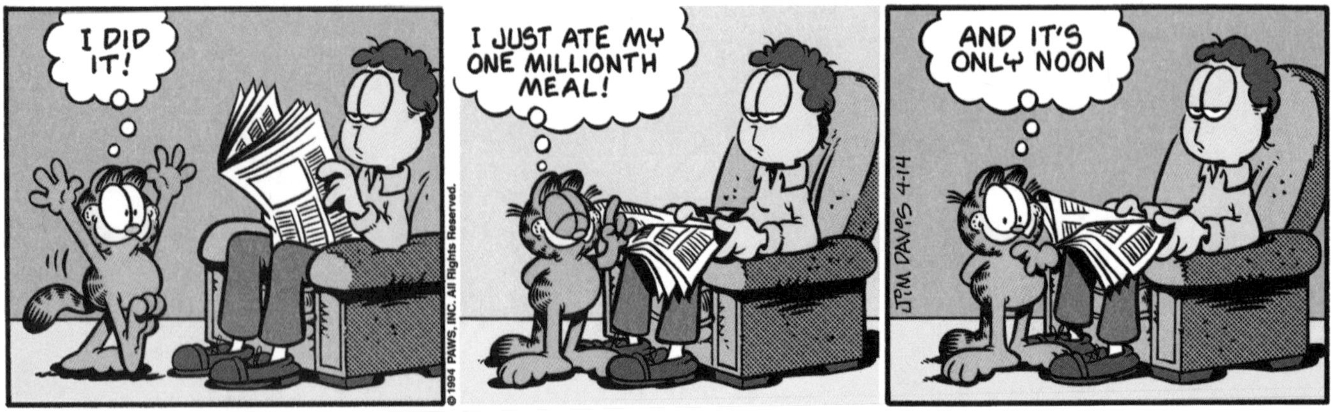
I DID IT!
I JUST ATE MY ONE MILLIONTH MEAL!
AND IT'S ONLY NOON
© 1994 PAWS, INC. All Rights Reserved.
JIM DAVIS 4-14

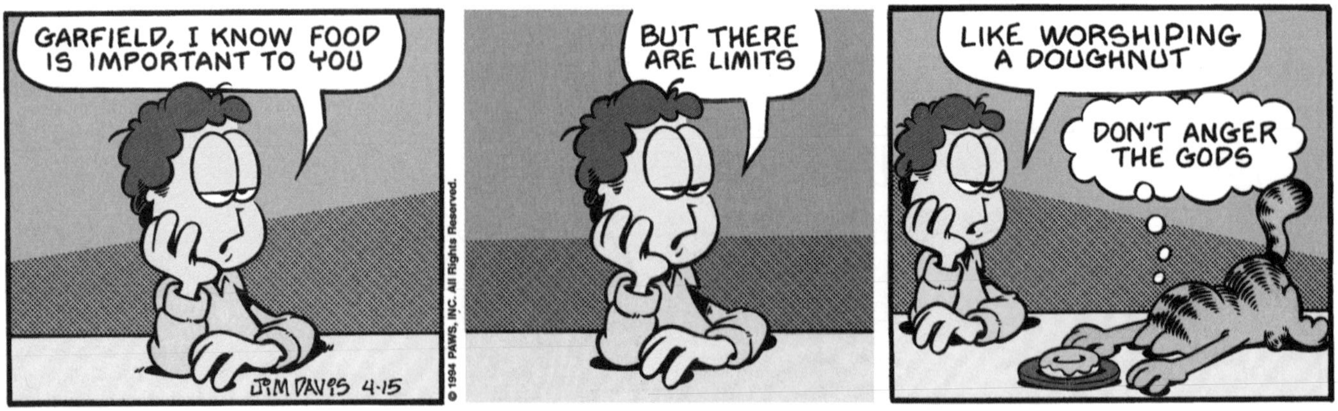
GARFIELD, I KNOW FOOD IS IMPORTANT TO YOU
BUT THERE ARE LIMITS
LIKE WORSHIPING A DOUGHNUT
DON'T ANGER THE GODS
© 1994 PAWS, INC. All Rights Reserved.
JIM DAVIS 4-15

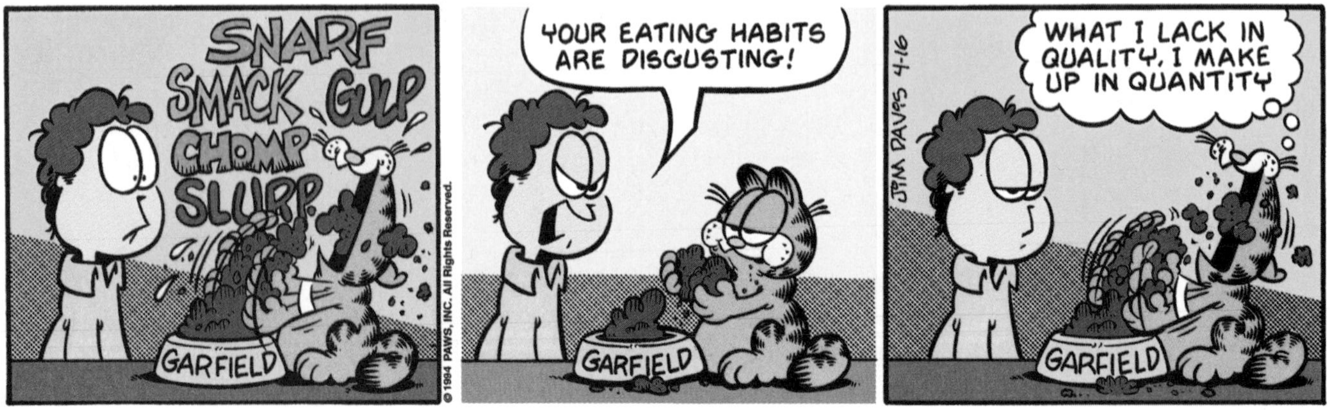
SNARF
SMACK
GULP
CHOMP
SLURP
GARFIELD
YOUR EATING HABITS ARE DISGUSTING!
GARFIELD
WHAT I LACK IN QUALITY, I MAKE UP IN QUANTITY
GARFIELD
© 1994 PAWS, INC. All Rights Reserved.
JIM DAVIS 4-16

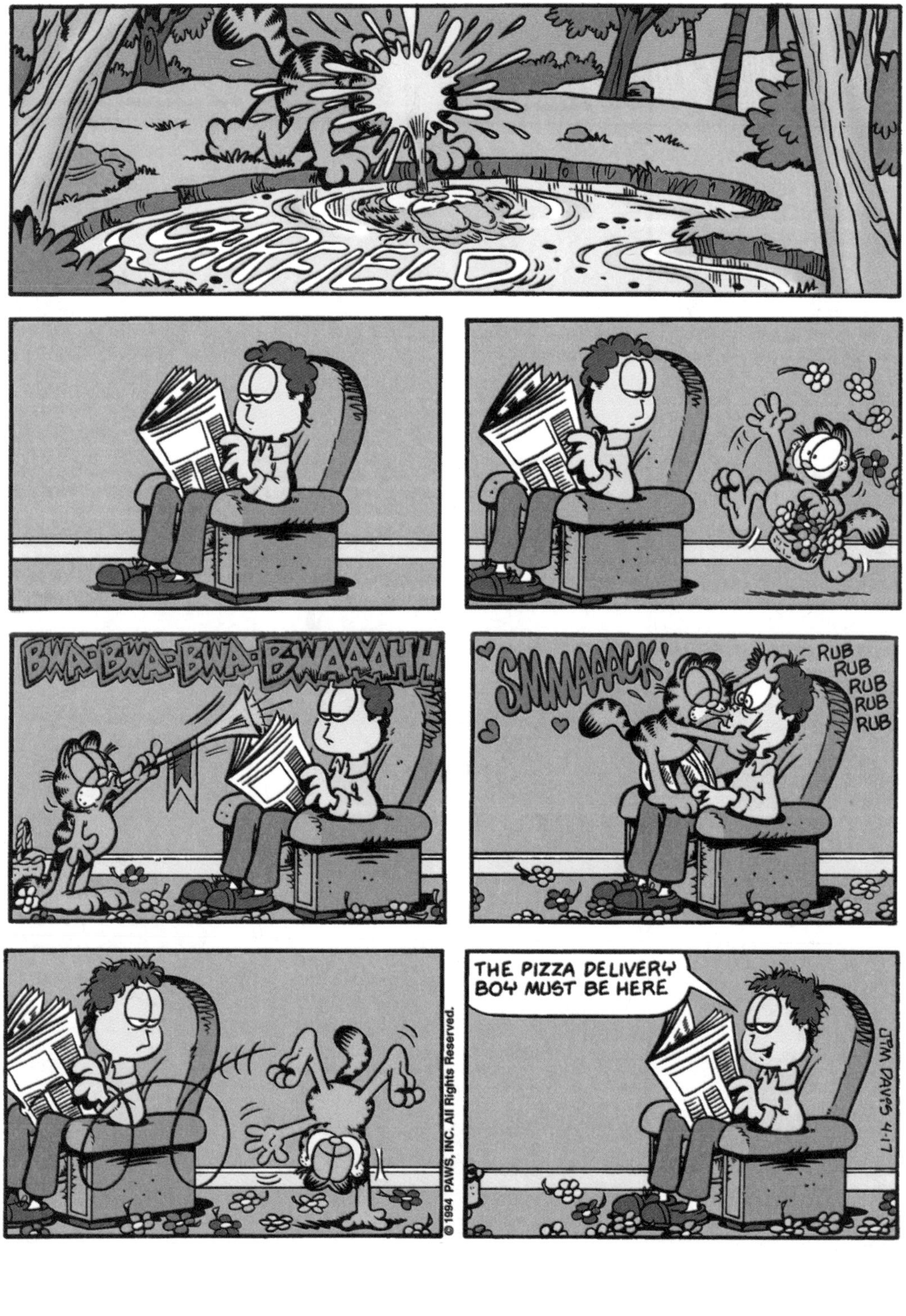
GARFIELD
BWA-BWA-BWA-BWAAAHH
SMMAAACK!
RUB RUB RUB RUB RUB
THE PIZZA DELIVERY BOY MUST BE HERE
JPM DAVIS 4-17

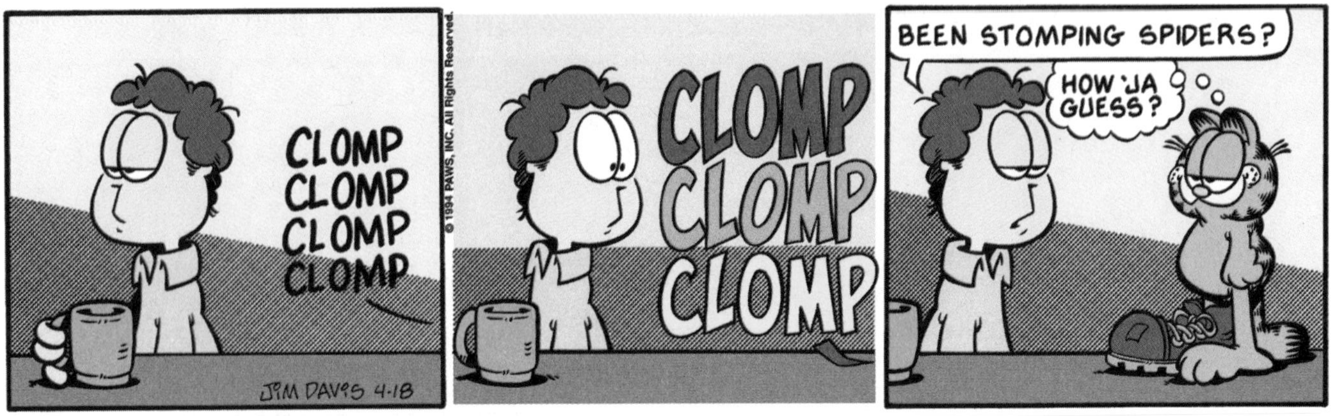
CLOMP
CLOMP
CLOMP
CLOMP
JIM DAVIS 4-18
© 1994 PAWS, INC. All Rights Reserved.
CLOMP
CLOMP
CLOMP
BEEN STOMPING SPIDERS?
HOW 'JA GUESS?

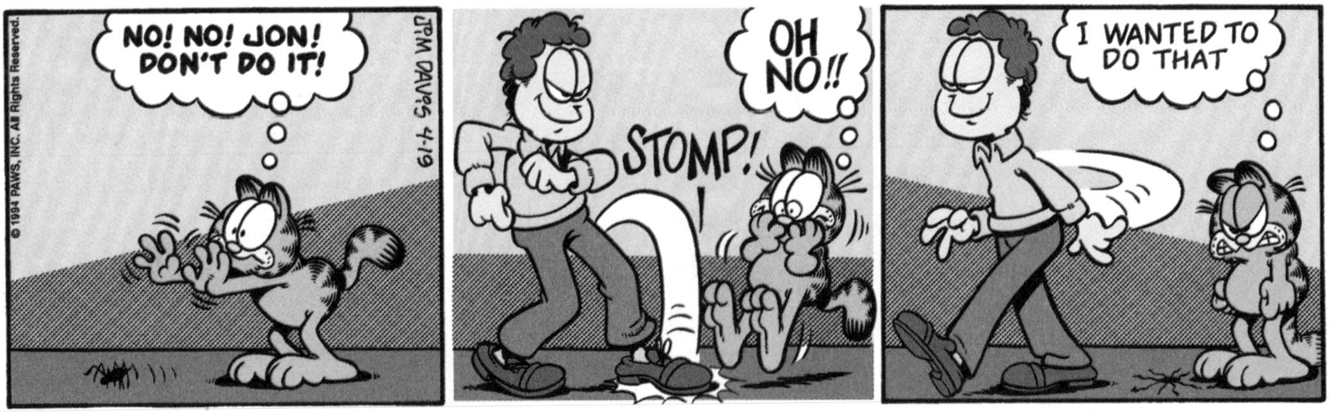
© 1994 PAWS, INC. All Rights Reserved.
NO! NO! JON! DON'T DO IT!
JIM DAVIS 4-19
OH NO!!
STOMP!
I WANTED TO DO THAT

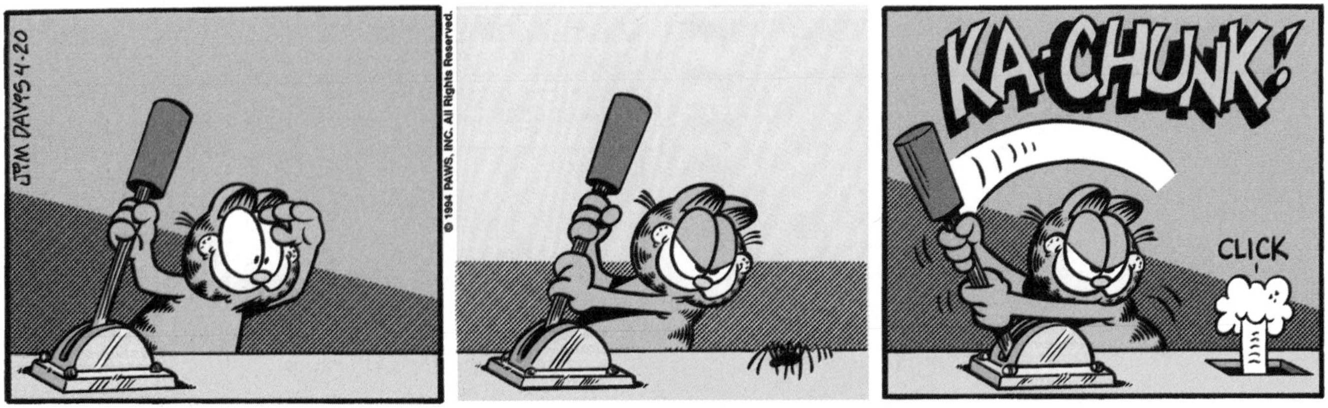
JIM DAVIS 4-20
© 1994 PAWS, INC. All Rights Reserved.
KA-CHUNK!
CLICK

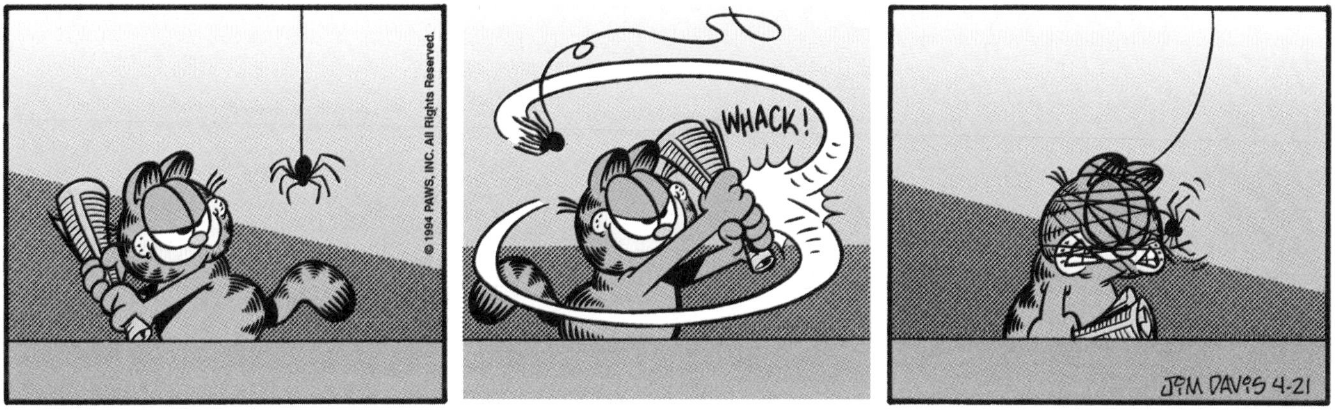
© 1994 PAWS, INC. All Rights Reserved.
WHACK!
JIM DAVIS 4-21

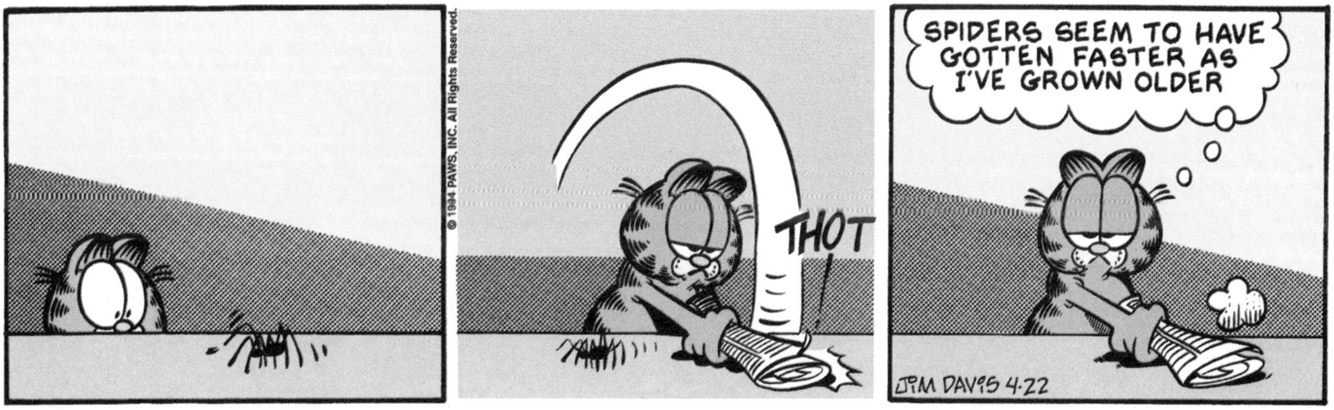
© 1994 PAWS, INC. All Rights Reserved.
THOT
SPIDERS SEEM TO HAVE GOTTEN FASTER AS I'VE GROWN OLDER
JIM DAVIS 4-22

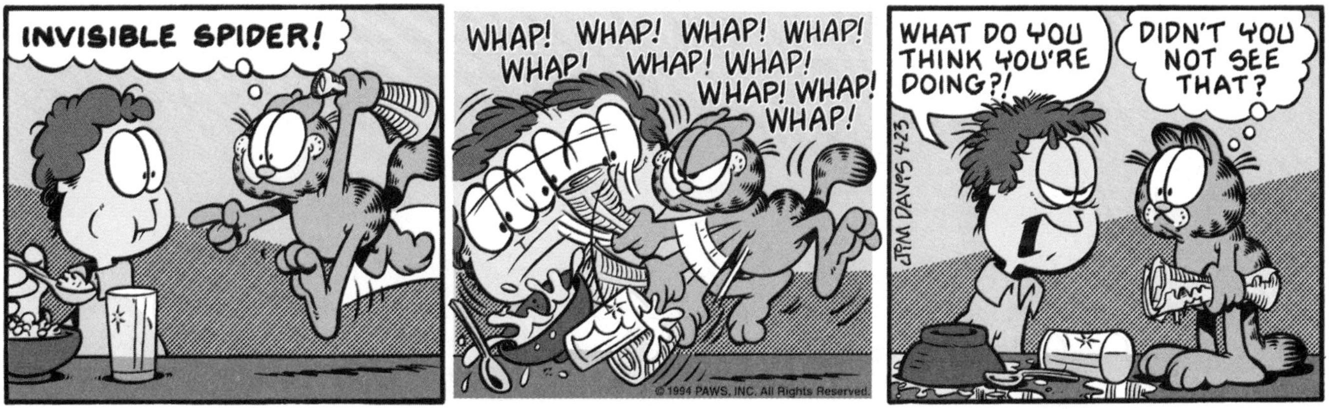
INVISIBLE SPIDER!
WHAP! WHAP! WHAP! WHAP! WHAP! WHAP! WHAP! WHAP! WHAP! WHAP!
© 1994 PAWS, INC. All Rights Reserved.
JIM DAVIS 4-23
WHAT DO YOU THINK YOU'RE DOING?!
DIDN'T YOU NOT SEE THAT?

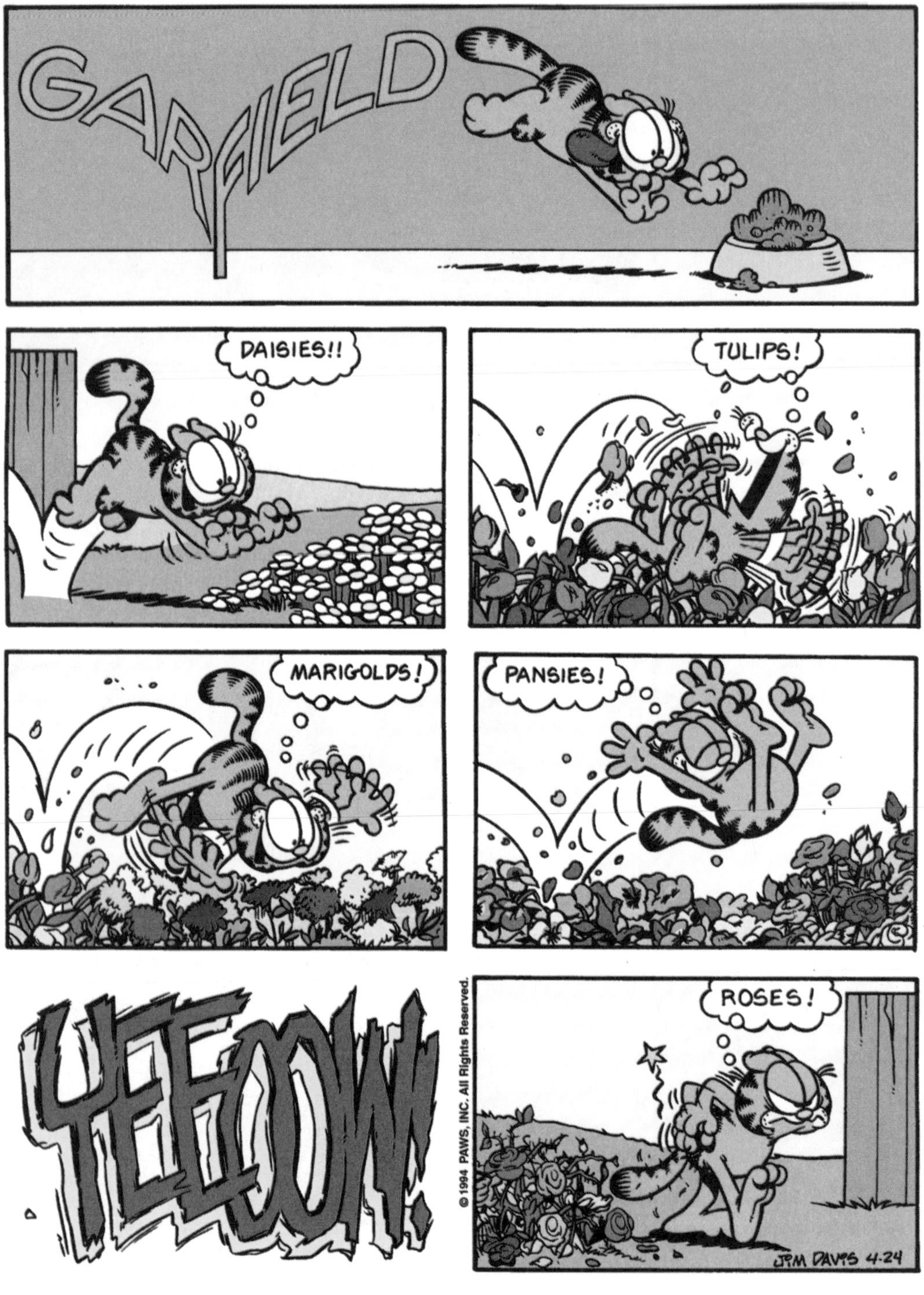
GARFIELD
DAISIES!!
TULIPS!
MARIGOLDS!
PANSIES!
YEEOOW!
ROSES!
JIM DAVIS 4-24

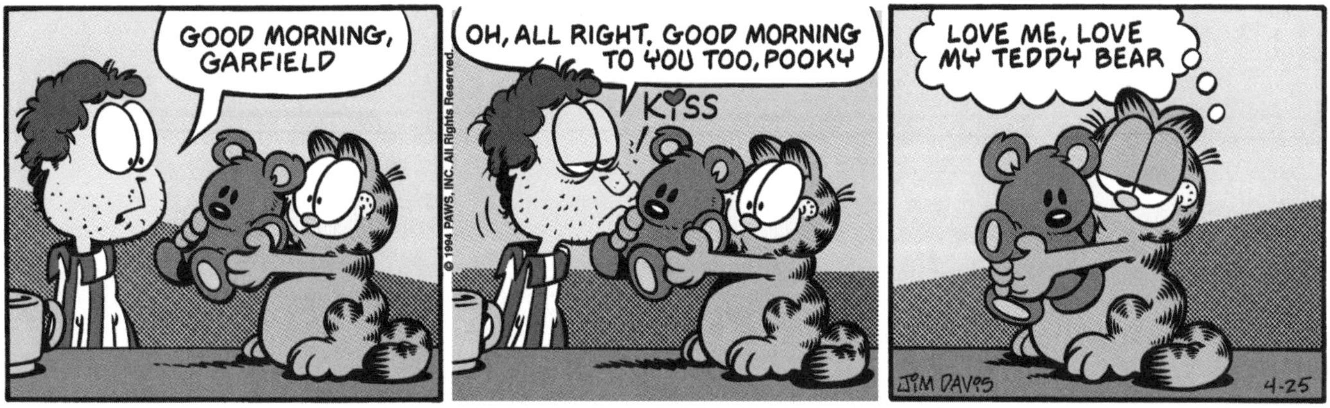
GOOD MORNING, GARFIELD
© 1994 PAWS, INC. All Rights Reserved.
OH, ALL RIGHT. GOOD MORNING TO YOU TOO, POOKY
KISS
LOVE ME, LOVE MY TEDDY BEAR
JIM DAVIS 4-25

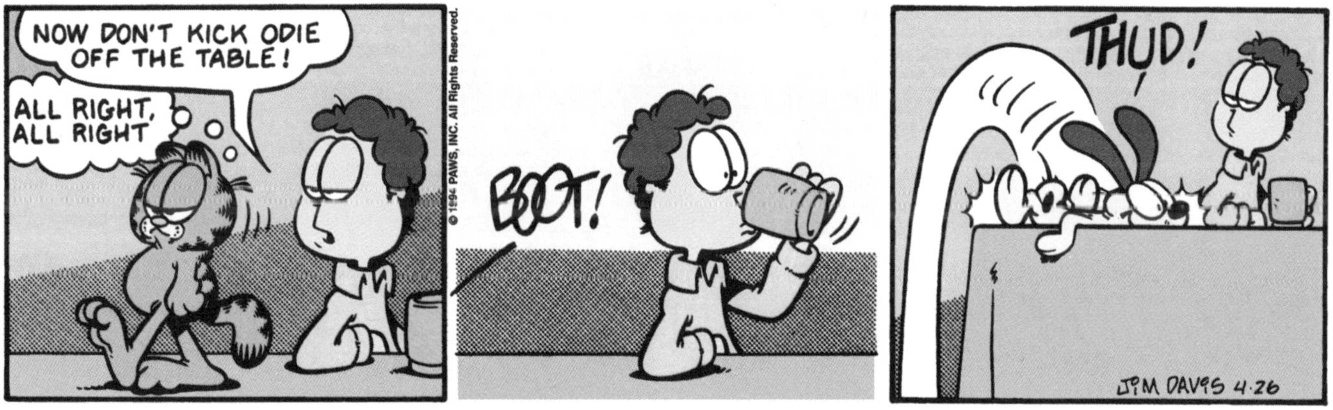
NOW DON'T KICK ODIE OFF THE TABLE!
ALL RIGHT, ALL RIGHT
© 1994 PAWS, INC. All Rights Reserved.
BOOT!
THUD!
JIM DAVIS 4-26

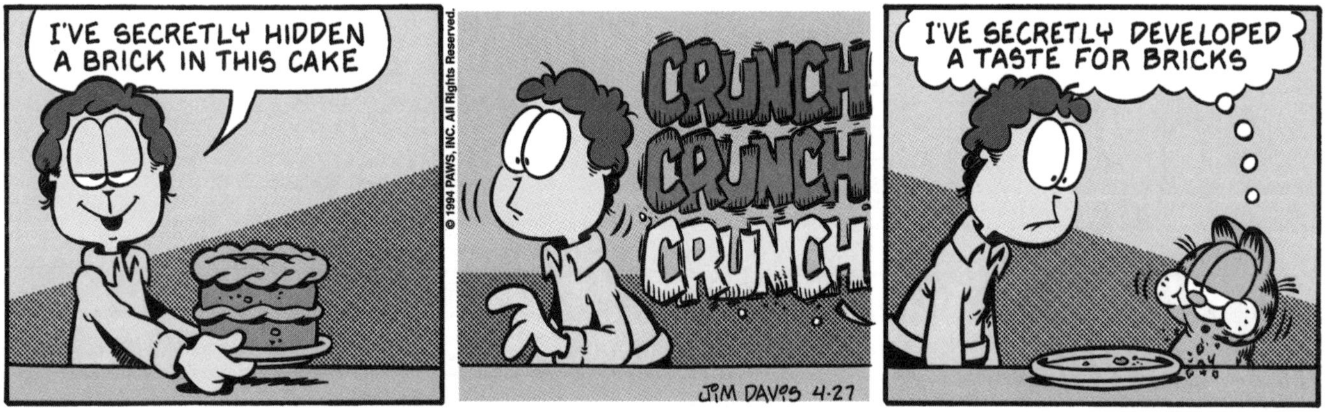
I'VE SECRETLY HIDDEN A BRICK IN THIS CAKE
© 1994 PAWS, INC. All Rights Reserved.
CRUNCH
CRUNCH
CRUNCH
JIM DAVIS 4-27
I'VE SECRETLY DEVELOPED A TASTE FOR BRICKS

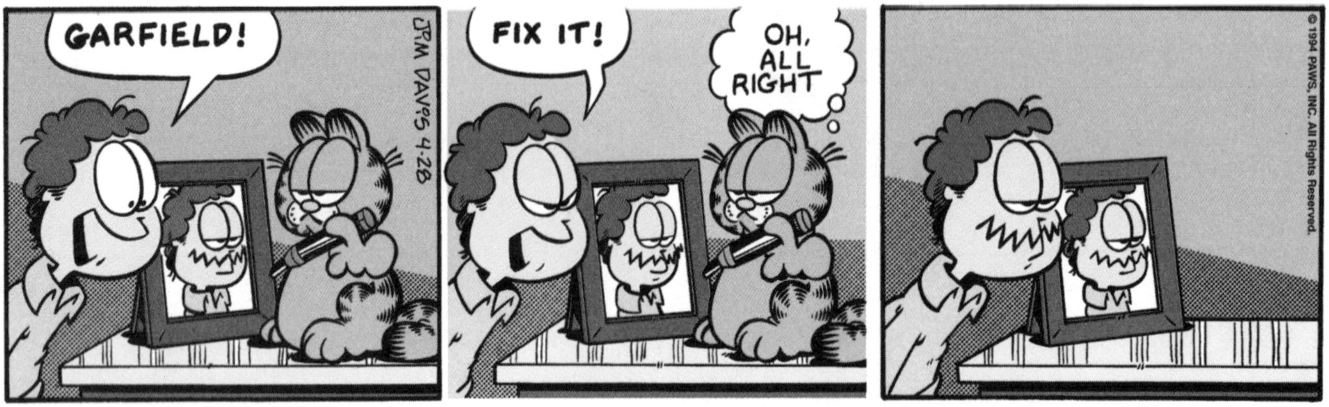
GARFIELD!
JIM DAVIS 4-28
FIX IT!
OH, ALL RIGHT
© 1994 PAWS, INC. All Rights Reserved.

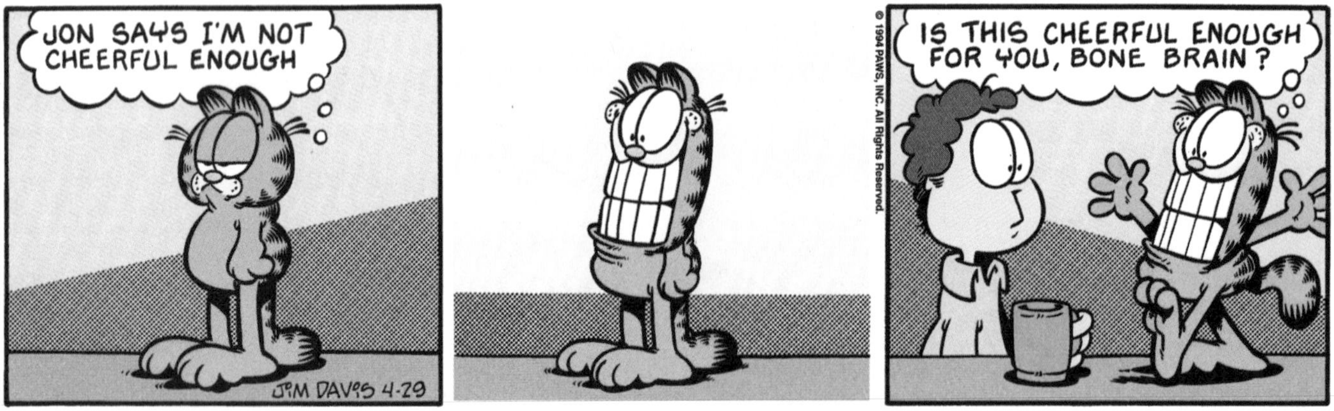
JON SAYS I'M NOT CHEERFUL ENOUGH
JIM DAVIS 4-29
© 1994 PAWS, INC. All Rights Reserved.
IS THIS CHEERFUL ENOUGH FOR YOU, BONE BRAIN?

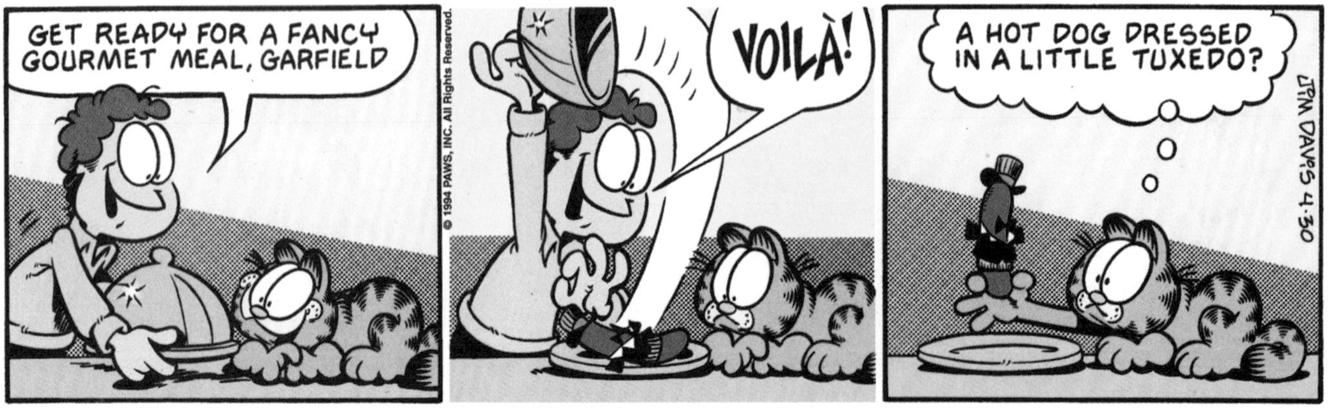
GET READY FOR A FANCY GOURMET MEAL, GARFIELD
© 1994 PAWS, INC. All Rights Reserved.
VOILÀ!
A HOT DOG DRESSED IN A LITTLE TUXEDO?
JIM DAVIS 4-30

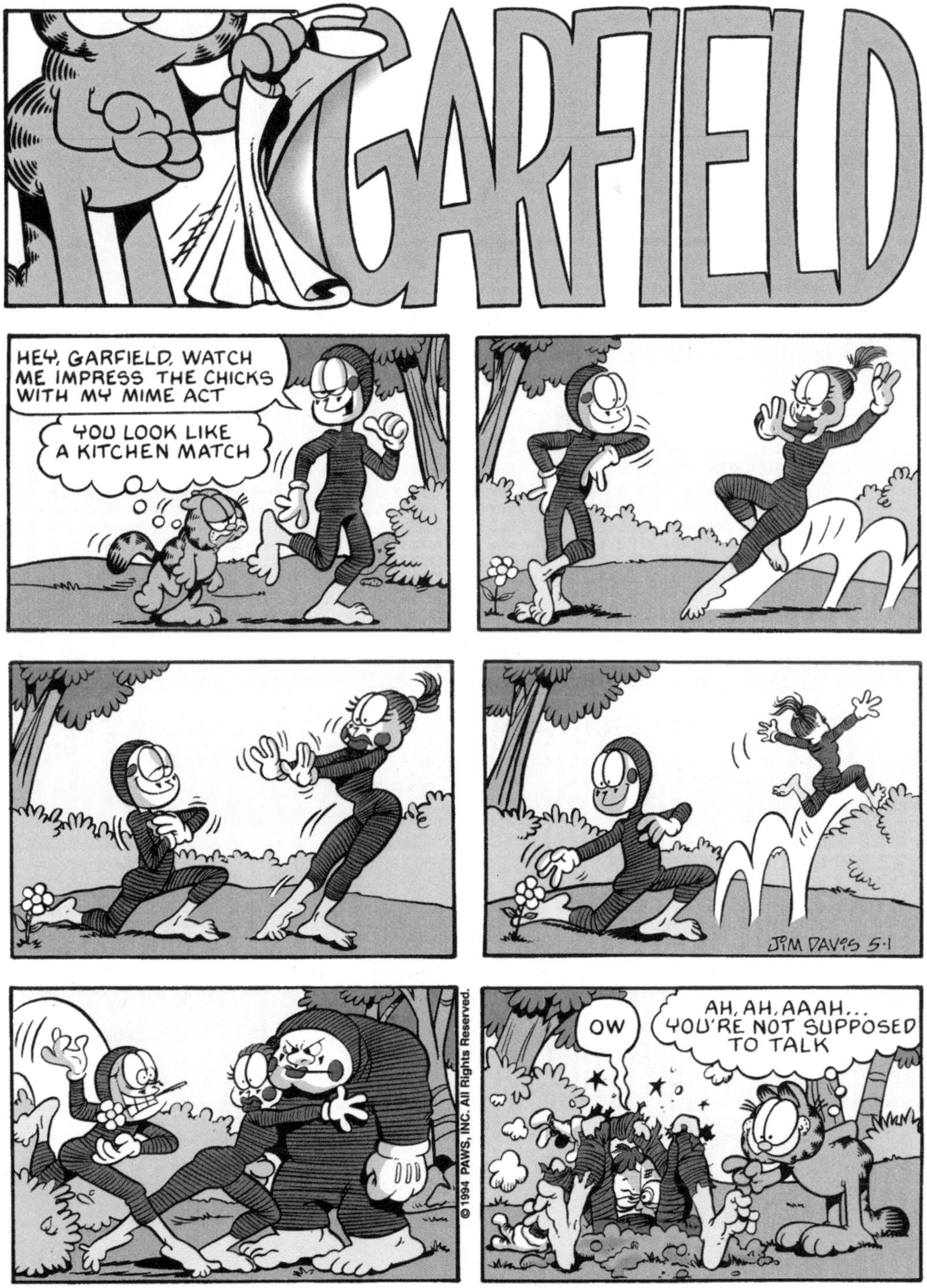
GARFIELD
HEY, GARFIELD, WATCH ME IMPRESS THE CHICKS WITH MY MIME ACT
YOU LOOK LIKE A KITCHEN MATCH
JIM DAVIS 5-1
© 1994 PAWS, INC. All Rights Reserved.
OW
AH, AH, AAAH... YOU'RE NOT SUPPOSED TO TALK

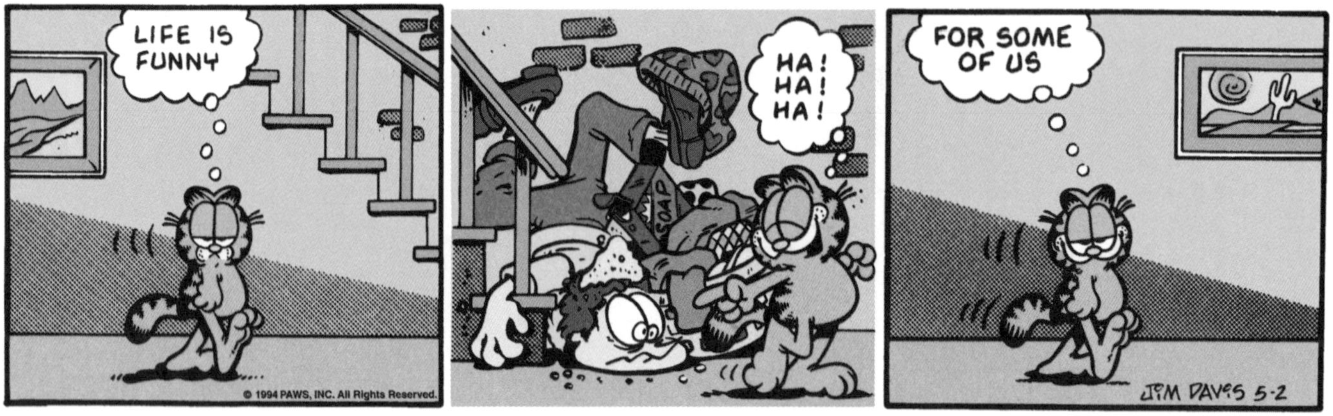
LIFE IS FUNNY
© 1994 PAWS, INC. All Rights Reserved.
SOAP
HA! HA! HA!
FOR SOME OF US
JIM DAVIS 5-2

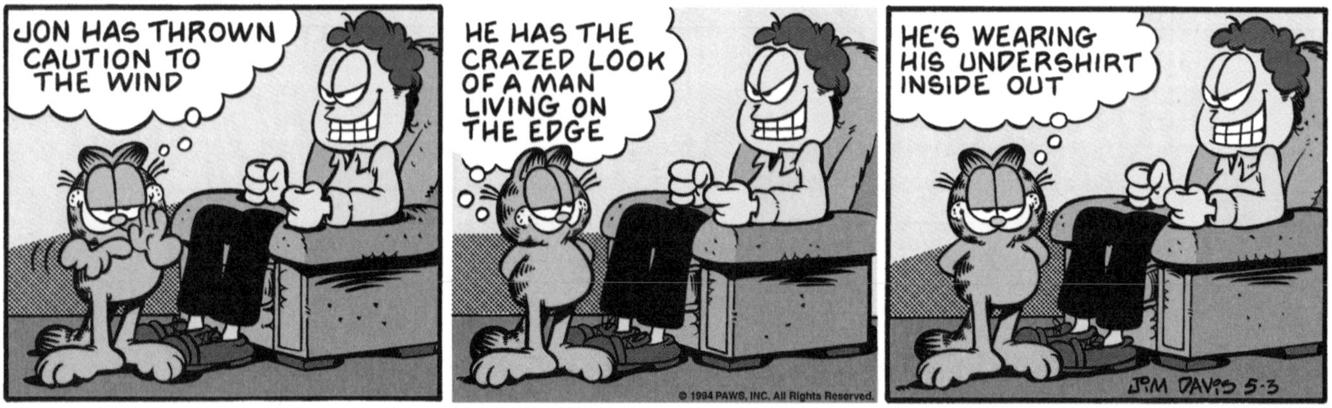
JON HAS THROWN CAUTION TO THE WIND
HE HAS THE CRAZED LOOK OF A MAN LIVING ON THE EDGE
© 1994 PAWS, INC. All Rights Reserved.
HE'S WEARING HIS UNDERSHIRT INSIDE OUT
JIM DAVIS 5-3

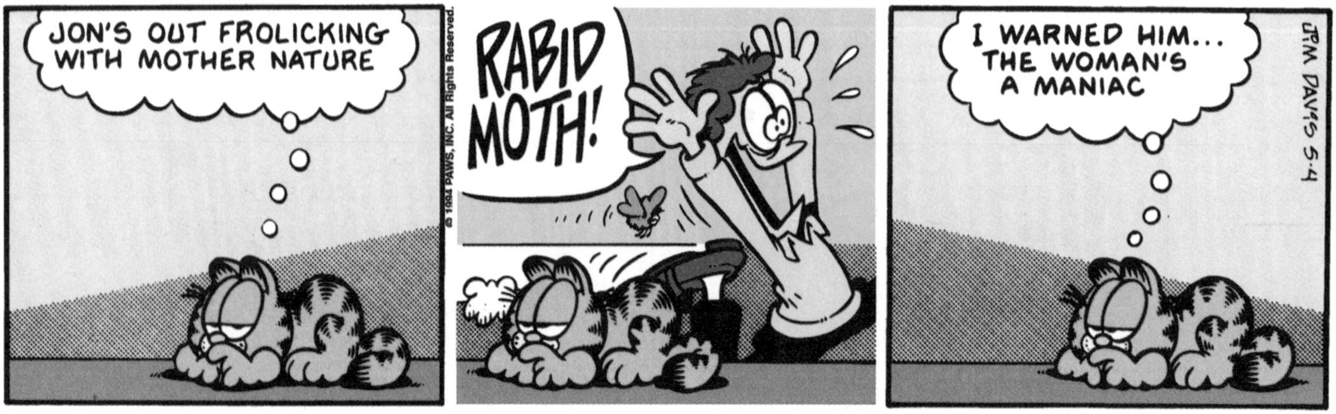
JON'S OUT FROLICKING WITH MOTHER NATURE
© 1994 PAWS, INC. All Rights Reserved.
RABID MOTH!
I WARNED HIM... THE WOMAN'S A MANIAC
JIM DAVIS 5-4

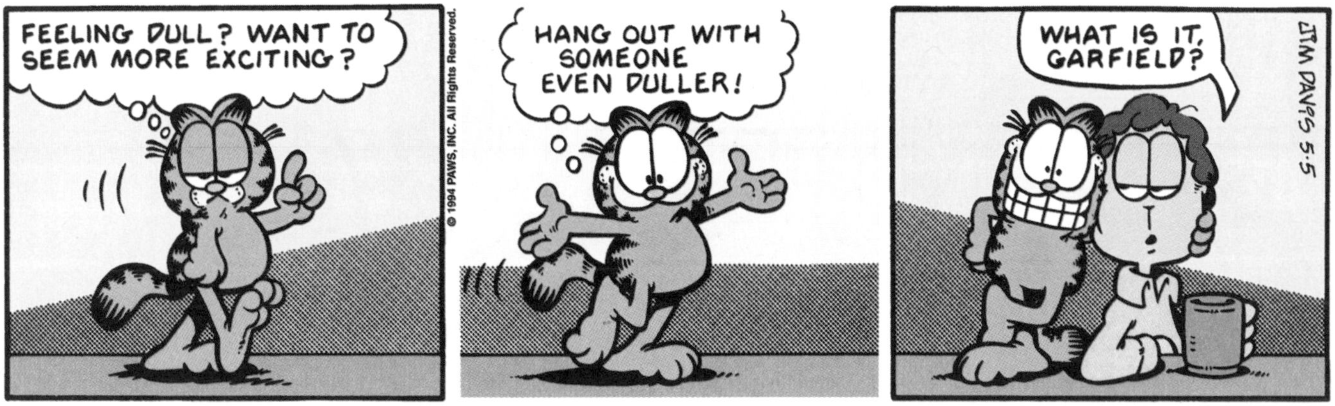
FEELING DULL? WANT TO SEEM MORE EXCITING?
© 1994 PAWS, INC. All Rights Reserved.
HANG OUT WITH SOMEONE EVEN DULLER!
WHAT IS IT, GARFIELD?
JIM DAVIS 5-5

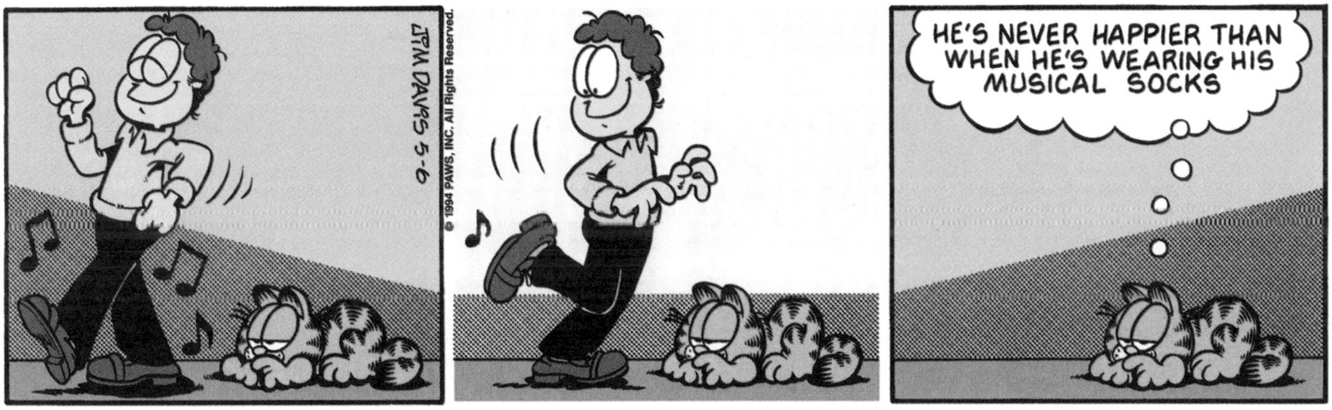
JIM DAVIS 5-6
© 1994 PAWS, INC. All Rights Reserved.
HE'S NEVER HAPPIER THAN WHEN HE'S WEARING HIS MUSICAL SOCKS

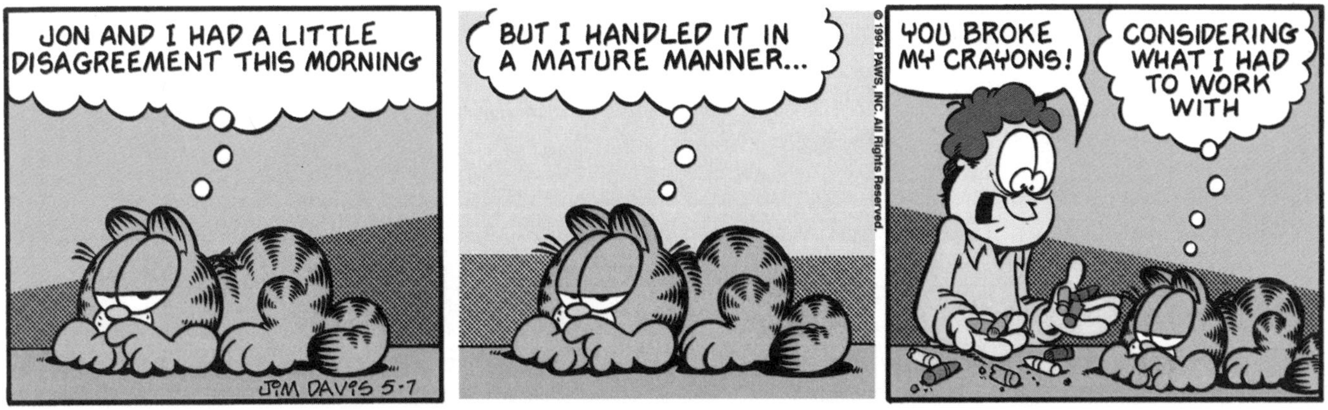
JON AND I HAD A LITTLE DISAGREEMENT THIS MORNING
JIM DAVIS 5-7
BUT I HANDLED IT IN A MATURE MANNER...
© 1994 PAWS, INC. All Rights Reserved.
YOU BROKE MY CRAYONS!
CONSIDERING WHAT I HAD TO WORK WITH

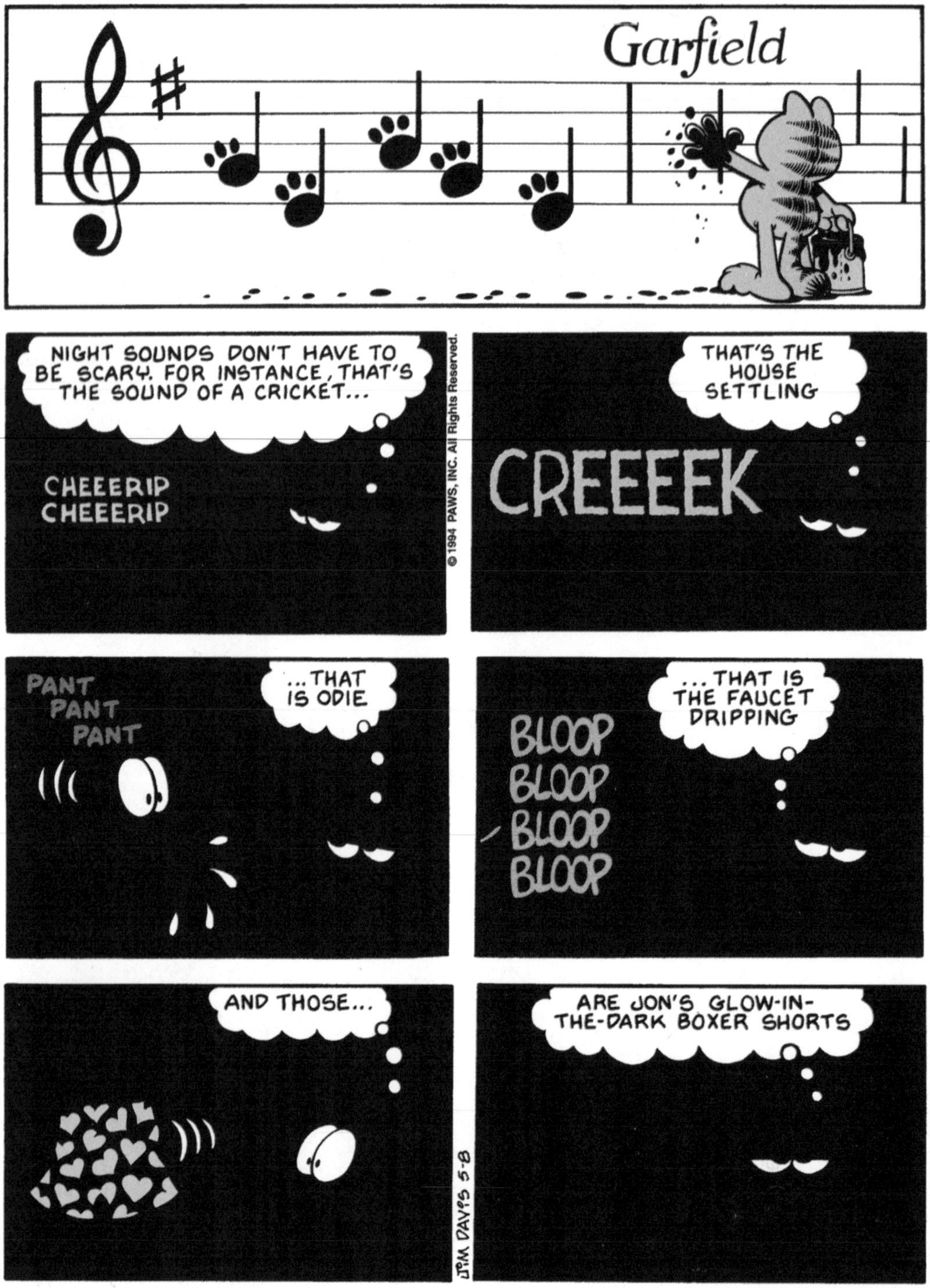
Garfield
NIGHT SOUNDS DON'T HAVE TO BE SCARY. FOR INSTANCE, THAT'S THE SOUND OF A CRICKET...
CHEEERIP CHEEERIP
© 1994 PAWS, INC. All Rights Reserved.
THAT'S THE HOUSE SETTLING
CREEEEK
PANT PANT PANT
...THAT IS ODIE
BLOOP BLOOP BLOOP BLOOP
...THAT IS THE FAUCET DRIPPING
AND THOSE...
JPM DAVPS 5-8
ARE JON'S GLOW-IN-THE-DARK BOXER SHORTS

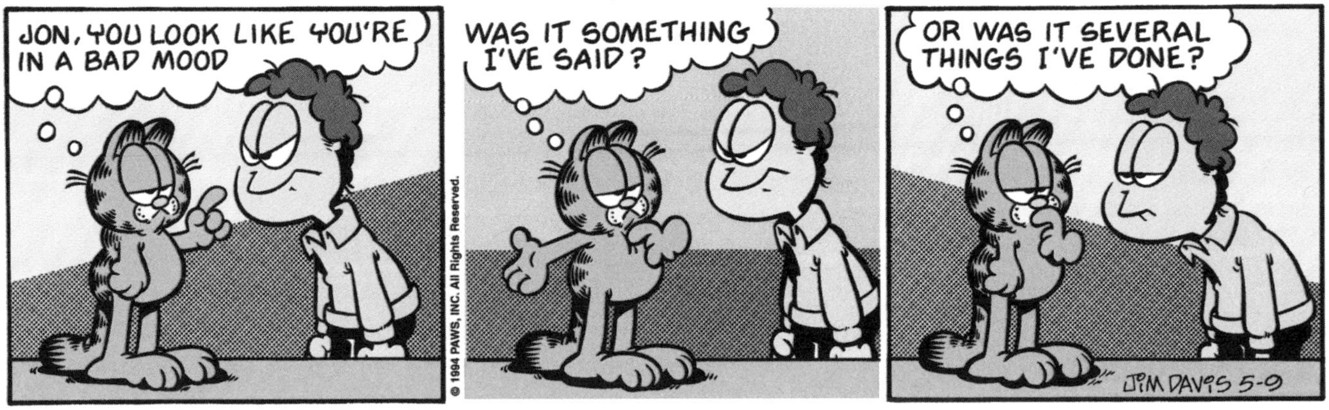
JON, YOU LOOK LIKE YOU'RE IN A BAD MOOD
© 1994 PAWS, INC. All Rights Reserved.
WAS IT SOMETHING I'VE SAID?
OR WAS IT SEVERAL THINGS I'VE DONE?
JIM DAVIS 5-9

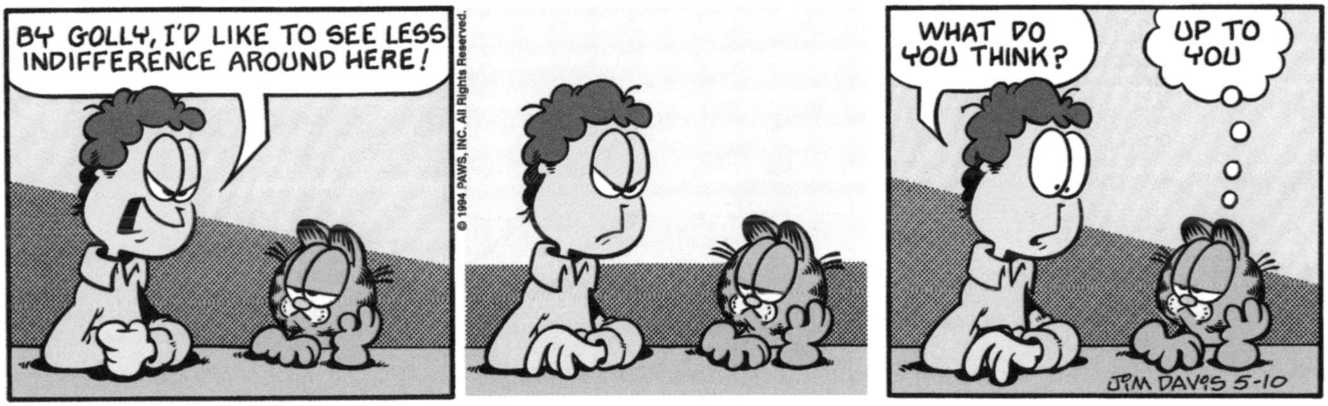
BY GOLLY, I'D LIKE TO SEE LESS INDIFFERENCE AROUND HERE!
© 1994 PAWS, INC. All Rights Reserved.
WHAT DO YOU THINK?
UP TO YOU
JIM DAVIS 5-10

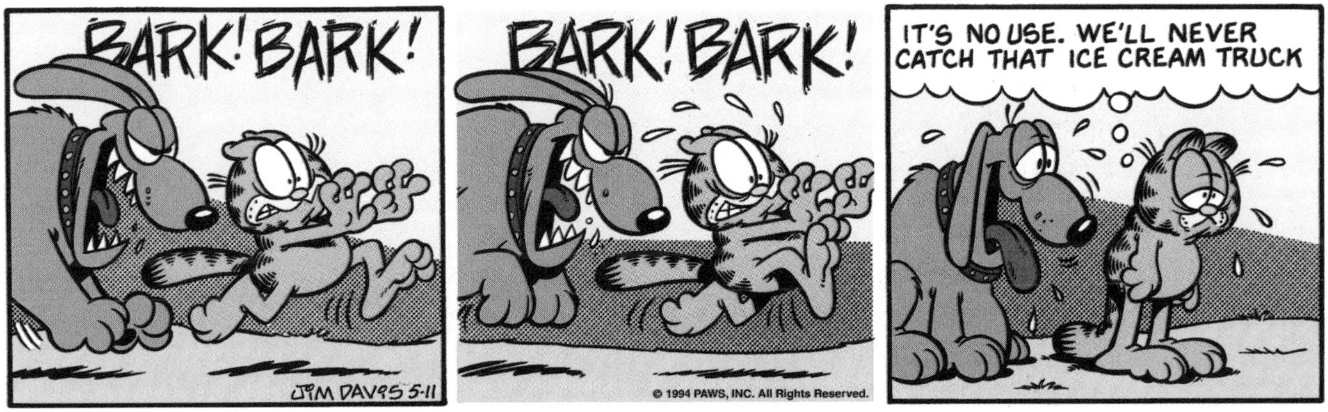
BARK! BARK!
JIM DAVIS 5-11
BARK! BARK!
© 1994 PAWS, INC. All Rights Reserved.
IT'S NO USE. WE'LL NEVER CATCH THAT ICE CREAM TRUCK

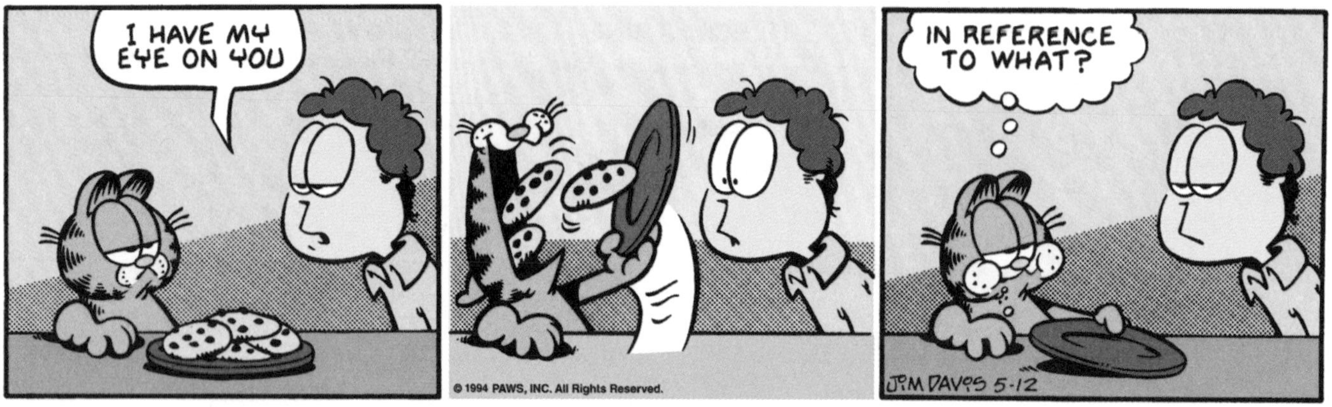
I HAVE MY EYE ON YOU
© 1994 PAWS, INC. All Rights Reserved.
IN REFERENCE TO WHAT?
JIM DAVIS 5-12

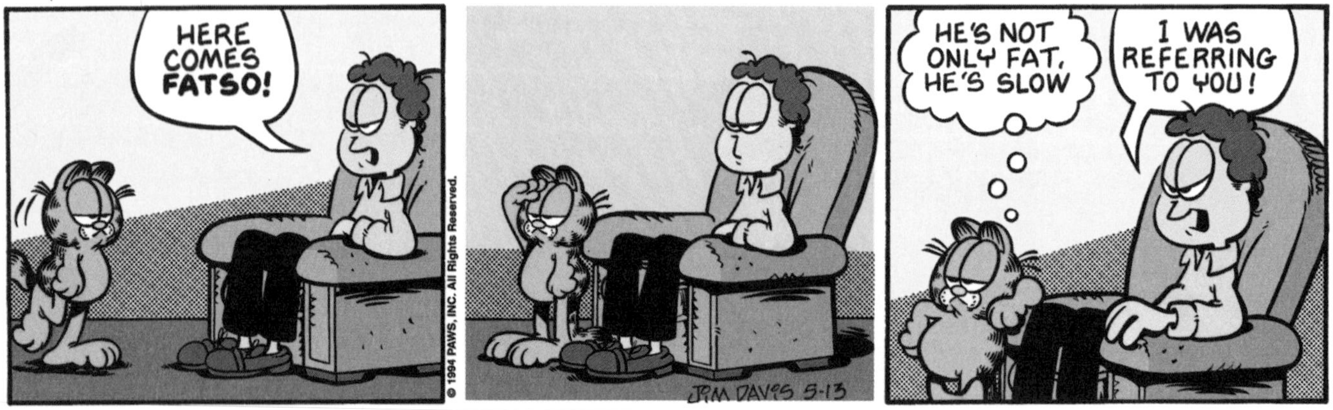
HERE COMES **FATSO!**
© 1994 PAWS, INC. All Rights Reserved.
JIM DAVIS 5-13
HE'S NOT ONLY FAT, HE'S SLOW
I WAS REFERRING TO YOU!

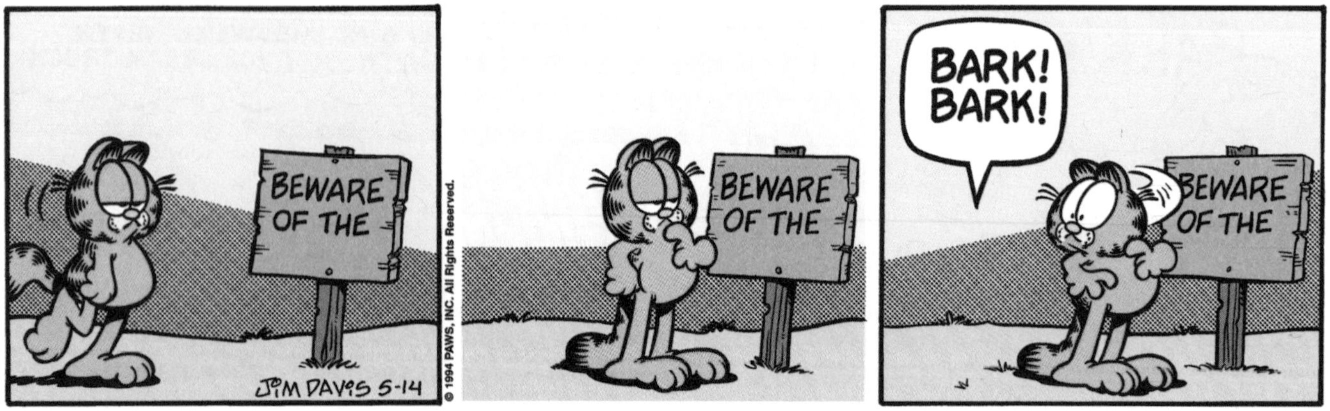
BEWARE OF THE
JIM DAVIS 5-14
© 1994 PAWS, INC. All Rights Reserved.
BEWARE OF THE
BARK! BARK!
BEWARE OF THE

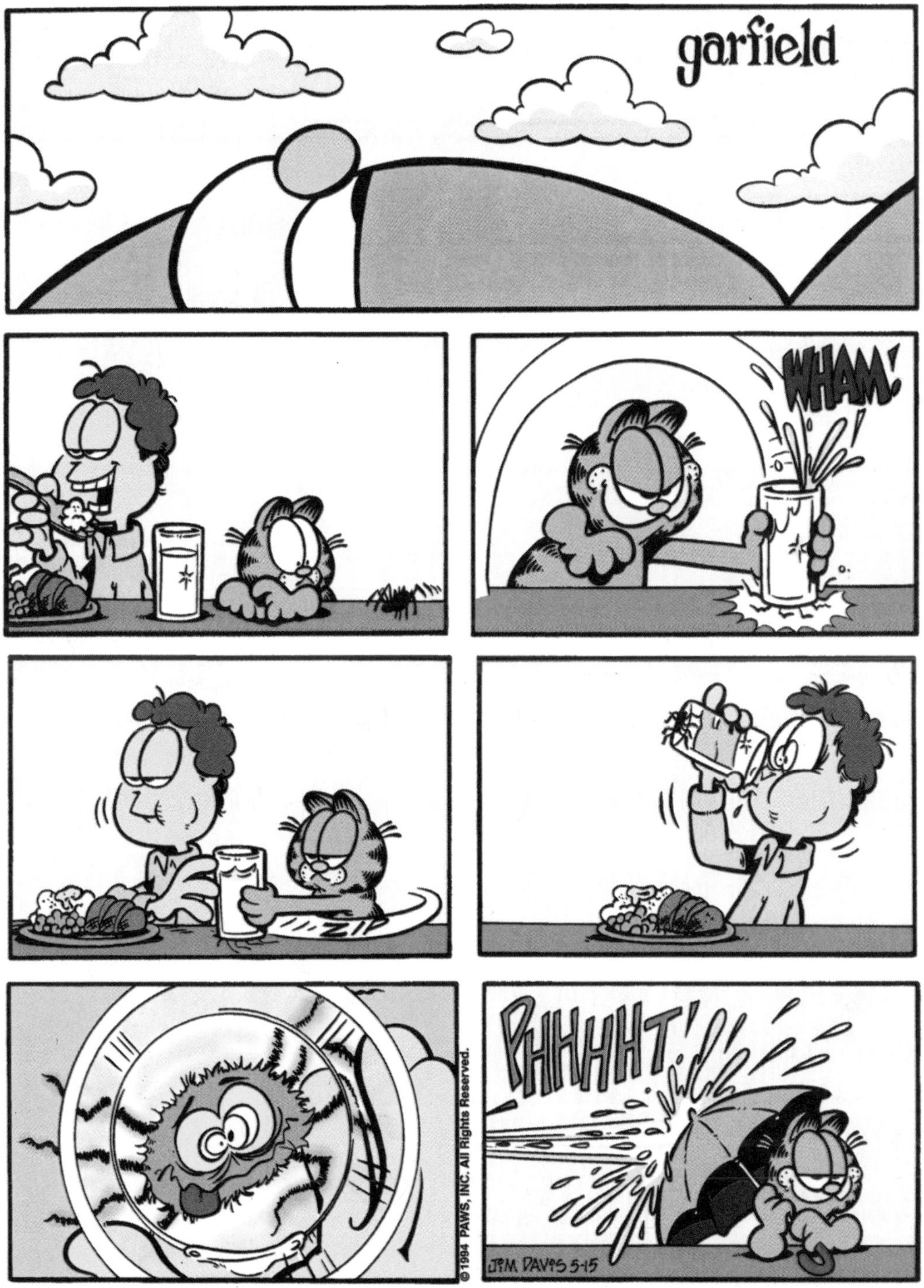
garfield
WHAM!
ZIP
PHHHT!
©1994 PAWS, INC. All Rights Reserved.
JIM DAVIS 5-15

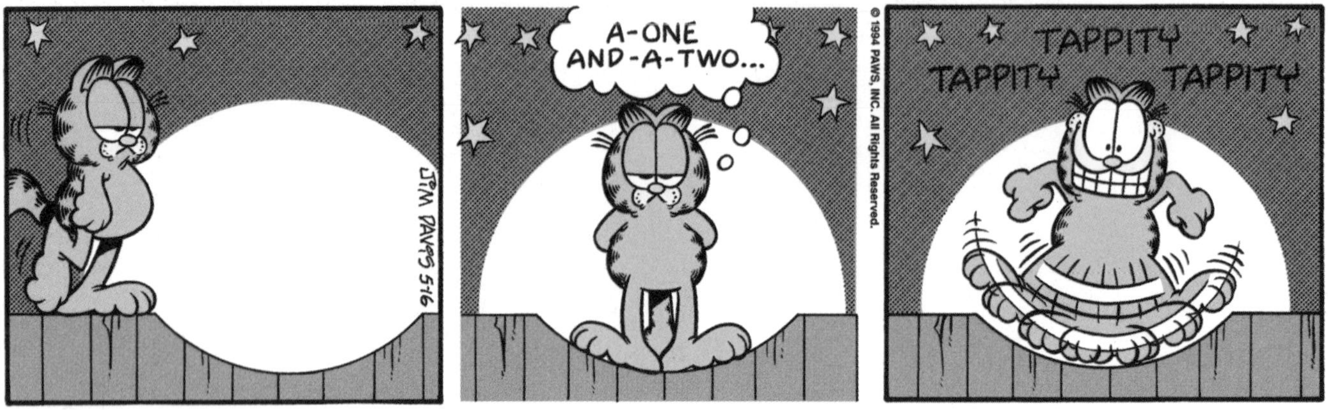
JIM DAVIS 5-16
A-ONE AND-A-TWO...
© 1994 PAWS, INC. All Rights Reserved.
TAPPITY TAPPITY TAPPITY

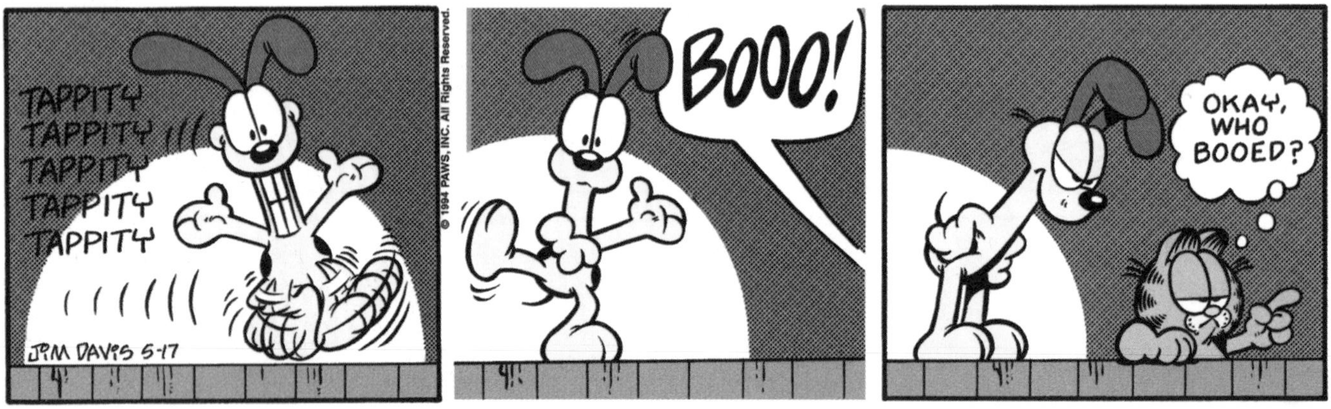
TAPPITY TAPPITY TAPPITY TAPPITY TAPPITY
JIM DAVIS 5-17
© 1994 PAWS, INC. All Rights Reserved.
BOOO!
OKAY, WHO BOOED?

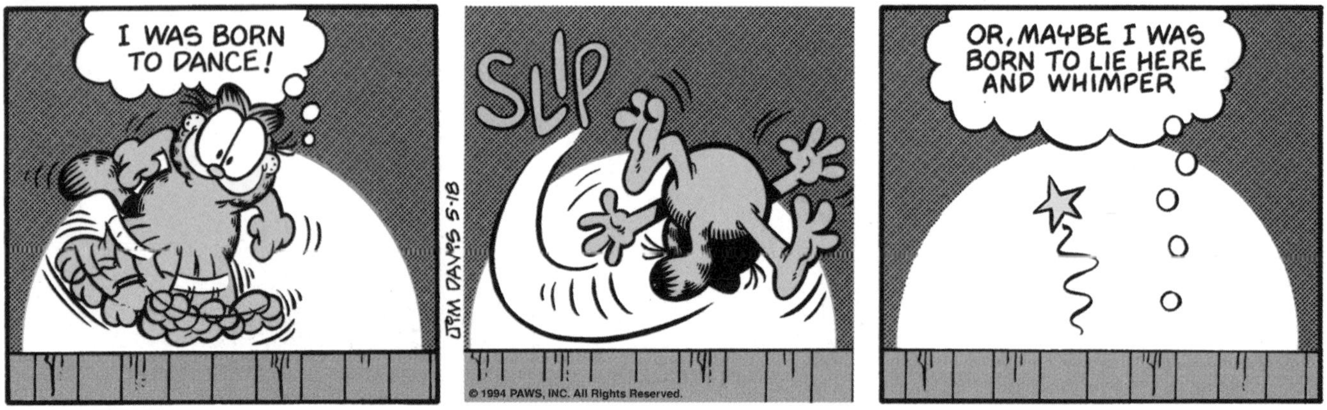
I WAS BORN TO DANCE!
JIM DAVIS 5-18
SLIP
© 1994 PAWS, INC. All Rights Reserved.
OR, MAYBE I WAS BORN TO LIE HERE AND WHIMPER

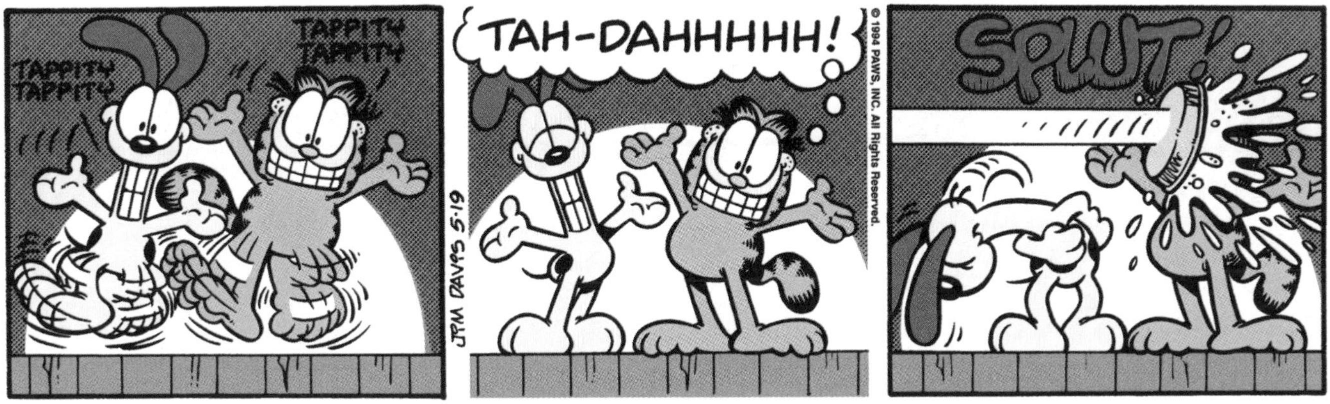
TAPPITY TAPPITY
TAPPITY TAPPITY
JIM DAVIS 5-19
TAH-DAHHHHH!
© 1994 PAWS, INC. All Rights Reserved.
SPLUT!

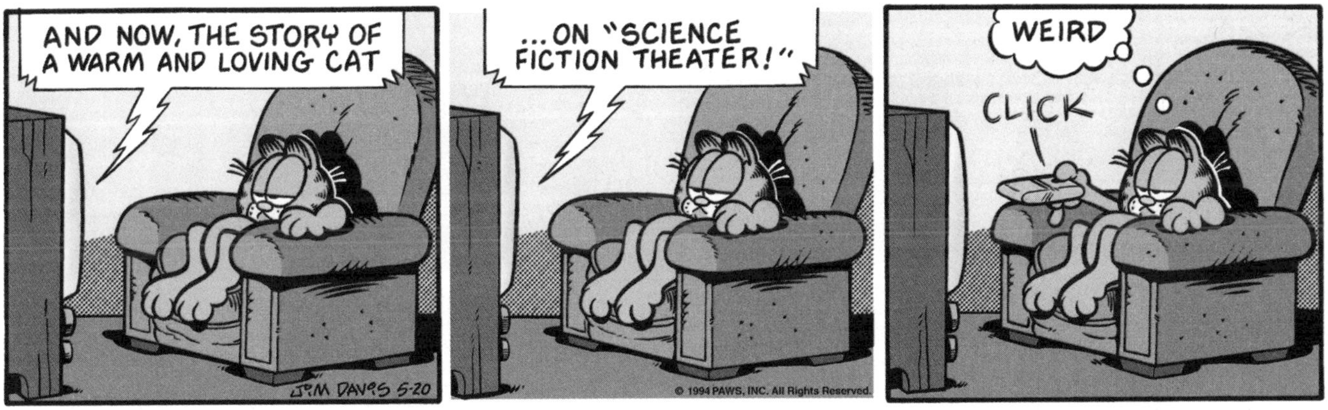
AND NOW, THE STORY OF A WARM AND LOVING CAT
JIM DAVIS 5-20
...ON "SCIENCE FICTION THEATER!"
© 1994 PAWS, INC. All Rights Reserved.
WEIRD
CLICK

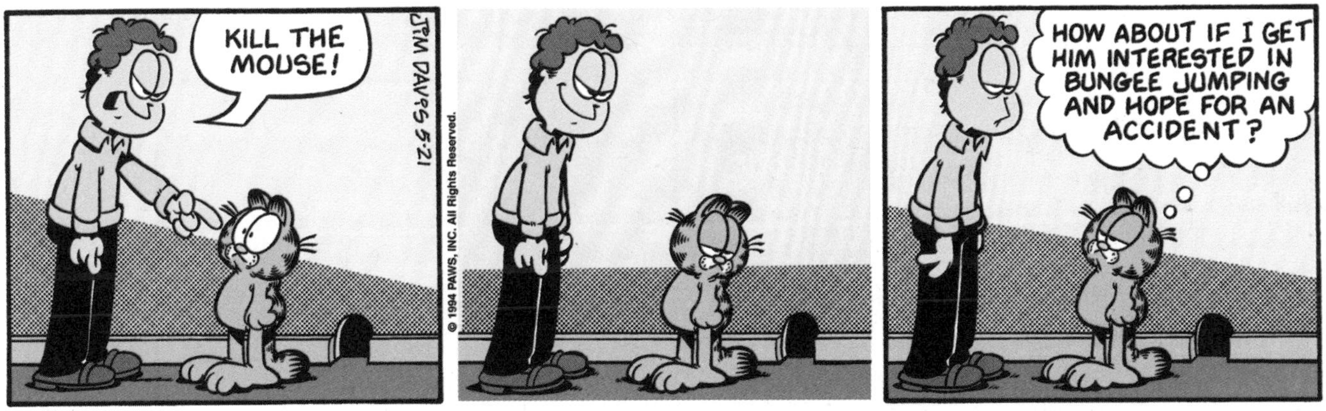
KILL THE MOUSE!
JIM DAVIS 5-21
© 1994 PAWS, INC. All Rights Reserved.
HOW ABOUT IF I GET HIM INTERESTED IN BUNGEE JUMPING AND HOPE FOR AN ACCIDENT?

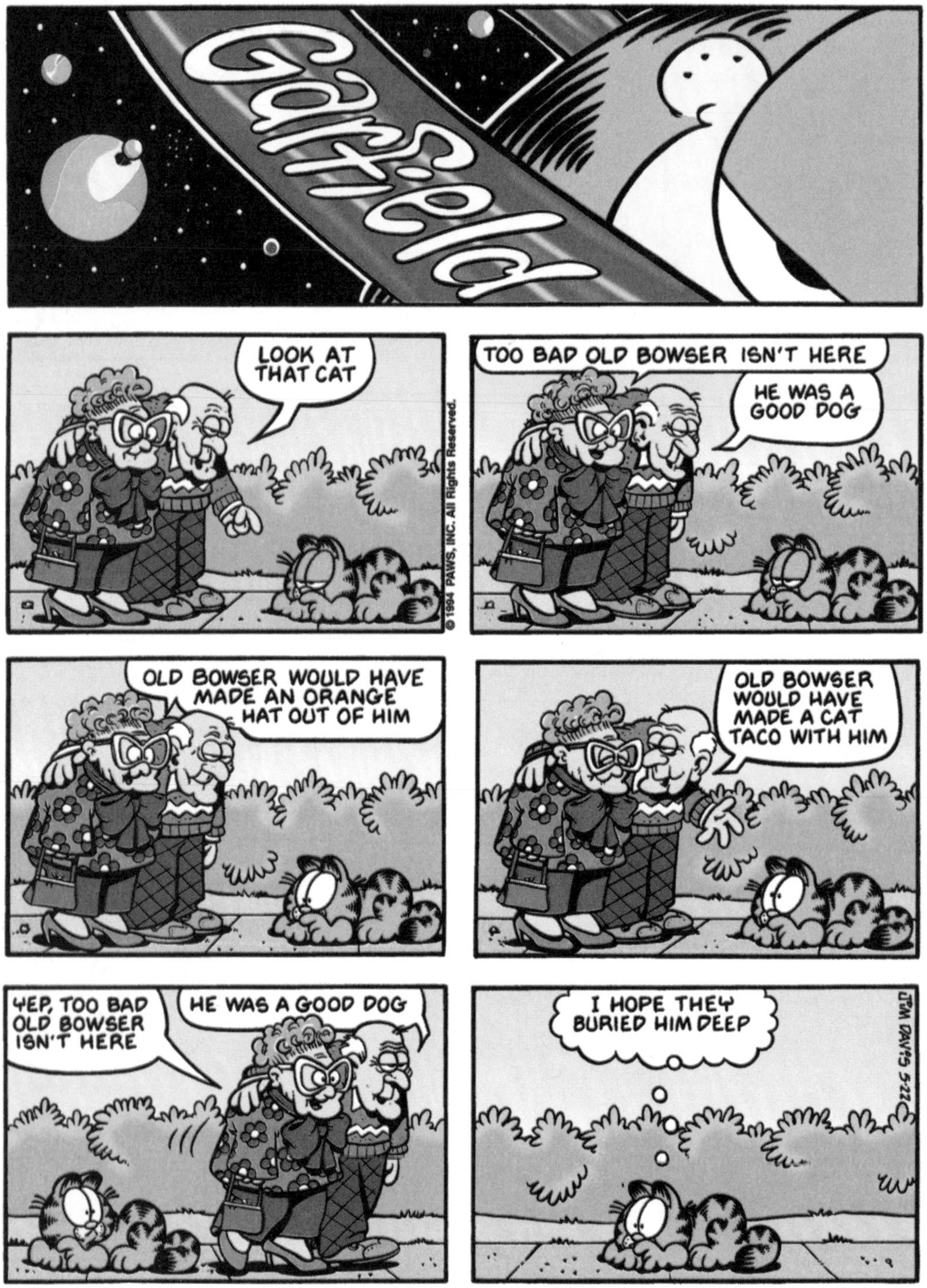
Garfield
LOOK AT THAT CAT
© 1994 PAWS, INC. All Rights Reserved.
TOO BAD OLD BOWSER ISN'T HERE
HE WAS A GOOD DOG
OLD BOWSER WOULD HAVE MADE AN ORANGE HAT OUT OF HIM
OLD BOWSER WOULD HAVE MADE A CAT TACO WITH HIM
YEP, TOO BAD OLD BOWSER ISN'T HERE
HE WAS A GOOD DOG
I HOPE THEY BURIED HIM DEEP
JIM DAVIS 5-22

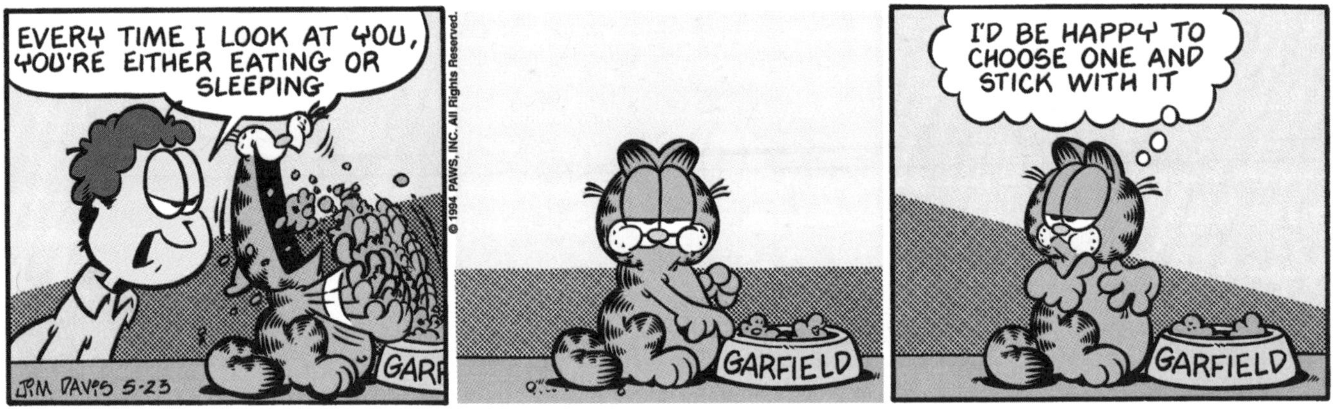
EVERY TIME I LOOK AT YOU, YOU'RE EITHER EATING OR SLEEPING
JIM DAVIS 5-23
GARF
GARFIELD
I'D BE HAPPY TO CHOOSE ONE AND STICK WITH IT
GARFIELD

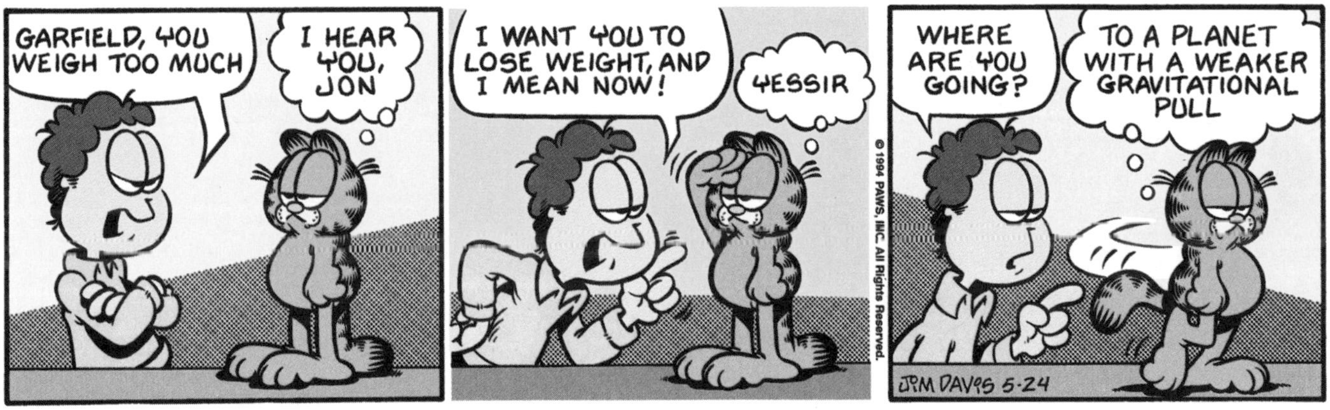
GARFIELD, YOU WEIGH TOO MUCH
I HEAR YOU, JON
I WANT YOU TO LOSE WEIGHT, AND I MEAN NOW!
YESSIR
WHERE ARE YOU GOING?
TO A PLANET WITH A WEAKER GRAVITATIONAL PULL
JIM DAVIS 5-24

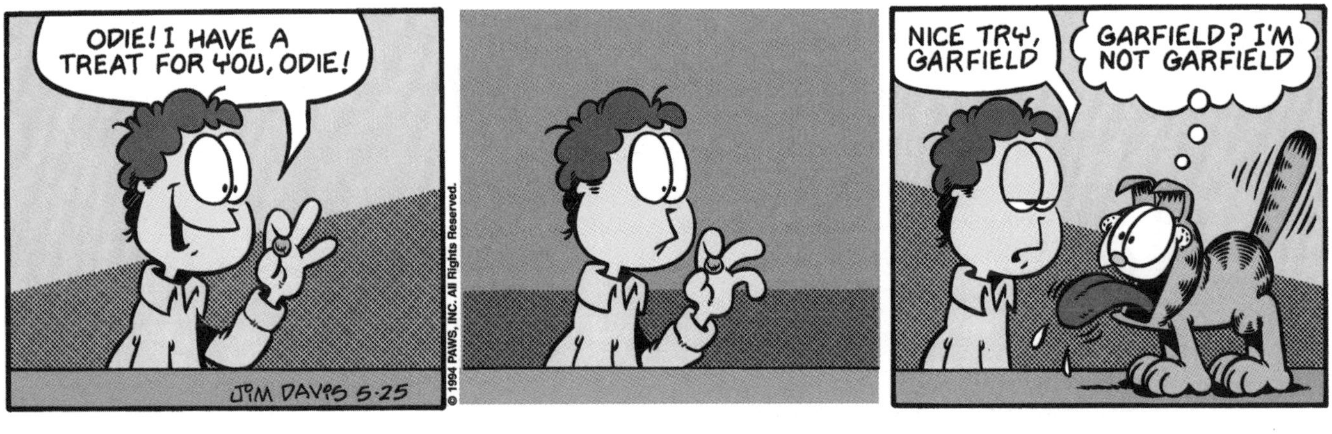
ODIE! I HAVE A TREAT FOR YOU, ODIE!
JIM DAVIS 5-25
NICE TRY, GARFIELD
GARFIELD? I'M NOT GARFIELD

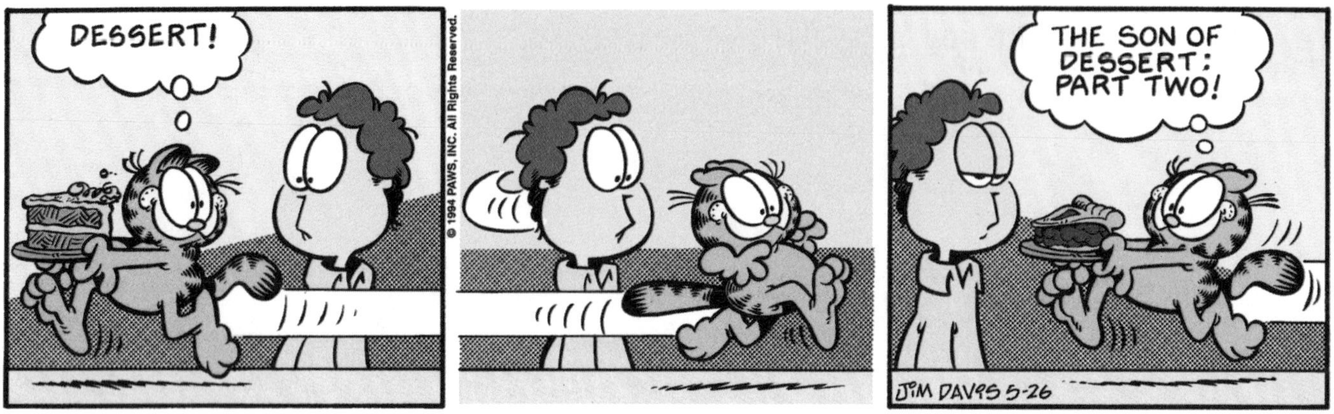
DESSERT!
© 1994 PAWS, INC. All Rights Reserved.
THE SON OF DESSERT: PART TWO!
JIM DAVIS 5-26

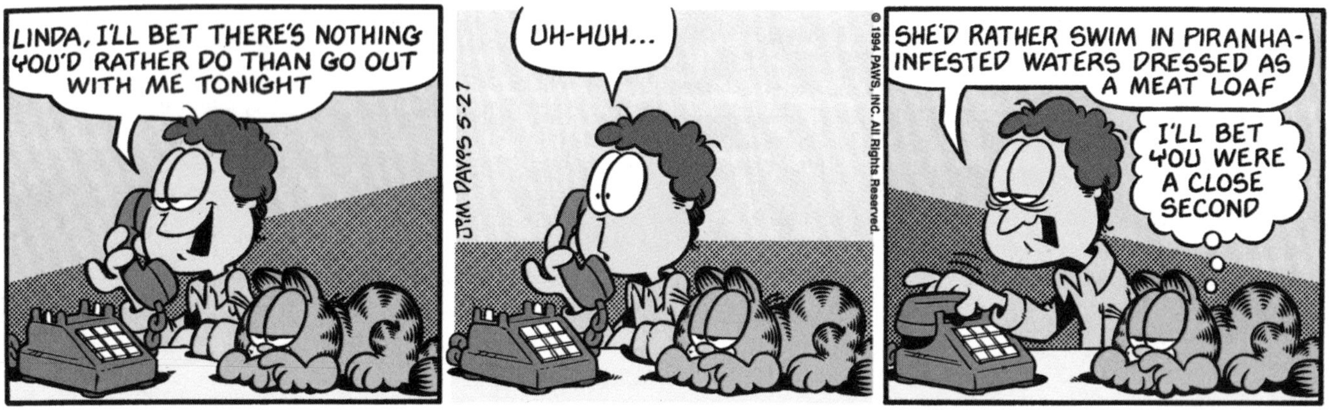
LINDA, I'LL BET THERE'S NOTHING YOU'D RATHER DO THAN GO OUT WITH ME TONIGHT
JIM DAVIS 5-27
UH-HUH...
© 1994 PAWS, INC. All Rights Reserved.
SHE'D RATHER SWIM IN PIRANHA-INFESTED WATERS DRESSED AS A MEAT LOAF
I'LL BET YOU WERE A CLOSE SECOND

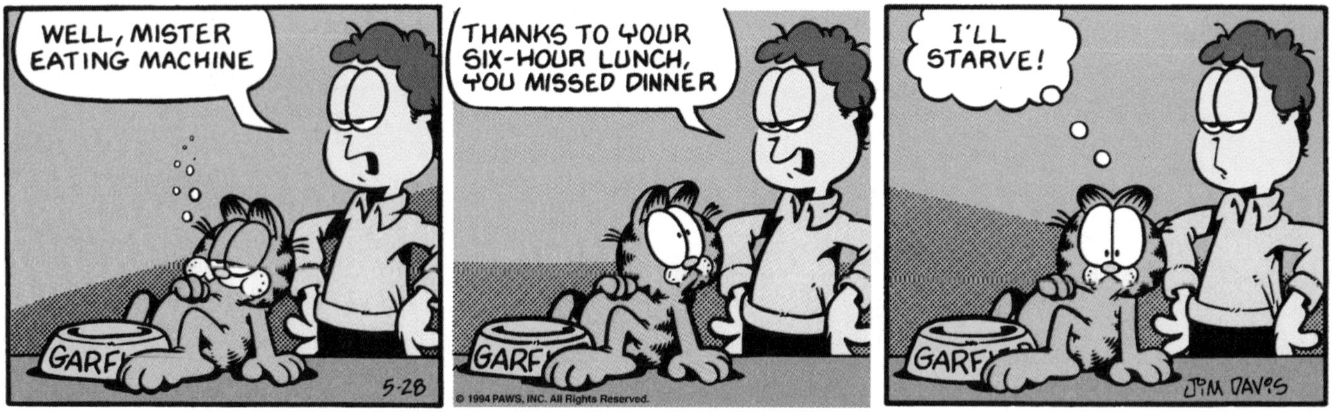
WELL, MISTER EATING MACHINE
GARF
5-28
THANKS TO YOUR SIX-HOUR LUNCH, YOU MISSED DINNER
GARF
© 1994 PAWS, INC. All Rights Reserved.
I'LL STARVE!
GARF
JIM DAVIS

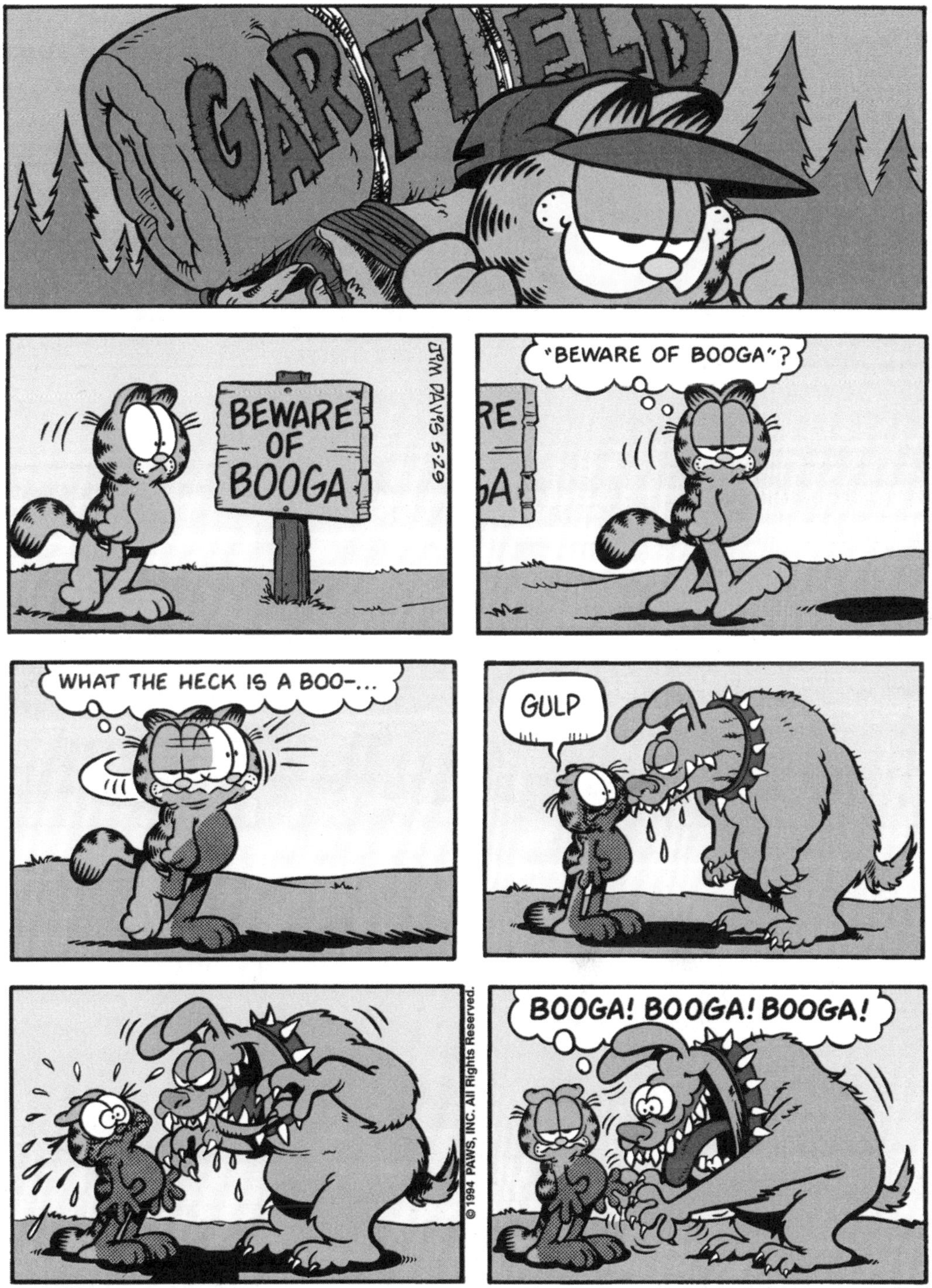
GARFIELD
JPM DAVIS 5-29
BEWARE OF BOOGA
"BEWARE OF BOOGA"?
WHAT THE HECK IS A BOO-...
GULP
© 1994 PAWS, INC. All Rights Reserved.
BOOGA! BOOGA! BOOGA!

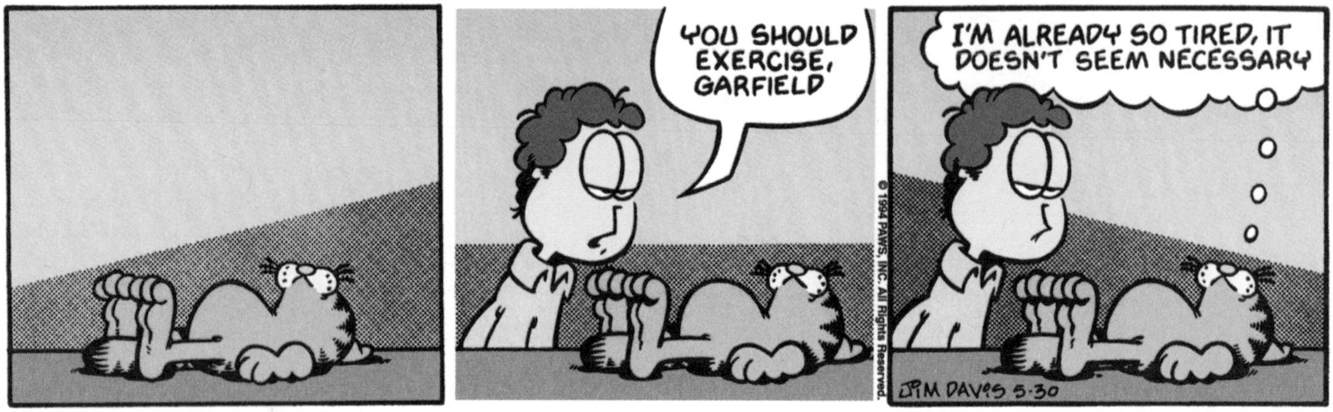
YOU SHOULD EXERCISE, GARFIELD
I'M ALREADY SO TIRED, IT DOESN'T SEEM NECESSARY
© 1994 PAWS, INC. All Rights Reserved.
JIM DAVIS 5-30

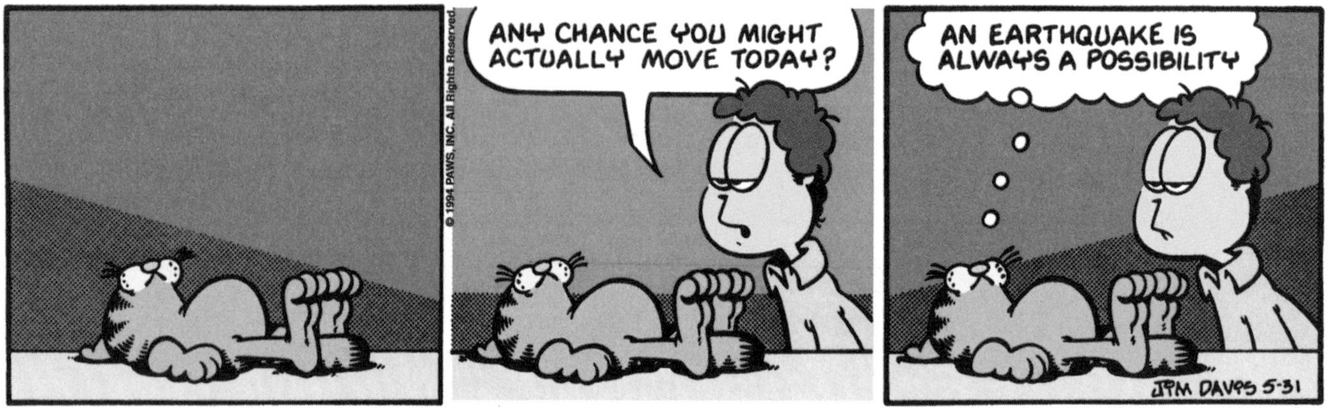
© 1994 PAWS, INC. All Rights Reserved.
ANY CHANCE YOU MIGHT ACTUALLY MOVE TODAY?
AN EARTHQUAKE IS ALWAYS A POSSIBILITY
JIM DAVIS 5-31

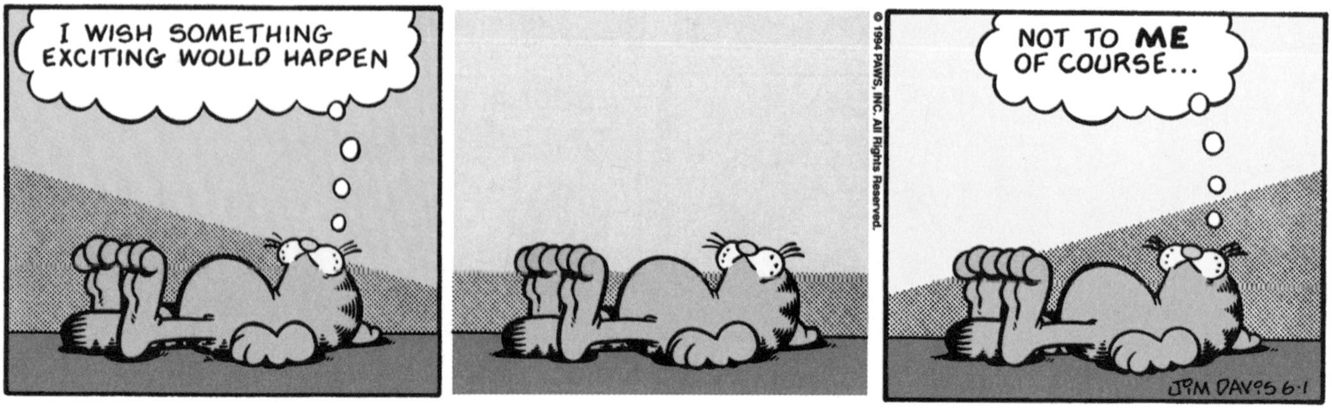
I WISH SOMETHING EXCITING WOULD HAPPEN
© 1994 PAWS, INC. All Rights Reserved.
NOT TO ME OF COURSE...
JIM DAVIS 6-1

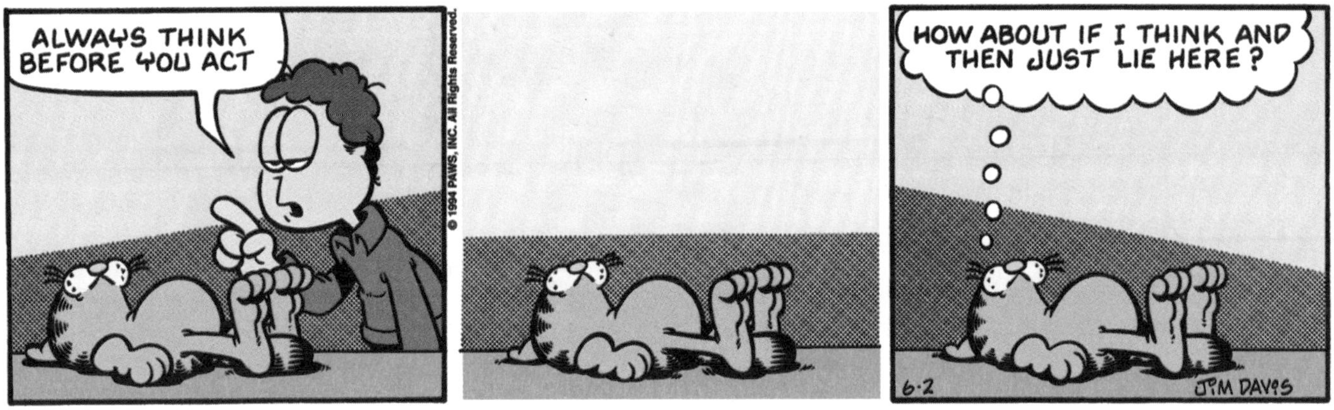
ALWAYS THINK BEFORE YOU ACT
© 1994 PAWS, INC. All Rights Reserved.
HOW ABOUT IF I THINK AND THEN JUST LIE HERE?
6·2
JIM DAVIS

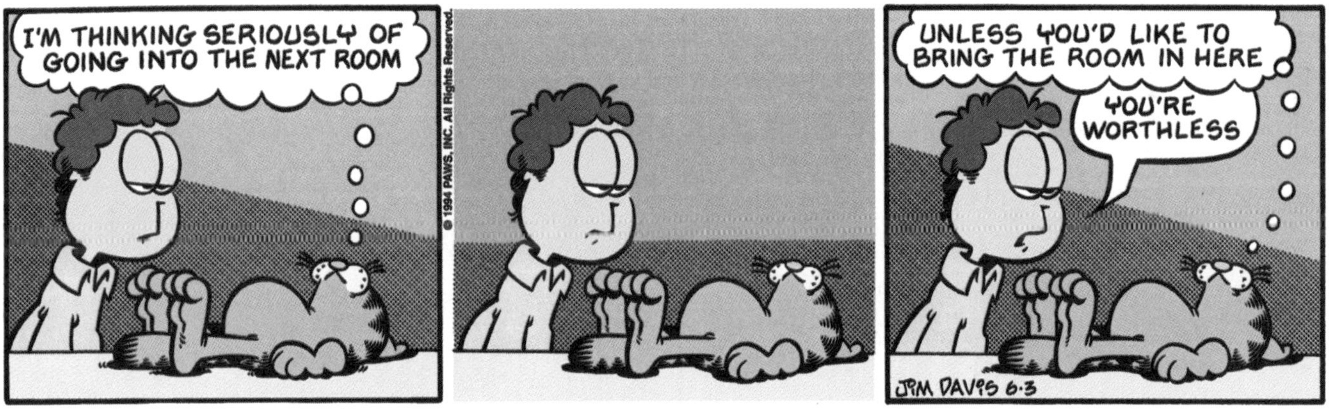
I'M THINKING SERIOUSLY OF GOING INTO THE NEXT ROOM
© 1994 PAWS, INC. All Rights Reserved.
UNLESS YOU'D LIKE TO BRING THE ROOM IN HERE
YOU'RE WORTHLESS
JIM DAVIS 6·3

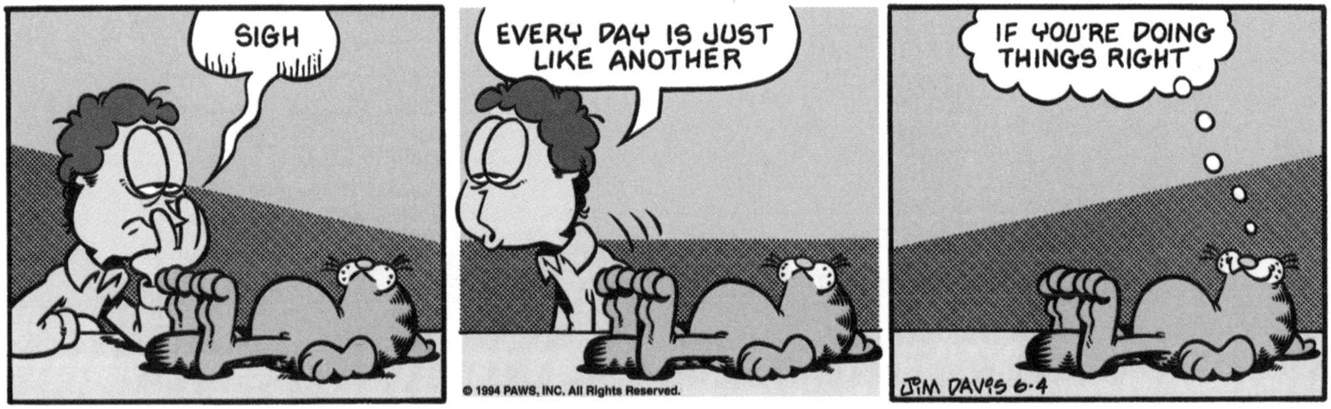
SIGH
EVERY DAY IS JUST LIKE ANOTHER
© 1994 PAWS, INC. All Rights Reserved.
IF YOU'RE DOING THINGS RIGHT
JIM DAVIS 6·4

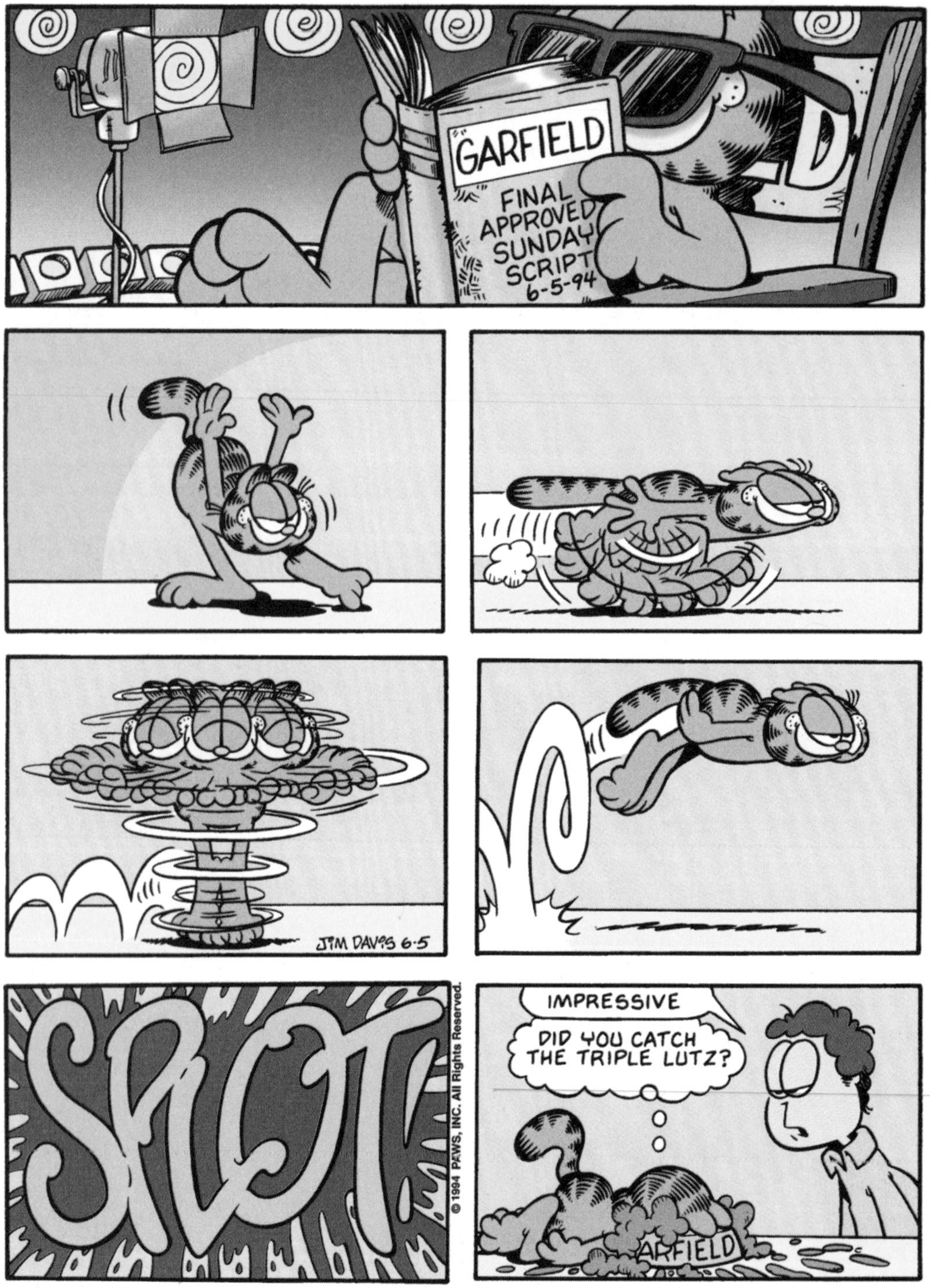
GARFIELD
FINAL APPROVED SUNDAY SCRIPT 6-5-94
JIM DAVIS 6-5
SPLOT!
IMPRESSIVE
DID YOU CATCH THE TRIPLE LUTZ?
ARFIELD

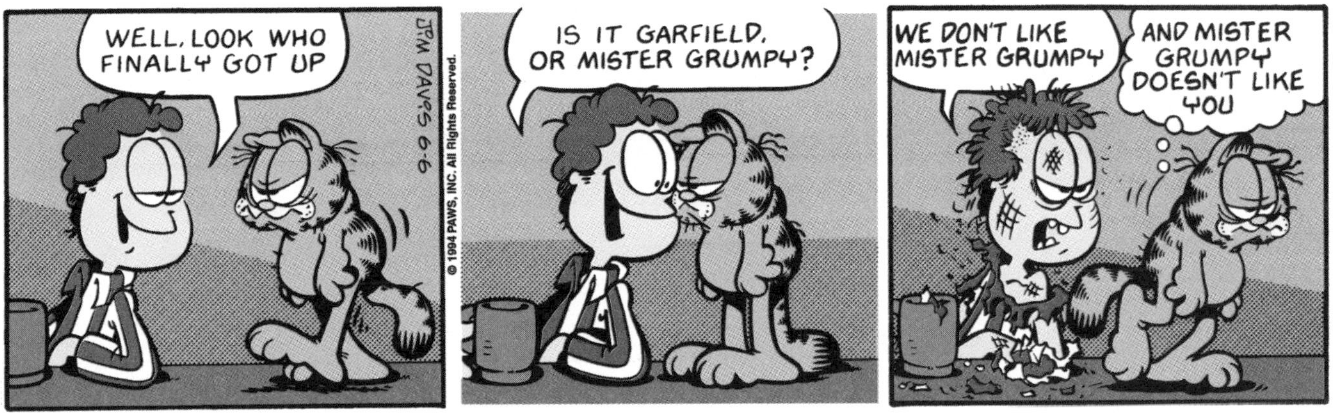
WELL, LOOK WHO FINALLY GOT UP
JIM DAVIS 6-6
© 1994 PAWS, INC. All Rights Reserved.
IS IT GARFIELD, OR MISTER GRUMPY?
WE DON'T LIKE MISTER GRUMPY
AND MISTER GRUMPY DOESN'T LIKE YOU

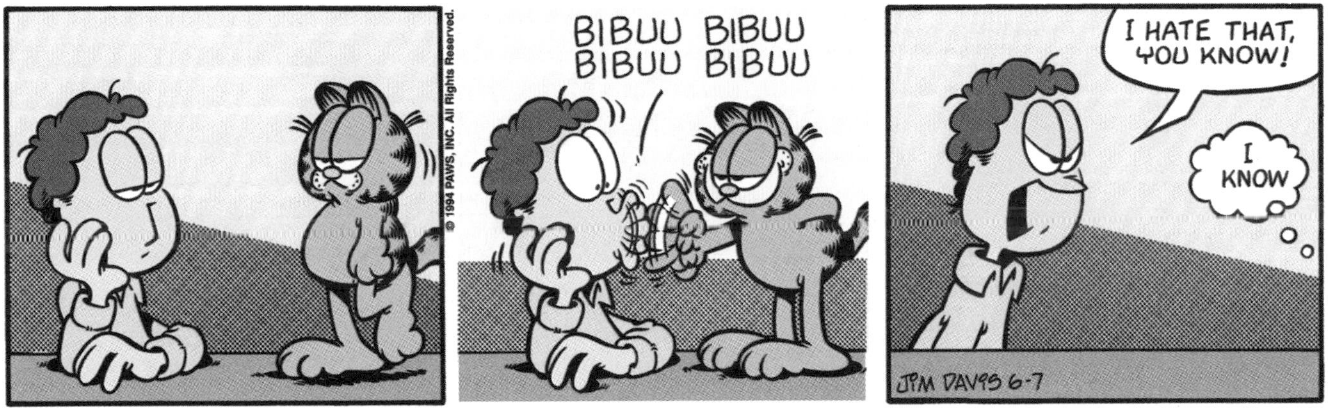
© 1994 PAWS, INC. All Rights Reserved.
BIBUU BIBUU BIBUU BIBUU
I HATE THAT, YOU KNOW!
I KNOW
JIM DAVIS 6-7

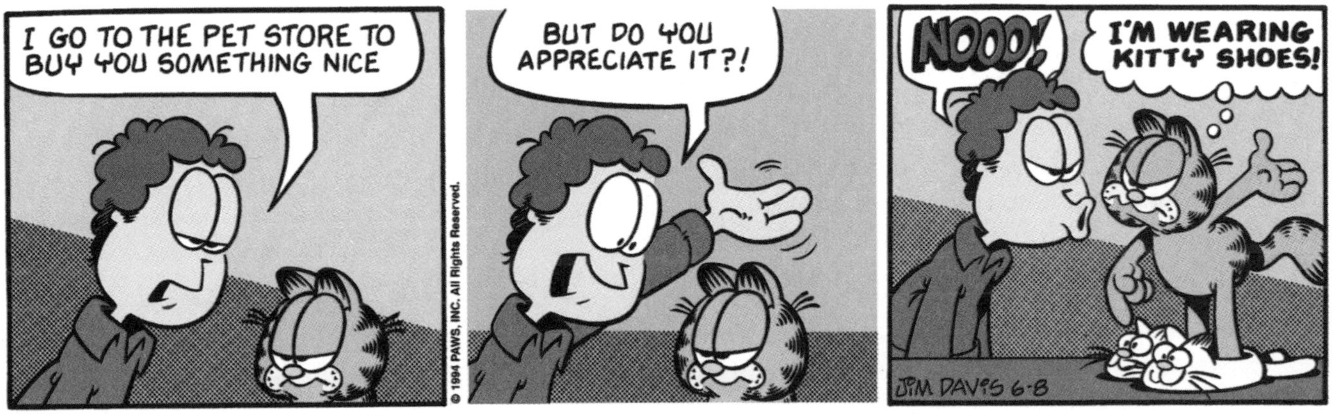
I GO TO THE PET STORE TO BUY YOU SOMETHING NICE
© 1994 PAWS, INC. All Rights Reserved.
BUT DO YOU APPRECIATE IT?!
NOOO!
I'M WEARING KITTY SHOES!
JIM DAVIS 6-8

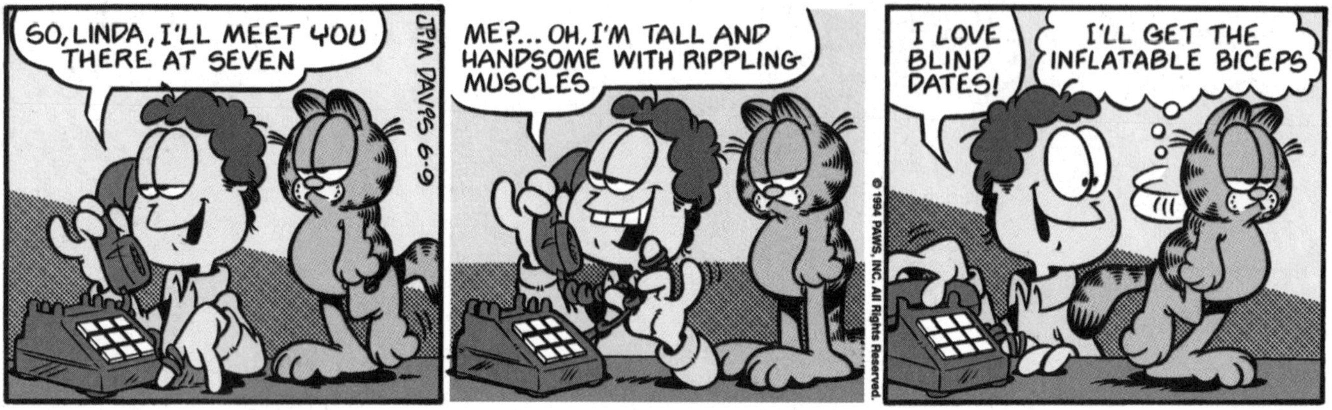
SO, LINDA, I'LL MEET YOU THERE AT SEVEN
JPM DAVPS 6-9
ME?... OH, I'M TALL AND HANDSOME WITH RIPPLING MUSCLES
© 1994 PAWS, INC. All Rights Reserved.
I LOVE BLIND DATES!
I'LL GET THE INFLATABLE BICEPS

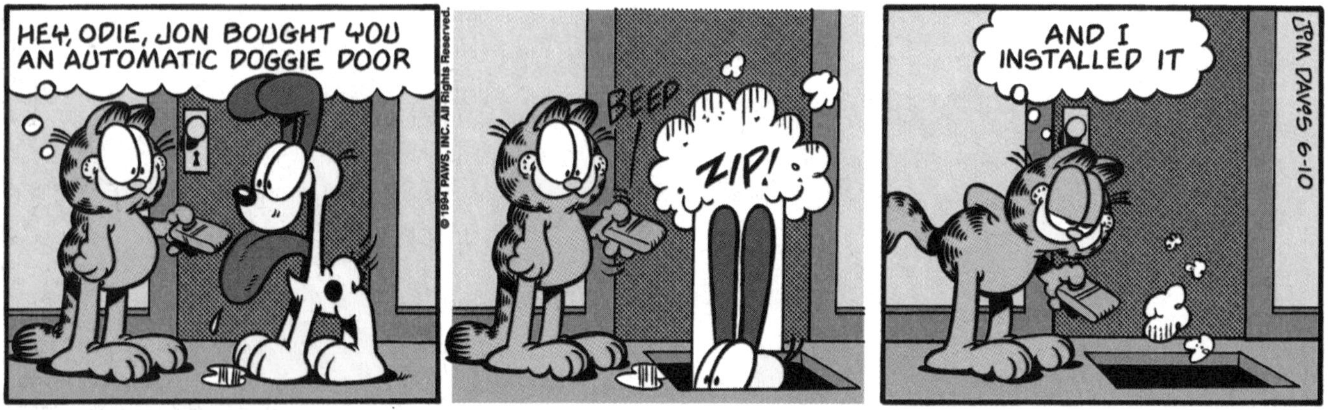
HEY, ODIE, JON BOUGHT YOU AN AUTOMATIC DOGGIE DOOR
© 1994 PAWS, INC. All Rights Reserved.
BEEP
ZIP!
AND I INSTALLED IT
JPM DAVPS 6-10

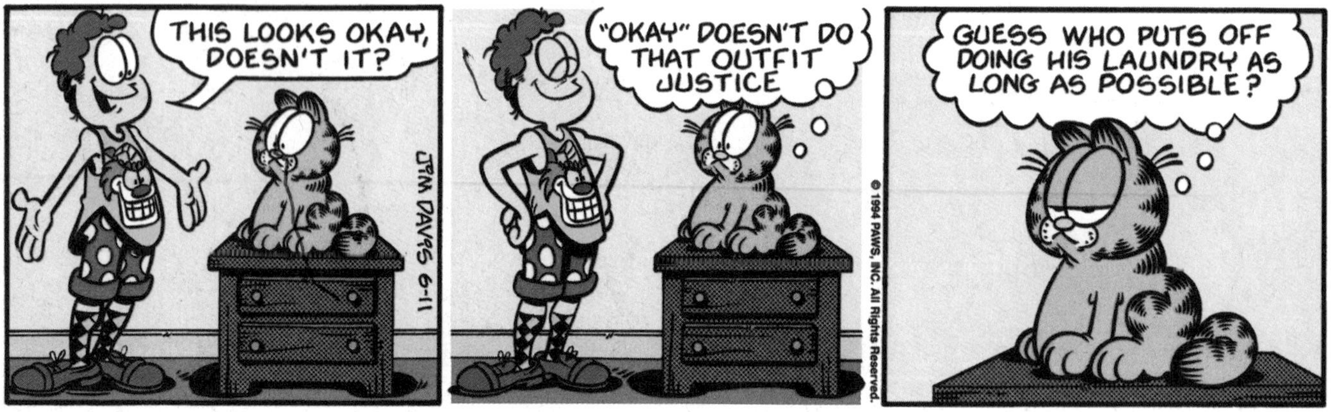
THIS LOOKS OKAY, DOESN'T IT?
JPM DAVPS 6-11
"OKAY" DOESN'T DO THAT OUTFIT JUSTICE
© 1994 PAWS, INC. All Rights Reserved.
GUESS WHO PUTS OFF DOING HIS LAUNDRY AS LONG AS POSSIBLE?

GARFIELD'S PARALLEL UNIVERSE

NIGHT IS DAY
AND BLACK IS WHITE...
BEHOLD A WORLD
OF INVERTED SIGHT!

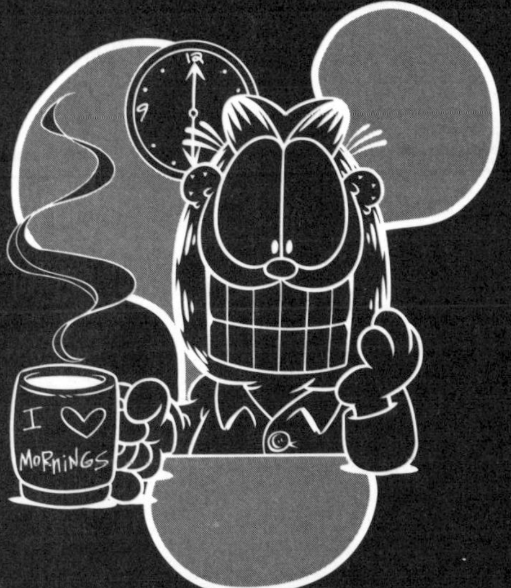
I ♥ MORNINGS

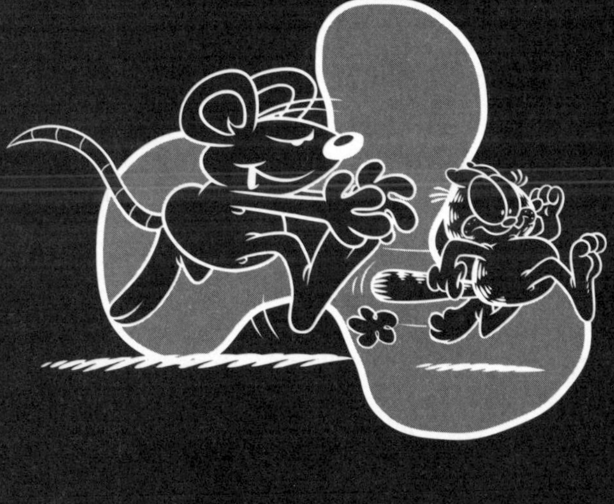

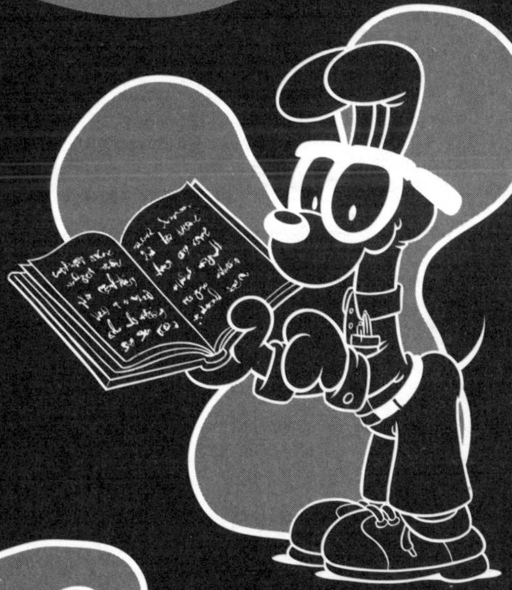

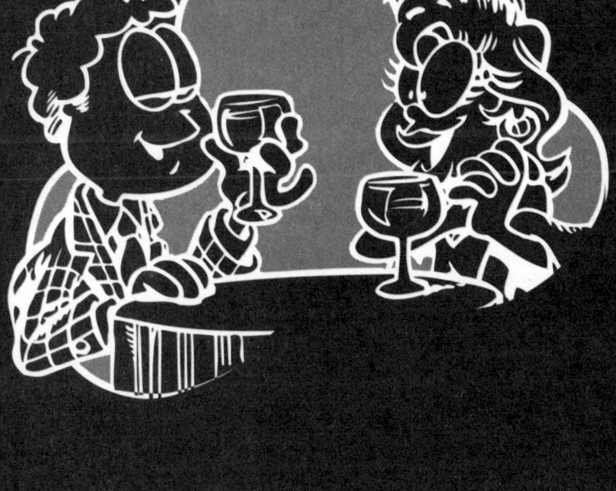

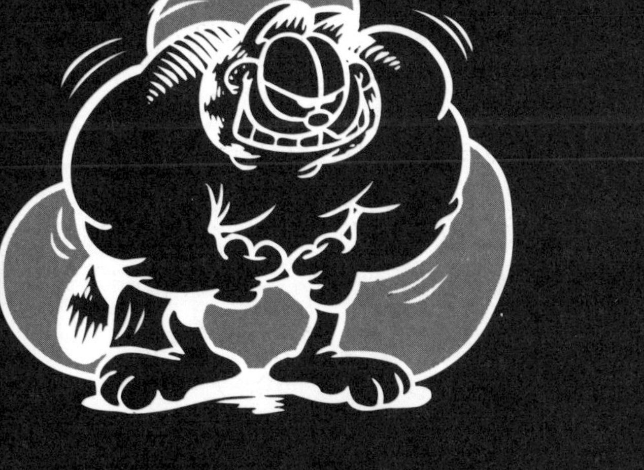

Watch. Read. Shop. Play.

DON'T FORGET THE SNACKS!

garfield.com

* **The Garfield Show**
  Catch Garfield and the rest of the gang on *The Garfield Show*, now airing on Cartoon Network and Boomerang!

* **The Comic Strip**
  Search & read thousands of GARFIELD® comic strips!

* **Garfield on Facebook & Twitter**
  Join millions of Garfield friends on Facebook. Get your daily dose of humor and connect with other fat cat fans!

* **Shop all the Garfield stores!**
  Original art & comic strips, books, apparel, personalized products, & more!

* **Play FREE online Garfield games!**
  Plus, check out all of the FREE Garfield apps available for your smartphone, tablet, and other mobile devices.